THE NETSIZE GUIDE 2010

MOBILE RENAISSANCE

8 SHARE THE WEALTH

12 ACTIVATION
- 17 Engulfed in an app store hysteria, Andreas Constantinou, VisionMobile
- 21 Making an (app) offer you can't refuse, Christopher David, Sony Ericsson
- 24 Applications for the masses, Patrick Mork, GetJar

28 INTERACTION
- 33 Taking the initiative, Rimma Perelmuter, Mobile Entertainment Forum
- 36 Flirting for fun and profit, Mark Curtis, Flirtomatic
- 39 Super model, Ian Henderson, Sony Music Entertainment

44 CONVERSATION
- 50 Call to action, Paul Berney, Mobile Marketing Association
- 53 Linking mobile, Internet and e-commerce, Jon Mew, Internet Advertising Bureau
- 56 Parlez-vous Mobile Internet?, Dimitri Dautel, Havas
- 59 High performance, Valérie Itey, Universal McCann
- 62 Mapping the future, Diana LaGattuta, NAVTEQ Media Solutions
- 64 (Best) practice makes perfect, Mark Wächter, MWC.mobi

68 TRANSACTION
- 74 The second wave of mobile payments, Chiel Liezenberg, Innopay
- 78 Let us entertain you, Elisabeth Trochet, UGC S.A.
- 80 Shop your way, Sienne Veit, M&S Direct
- 83 Tour de France, Olivier Céchura, SFR
- 86 Converting readers into shoppers, Scott Dunlap, NearbyNow
- 89 See it, click it, get it, Jonathan Bulkeley, Scanbuy
- 92 All systems go!, Francesco Rovetta, Paypal

96 TRANSFORMATION
- 104 Mind the gap, Susan Dray, Dray & Associates
- 107 Browse the world, Maarten Lens-FitzGerald, Layar
- 110 Finding not tracking, James E. (Jim) Nalley, EmFinders
- 113 Pointing to profits, John Ellenby, GeoVector
- 116 Read my mind, Phil Libin, Evernote

119 VIEWPOINTS
- 120 The global regulatory challenge, Suhail Bhat, Mobile Entertainment Forum
- 124 The appetite for Mobile Internet, Jamie Gavin & Alistair Hill, comScore
- 128 The conquest of mobile, the conquest of space, Christophe Romei, Memodia

131 ABOUT NETSIZE

143 MOBILE TRENDS SURVEY 2010

156 COUNTRY DATA
- 156 The mobile content market in 2010, Mark Newman, Informa Telecoms & Media
- 162 About the Country Data

287 SPECIAL THANKS

290 ABOUT GEMALTO

SHARE THE WEALTH

In the Old Economy, if something was scarce it was valuable. Executives played the role of gatekeepers, shoring up the boundaries of the company both internally, by creating hierarchies, and externally, by remaining largely unconnected with the outside world. The company was free to function at the center of its universe.

In our century the tables have turned and it's openness and availability that drive value. The more people who have access to a product or an idea the better.

While we may like to think that we are all part of a value chain, the reality is quite different. We are all linked in a value web with stakeholders, shareholders, customers and partners, where collaboration is crucial. In this new ecosystem strength is in numbers and only members of the ecosystem that have the right connections can achieve great things.

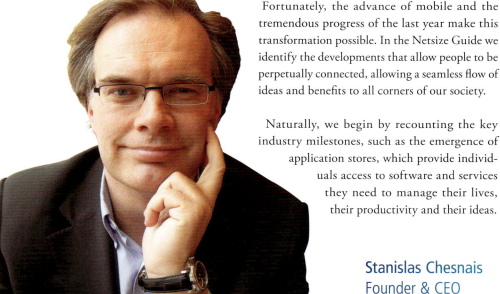

Fortunately, the advance of mobile and the tremendous progress of the last year make this transformation possible. In the Netsize Guide we identify the developments that allow people to be perpetually connected, allowing a seamless flow of ideas and benefits to all corners of our society.

Naturally, we begin by recounting the key industry milestones, such as the emergence of application stores, which provide individuals access to software and services they need to manage their lives, their productivity and their ideas.

Stanislas Chesnais
Founder & CEO
of Netsize

But we didn't stop there. We also surveyed professionals and practitioners for their pick of mobile trends and their views on the future of mobile. Their ideas and insights are part of the final chapter, aptly titled Transformation. In the same chapter we examine the role of mobile in our lives and in our society.

From new services aimed at achieving socioeconomic development goals in emerging markets, to the advance of mobile into new vertical industry sectors and disciplines, to the emergence of Augmented Reality applications that blend the physical and digital worlds around us. It is clear that mobile is the global catalyst for significant change and improvement.

Indeed, mobile allows us to collaborate, communicate, and connect with diverse networks of people, breaking down the walls between cultures, professions and fields of knowledge. Mobile also allows us to share and leverage a wealth of good ideas, involving everyone everywhere in the process.

In my view, mobile is the medium that paves the way for a new Renaissance, unleashing our collective potential and empowering us to affect change for the good.

Read and enjoy!

ACTIVATION

APPLICATIONS
STORES
ACTIVATE
EXPERIENCE
EXTEND
PROMOTION
DISCOVERY
PAYMENT

Mobile in 2010 is ACTIVATION: The mobile becomes a platform for applications, user engagement, a launch pad for Long Tail services and a marketplace for a plethora of application stores and developer ecosystems.

With mobile phones outnumbering PCs around the world by a ratio of 4:1, mobile applications represent a huge opportunity for the mobile industry, much bigger than the explosion of content and services that accompanied the growth of the fixed-line Internet just over a decade ago.

And the timing couldn't be better. The advance of smartphones and the arrival of applications ('apps') and services have effectively reinvigorated the mobile content and services market, paving the way for new content genres and even boosting interest in mobile video. The Apple iPhone App Store, for example, currently counts a whopping 20 content categories, ranging from games, music and social networking to productivity apps that help consumers find nearby businesses, comparison shop and simplify their daily routines.

But the App Store model, which effectively distintermediates mobile operators, streamlines commerce and guarantees developers a 70/30 revenue split on paid-for apps, has not only jumpstarted the market. It has transformed the mobile value chain, clearing the way for media companies and garage developers alike to introduce an avalanche of innovative and functional apps into the world of mobile applications. In 2009 Apple announced that more than two billion apps had been downloaded from its App Store. In total more than 85,000 apps were available to the more than 50 million iPhone and iPod touch customers worldwide, and the iPhone Developer Program had grown to over 125,000 developers. Analyst firm IDC predicts the number of iPhone apps will rise to a staggering 300,000 by end-2010, compared to 75,000 apps on the Android platform.

Abundant growth

Despite the excitement about the iPhone, figures from mobile application analytics firm Flurry remind us that Google's Android Market growth, while not as fast or furious as Apple's App Store, is nonetheless significant. Flurry estimates that Google will have between 100,000 and as many as 150,000 apps by end-2010, a number that could skyrocket as developers join the Android platform encouraged by the positive consumer response to Android devices such as Motorola's Droid and HTC's G1 and Magic. Not to be outdone, Google started 2010 with a bang, stepping into the device manufacturing fray to produce Nexus One, a device market research firm ABI Research claims will make 2010 "the year of Android."

In 2010 market research firm Forrester Research is estimating that Google Android will have a 10 percent market share of the mobile device market. Meanwhile, research firm Gartner reckons the seven million iPhones sold by Apple in Q3 2009 earned it a 17.1 percent share of the global smartphone market. Nokia managed to hold its lead with 39 percent market share, a drop from 45 percent in Q2 2009, while Research in Motion's BlackBerry device reach 20 percent market share, it's highest yet.

Predictably, the breakout success of Apple's App Store made it inevitable that rivals would introduce their own app stores. But few were prepared for the deluge of branded mobile content storefronts and apps that flooded the market. Nokia and Microsoft were first to announce their app store offers, the Nokia Ovi Store and Windows Marketplace for Mobile (although Microsoft didn't open for business until October 2009).

The following months saw Research In Motion unveil its BlackBerry App World and Sony Ericsson team up with independent app portal GetJar, a move that Christopher David, Sony Ericsson Head of Developer and Partner Engagement, tells us allows the handset vendor to focus on forging closer relationships with fewer developers, thus ensuring a supply of quality apps that "leverage the innovation that Sony Ericsson puts around and on top of the core platform," leaving GetJar to provide the Long Tail of more mainstream apps. **See Interview, page 21**. Surprisingly, GetJar has quietly emerged as the App Store's biggest rival, counting more than half a billion downloads and 50,000 mobile applications available in more than 200 different countries and optimized across roughly 1,700 handsets. **See Interview, page 24**. And the list goes on.

At the other end of the spectrum, mobile operators worldwide including Vodafone, Telefónica, Orange, TIM, T-Mobile, Verizon Wireless, Sprint, China Mobile and SK Telecom are moving full-steam ahead on their own app store strategies.

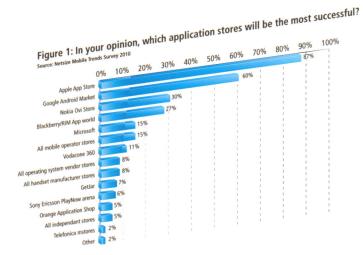

Figure 1: In your opinion, which application stores will be the most successful?
Source: Netsize Mobile Trends Survey 2010

- Apple App Store — 87%
- Google Android Market — 60%
- Nokia Ovi Store — 30%
- Blackberry/RIM App world — 27%
- Microsoft — 15%
- All mobile operator stores — 15%
- Vodacone 360 — 11%
- All operating system vendor stores — 8%
- All handset manufacturer stores — 8%
- GetJar — 7%
- Sony Ericsson PlayNow arena — 6%
- Orange Application Shop — 5%
- All independant stores — 5%
- Telefonica mstores — 2%
- Other — 2%

Models and approaches differ widely, but analyst firm Wireless Expertise Ltd. believes mobile operators will ultimately have to adopt a dual app store strategy, which pairs the proven app store with a browser-based widget store.

Leader of the (app) pack

Which companies will operate the most successful app stores and what will separate the leaders from the also-rans? The Netsize Mobile Trends Survey 2010 asked 1,000 mobile professionals, executives and influencers for their pick. In total 87 percent of respondents believe the Apple App Store will be the most successful, followed by Google Android Market with 60 percent. Nokia comes in a distant third with 30 percent, and mobile operators follow with 15 percent.

As one respondent put it: "The only real success … is the Apple App Store. None of the others is anywhere near the horizon in terms of usage…. Activation will be a real challenge unless handset usability with app stores dramatically increases. That [fit] is the primary factor driving Apple's success." **See Figure 1**

We also asked respondents to share what it is about app stores that make them a leading destination for software applications. The four C's – Convenience, Compatibility, Choice and Charging – are the main selling points, with 65 percent giving Convenience (everything you need to manage you mobile life in one place) a top-notch spot.

Convenience is also the focus of Netsize's Smart Billing and mPayment solutions with the objective to simplify mobile commerce for developers, application stores and online storefronts through secured payment transactions.

Figure 2: Loyalty by Application Category (Source: Flurry)

CATEGORY	30 DAY RETENTION	60 DAY RETENTION	90 DAY RETENTION	FREQUENCY OF USE / WEEK
News	74%	57%	43%	11.00
Medical	72%	55%	43%	3.0
Reference	70%	55%	42%	10.7
Productivity	72%	38%	35%	6.0
Navigation	73%	33%	30%	6.0
Health & Fitness	85%	35%	30%	7.0
Education	72%	34%	30%	4.0
Weather	74%	38%	30%	10.5
Business	71%	33%	27%	5.0
Music	65%	32%	26%	5.0
Finance	71%	33%	26%	6.0
Sports	73%	30%	21%	4.0
Travel	61%	25%	20%	7.0
Utilities	55%	19%	17%	7.7
Games	72%	23%	16%	7.4
Social Networking	61%	19%	14%	6.0
Entertainment	51%	15%	12%	2.6
Books	72%	23%	12%	10.0
Lifestyle	50%	8%	5%	8.0
AVERAGE	**67%**	**32%**	**25%**	**6.7**

Where's the money?

Between year-end 2008 and year-end 2014 technology consultancy Ovum estimates the total number of app downloads, including both free and paid-for apps, will grow from $491 million to $18.6 billion worldwide. This represents a CAGR of 83 percent over the forecast period.

However, figures that quantify the value of the billions of iPhone App Store downloads are sketchy at best. Market research firm Yankee group pegs the U.S. market at just $343 million in revenue in 2009; a number it predicts will grow to $4.2 billion by 2013. Drivers are an increase in smartphone adoption overall and a slight uptick in the average selling price for a majority of apps from today's price tag of $1.95 to roughly $2.37 in 2013.

Meanwhile, analyst firm Wireless Expertise Ltd. is the latest to estimate the future growth of the global app market, claiming that its worth will skyrocket from $4.6 billion in 2009 to $16.6 billion by 2013.

However, before we break out the champagne to mark the massive growth potential of mobile apps, mobile pundit and author Tomi Ahonen reminds us that apps – regardless whether they come to market via handset makers, platform providers or mobile operators – may only be a "trivial sideshow."

The action, he says, is in the more traditional mobile content and services market, which generates more revenues and consumer interest than all the app stores put together. In fact, market research firm Portico reports the global value of "non-messaging" premium content -- content including games, music and information – downloaded and consumed on mobile devices in 2009 hit a record $85 billion.

Another word of caution comes from Martin Wilson, founder of the independent consultancy Indigo 102, specializing in mobile strategy. It analyzes user retention rates as reported by mobile analytics companies Flurry and comScore and concludes the hard numbers paint a "shocking picture" of the iPhone and Android app marketplaces. **See Table**

Specifically, Wilson says, the figures indicate that apps – like the first fad ringtones that characterized the mobile content marketplace over a decade ago – have degraded into a string of "one-off offers." Assuming $3 per user in customer acquisition costs, and considering that some 70 percent of users loose interest in their apps after 60 days, the numbers simply don't add up for a sustainable business model. Acquisition costs will rise quickly as the number of offered apps explodes. "Apps appear to be being brought to market with little strategic view towards evolution and providing ongoing consumer engagement." Moving forward, companies are advised to shift their efforts away from one-hit wonders and focus on meeting the specific needs of consumers for functional and innovative apps and deepening their relationship with customers.

Long tail returns

A sharper focus on delighting the customer could result in more than return sales and increased loyalty. It could also mark the emergence of a long tail of vertical and niche app stores, catering to the needs of specific customer segments. Even better if the app store harnesses mobile CRM tools to fulfill the first rule of retail: listen to the customer.

App stores for healthcare professionals, app stores for musicians and even app stores for children. But it won't stop there. Andreas Constantinou, Research Director at VisionMobile, an industry analysis firm specializing in mobile software strategy, predicts this wave of specialized app stores will also be accompanied by an explosion in app stores offering localized content such as French-language news or Indian Bollywood film fanzines.

Moving forward, the possibilities – like our passions – are endless.

ENGULFED IN AN APP STORE HYSTERIA

The avalanche of applications stores coming online this year signals a seismic shift in the way software and services are promoted and monetized and by whom. Operators, handset manufacturers and platform providers are all jockeying for position but this time size and scope is no guarantee of success. Andreas Constantinou, Research Director at VisionMobile – an industry analysis firm specializing in mobile software strategy – describes the current state of the market and delves into how companies can play in the complex app store market.

From operators to platform providers, to all the wanabe players in-between, the mobile industry is engulfed in application store hysteria. Everyone is convinced that opening one of these software super-malls is a sure-fire way to secure a central – and profitable – position in this emerging business ecosystem. But nothing could be further from the truth.

To understand what lies ahead for the dozens of companies competing for our attention and our wallets, we need to go back in mobile software history. Nearly a decade ago, platforms such as BREW, Symbian, Windows Mobile and Palm introduced APIs (Application Programming Interfaces), allowing third-parties to develop content and services on top of their platforms.

However, the focus of these 'open' platforms was more on technology and less on the commercial tools that would allow developers to make money. These open platforms made developers jump through hoops in order to reach direct to consumers. In retrospect it took Symbian six years to reach 10,000 applications. Fast forward, and it took Apple only six months to achieve the same results. In fact, in the first year of operation, Apple's App Store counted 65,000 apps, 100,000 registered developers and 1.5 billion application downloads.

How did Apple do so much better than its predecessors? Apple figured that streamlining the commercial route to market was more important than opening up APIs. On the developer end, Apple reduced the number of middlemen, taking out the operators, content aggregators and content retailers who were eating 60 percent or more of the retail price. On the consumer end Apple took out the obstacles for application discovery and enabled one-click purchase. What better way

ANDREAS CONSTANTINOU

Research Director,
VisionMobile

Mobile Application Stores (end- 2009)
Source: VisionMobile research

FUNDAMENTALS	APP STORE	ANDROID MARKET	OVI STORE	HANDANGO	GETJAR
Owner	Apple	Google	Nokia	Handango	Getjar Networks
Distribution model	via App Store on iPhone and iPod Touch	via Market on Android devices (closed source)	via download, and preloaded from 4Q09	via web mostly (direct + white label)	via web only (direct + white label)
Platforms	OSX	Android	S60, S40	Java, S60, RIM, WinMo, Palm, Android	Java, Flash, Android, RIM, WinMo, Palm, Android
KEY FIGURES					
Installed base of on-device storefront (2009 est.)	60M	5M	2M (preload on S60 + some S40 from 4Q09)	< 1M	0 (plans to pre-load icon shortcut on phones)
Downloads per month as of end of 2009 (est.)	200M	30M	5M	3M	50M
Applications to end of 2009 (est.)	110,000	16,000	4,000 apps 1,500 themes	140,000 apps	50,000 apps
Annual revenues (2009 est.)	$700M/year	$20M/year	N/A	N/A	N/A
Revenue model	70% to developer	70% to developer 30% optional to operator	70% to developer (less w/ carrier billing)	30-40% to developer + rev share to channel	Ad-based apps + paid placement

to win developers and secure a growing demand for apps?

Crowded house

Of course, Apple now has company.

At VisionMobile we have analyzed the five most prominent app stores (App Store, Android Market, Ovi Store, Handango and GetJar). We also identified an additional 19 white label application store enablers and vendors. They have emerged over the last months in response to companies across the ecosystem – including chipset vendors and media companies – clamoring for the tools and technologies to set up shop. These white label providers include: Amdocs, Cellmania, Comverse, Ericsson, Everypoint, GetJar, Handango, Handmark, Ideaworks 3D, Javaground, Mobango, PocketGear, Ondeego, OnMobile, Qualcomm, SlideME, Sun Microsystems and Tanla.

The chart above sheds light of the key performance indicators that characterize the size and scope of each app store. However, winning is not about size; it's about orchestrating capabilities and partnering to fill the gaps within the complex app store recipe.

At first glance, the formula for any company that wants to follow Apple's lead seems simple enough. They must provide a go-to-market vehicle for allowing developers to distribute and retail their applications directly to end-consumers, and be sure to remove the middlemen from distribution and retail along the way. An on-device app store would be nice, too. Right?

Wrong – if only it were that simple.

Building a business

At VisionMobile, we have identified five key building blocks that define a winning app store model. These are:

1. **Developer Marketplace**, i.e. the process for submission, certification, targeting and pricing

Key building blocks

Source: VisionMobile research

Building block	DEVELOPER MARKET	BILLING & SETTLEMENT	DISTRIBUTION SURFACE	DELIVERY & INLIFE MGMT	RETAILING & MERCHANDISING
Description	process for submission, certification, targeting and pricing of applications	mechanism for billing, settlement and reporting of application sales	size of addressable market across handset OEMs, operators and regions	app download, silent install, in-place access, app licensing and in-life app management	app discovery, app promotion, premium placement, search and recommendations
Evolution					
2000-7 open APIs, closed route to market	complex, undocumented & fragmented approach for certification and pricing	developers had to set up own billing or use premium SMS with only 10%-50% going to developer	distribution done on region by region AND handset by handset basis	download separate from access, lack of updates, no rights management	app promotions and discovery via complex shortcodes and scattered website ads
2008-9 the iTunes Store cloning era	single websites for submission, certification, targeting and pricing of applications	credit-card billing, fast time to settlement, 70% rev share as the norm	global distribution on a perplatform basis (OSX, S60, Blackberry, etc)	transparent app download, install, access and in-life app updating	on-device app discovery, 1- click purchase, automated recommendations
2010-2012 the app stores everywhere era	10s of marketplaces, emergence of marketplace aggregators	ubiquitous operator billing approaching 70% rev share, and multitude of revenue models	global distribution on perplatform OR per-operator basis	app delivery extends to B2B apps and middleware that can be backgrounddown-loaded & installed	segment-specific retailing of apps, social recommendations and developer back-channel
Roles					
MNO unique value add	none	established billing relationship and credit line	none	none	can aggregate apps across devices/stores and promote 'preferred' apps
OEM unique value add	platform certification, developer tools, developer communities	none	cross-operator and crossregional distribution	on-device integration for transparent app install, access & lifecycle mgmt	none

of applications.

2. **Billing & Settlement**, i.e. providing mechanisms for billing, settlement and reporting of application sales, as well more imaginative monetization models such as subscription, gifting, and cross-app billing (where the credit paid through one app is valid for use in another app).

3. **Distribution Surface**, i.e. the addressable market for an app store that spans handset OEMs, operators and geographical regions and the ability to provide application distribution across all of these points.

4. **Delivery & In-Life Management**, i.e. the mechanisms enabling app download, silent install, in-place access, app licensing and in-life app management ensuring that apps can be downloaded, activated and updated auto-magically.

5. **Retailing & Merchandizing**, which covers the gamut of tools and technologies around application discovery, promotion, premium placement, personalization, recommendation and search.

How is this new business ecosystem shaping up? And what roles and responsibilities will each player have in this value creation web?

Hidden talents

There are no easy answers, but our analysis highlights the key areas where players can add value and should therefore focus their efforts.

It should come as no surprise that mobile operators, based on their billing relationship with the customer and their insights into customer data including profiles, preferences, purchases and browsing patterns, have an important role to play. Specifically, they bring two building blocks to the table: Billing & Settlement and Retailing & Merchandizing. However, operators are weak on all other fronts.

Against this backdrop, the Joint Innovation Labs (JIL) – a joint venture between Vodafone, Verizon Wireless, China Mobile and Softbank Mobile to develop a one-size-fits-all super store – is far too ambitious.

Why? Because JIL and efforts like it are trying to extract value where they cannot add value. For example, operators should not meddle with running developer marketplaces as they are worst suited in understanding and attracting developers.

At the other end of the spectrum, OEMs and platform providers are indeed well-positioned to create and cultivate developer communities. They have tools, platforms and a long-established process for submitting and certifying apps. Distribution is also a core strength. While operators can distribute across their footprint (often up to a third of regional subscribers), handset makers and platform providers are global. OEMs can integrate apps within the device, easily distribute these across multiple regions and manage all the 'magic' happening in the background when a user downloads/installs an app.

What can we expect in the coming months? The previous table summarizes our expectations for how each ingredient in the app store recipe will evolve. One of the most untapped areas of app store value is in the final piece of the chain; Retailing and Merchandising. This would explain why so many startups have emerged in the last six months to play in this arena. Among these: Apppopular, Appolicious, Appsfire, Chorus, Mplayit and Yappler.

We also see a business opportunity for companies to extend their offer beyond B2C apps to B2B middleware. Pursuing such a strategy will enable app store operators to monetize on a per-activation basis or perform bug fixes on behalf of operators, OEMs and/or enterprise customers.

However, the most exciting development may be the emergence of a long tail of app stores. In addition to offering a diverse assortment of apps, these app stores will also co-exist on the same platforms and devices. Case in point: LG and Samsung phones which shipped in Q4 2009 come with four app stores co-existing within the same handset; one from the OEM, one from the platform provider (Windows Mobile) and two from the South Korean operator SK Telecom.

Team(s) work

Our conclusion: Apple's recipe cannot be photocopied.

Moving forward, no single mobile operator, handset maker or platform provider will be able to dominate the value chain or run a one-stop app shop. This is because no single player will have the expertise to excel in all five areas – or building blocks – critical to achieving high performance. All players will need to collaborate and cooperate based on their core strengths and capabilities.

MAKING AN (APP) OFFER YOU CAN'T REFUSE

In 2009 Sony Ericsson took the wraps off a new app store coupled with a progressive framework to accelerate the creation of compelling apps for Sony Ericsson devices. In practice, Sony Ericsson handles all billing and then passes 70 percent of revenues back to developers. Other tangible benefits for developers include access to tools, distribution, marketing and top-notch placement in the app store. While there is a sharp focus on apps written for Java and Symbian, Sony Ericsson also recently expanded support to other platforms such as Android. Christopher David talks about app store strategy, partnerships and the content discovery dilemma.

How did the decision to launch an app store originate and how do you avoid a head-on confrontation with competitors?

Sony Ericsson has always been centered on bringing quality entertainment and content to consumers. To do that we also created long-term sustainable relationships with developers. This has evolved and, in 2009, we decided to take it all to a new level.

We opened up the marketplace to allow more people within the community to participate and launched submit.sonyericcson.com. When we did this we probably did not do a good enough marketing job. At the same time, others in the industry had made a much bigger push around apps. So, we had to think hard about how we would avoid being a 'me-too' app store.

We concluded there were things we had to do to raise the bar. We had to make it simple and easy for developers to get involved. There had to be low barrier of entry for the developers and the application providers with no submission fee, no membership fee, no annual fee and no hidden costs. But we also didn't want to just open up a floodgate; we wanted to ensure a wide range of quality content.

How do you maintain a balance in the quality and quantity of apps in the store?

First, the submission process ensures quality. We have a set of competent policy guidelines and a review process. We don't only look at whether apps function. We examine if they have the right UX [user experience] and if they make the best use of the screen. We also consider if they really benefit the consumer.

CHRISTOPHER DAVID

Head of Developer and Partner Engagement, Sony Ericsson

We asked ourselves: 'Does the consumer need 15 Sudoku apps or do they want one relevant Sudoku app.' We opted for the latter.

It's not about providing thousands of apps; it's about providing consumers access to a couple of hundred relevant apps and keeping it fresh. The focus is to have around 100 apps and will not be much more than that. That said, to keep this number of apps fresh for the consumer requires us to turn around a much bigger number than that. I would say it needs to be 10X more and – from that – we pick and chose what gets shown to the consumers.

The idea seems to be to forge closer relationships with fewer developers. Is that what you're doing here?

Absolutely. And this approach is reflected in the categories of apps. We currently classify apps in three categories.

Category One is being a good citizen to a non-fragmented platform. What I mean here is compliancy. Whether it's for a Java platform or a Symbian platform or a Windows Mobile platform, we are always going to be compliant and make sure we're not fragmenting the core foundation of our ecosystem. Therefore, any application developer that wants to make use of the core, the API set and the features of that platform will find these applications will run 'as is' on our phones, requiring a minimum effort to adapt navigational keys, touch and non-touch, and things like that.

And it's this category that you provide consumers access to through partnerships such as the agreement you have with GetJar, an independent app store with 50,000+ applications on offer.

Yes. We figure why make it even more complicated for the developers? We're looking at this much more in terms of it being complimentary. So, Category One apps is the focus area of GetJar.

What is your focus as Sony Ericsson?

Our focus is on Category Two and Category Three apps. Category Two type apps are apps that could potentially run across the Sony Ericsson portfolio, independent of platform. Put another way, there are apps that would leverage the innovation that Sony Ericsson puts around and on top of the core platform. Examples could be apps that harness the advanced imaging capabilities in our phones, make use of face recognition technique, or utilize the OpenGLES and 2.0 3-D environments that we have in all our phones right now.

Category Three are apps that are much more optimal, much more unique and targeted for a specific Sony Ericsson phone. Here we look for third party applications that could potentially integrate well with that UX [user experience] and further enhance the overall proposition of a phone.

How do you encourage sales, which benefits developers, and discovery, to satisfy consumers?

Many developers are starting to re-think. Do they go for big, with the probability of being discovered very low, or do they go for a lower volume with a much higher probability of being discovered. The developer community is split.

Most users won't look beyond a top ten list when they're searching for apps. We're trying to change that by understanding what the consumers are doing. If they've seen an app several times and not picked it, then we want to present the consumer with an app that is more interesting, fresher. We're also trying to understand what's viral and what consumers are recommending.

What is the impact of app stores on the value chain?

I think we're a the starting point of all the crazy things people will do and it's not only what the developers will do but what the individual users will do. The value chain in itself I think it is pretty straight forward in terms of the players and what they do.

I believe that, over time, we will see scenarios where anyone can create applications. As that happens, and it's already happening on the Internet today, the mobile phone will become a place where a lot of us can make what we want. That will push the industry toward building more components and building things in a way that allows people to integrate those components.

What is the role of mobile operators?

One development is clear, even if it's slow: the industry is going toward a much more open approach, much more embracing. It's all about operators allowing others to participate much more in their ecosystem.

Operators will have an important role to play as a facilitator and this will allow them to play several roles. Can they be a billing provider? Can they be an identity provider? Can they be a channel to content and media? They can do a lot of things, but they also have to open up and allow for more people to participate on equal grounds and equal terms. I would not say may the best man win, but rather the consumer will choose.

APPLICATIONS FOR THE MASSES

GetJar is the world's largest cross-platform app store with over a half billion downloads to date. The company provides more than 50,000 mobile applications across all major handsets and platforms to consumers in more than 200 countries. In addition to distributing content directly to consumers, GetJar also works with a select number of distribution partners including but not limited to Sony Ericsson, Sprint, Opera, Vodafone, 3UK and Virgin Mobile. Patrick Mork discusses the models and monetization schemes that will transform app stores into software malls.

Let's start with the high-level view. What is the download traffic and what can you tell us about the trends you're seeing.

As you know, we support BlackBerry, Android, Symbian, Flash and Palm [operating systems] and we're seeing robust growth across all the platforms. A year ago, when I joined the company, we counted about 15 million downloads a month. In August [2009] we hit 55 million downloads a month. So, we're doing anywhere from 15 to 16 million downloads every week now, and the growth has been pretty significant over the past 12 months. We're distributing content to consumers in over 200 countries.

In the catalog, I think we have about 53,000 apps live across all the different platforms. Over half are Java apps, which continues to be the dominant platform. Obviously, the other platforms are gaining momentum on Java, so the issue is going to be how the numbers shift with the introduction of Android, the introduction of Windows Mobile 7 and all the efforts being made by Adobe. My guess is Java will lose weight next year.

Some critics warn the avalanche of app stores could confuse and overwhelm consumers. Do you expect a shift there?

It's early days, but I predict 75 to 80 percent of these app stores are going to fail over the next 24 months. The numbers are going to be high because there's a lot of hype around app stores, which has got a lot of players excited about getting into apps without knowing what is involved and the time and resources needed.

It's not a core competency for most companies and they don't realize how difficult

PATRICK MORK

Vice President Marketing, GetJar

Activation _ Applications for the masses

it is to moderate content, for example. The excitement around apps is a lot like the hype we saw around games in 2005. A lot of companies crashed and burned and I think a lot of app store initiatives are going to crash and burn.

Let's talk about GetJar's partnership with Sony Ericsson. In your view, is this the text book model for the future?
I think that it's going to be a model for a number of handset makers, particularly companies that lack the dedicated resources to build and maintain an app store. I think it's also going to be the model for a lot of carriers.
But that's not to say that independent app stores won't be successful. I think you'll have two polar extremes. At one end, you'll have an extremely open, fluid and democratic ecosystem, which is where you can find a GetJar or an Android. At the other end of the spectrum, you will have the super-closed, extremely rigid – yet very well oiled machine. An example here is the Apple App Store.
The guys who are really going to have a rough time are the ones in the middle. They don't have the size of an Android or a GetJar, nor do they have the quality experience and richness of the applications of an Apple. For the companies in the middle to be successful the solution will be a model like Sony Ericsson's, one that allows they to focus on their core competency - whether it's running networks or building handsets - and let the guys who understand content actually manage the content.

The partnership with Sony Ericsson is non-exclusive. Will you do more partnership deals in 2010?

Without giving away confidential information I can tell you that we're in a number of discussions with other equally important partners to do something very similar. In the next four to six weeks [interview conducted October 2009] you will hear of a significant partnership with a major U.S. carrier, which will be our first.
So, the GetJar strategy, as it unfolds, is going to be two pronged. The main focus will in terms of traffic and downloads will continue to be direct-to-consumer, which accounts for 95 percent of our traffic. The other focus will be to build and extend GetJar's distribution, as either a co-branded or a white-label solution, through partnerships like Sony Ericsson or with carriers.

What is the role of the mobile operator in the application value chain? Based on what we saw in the on-portal space many argue operators are not suited to retail content or apps.

I believe operators can play a fundamental role and there are many ways they can do this. Part of what they can do is make sure the interface of the handsets is more conducive to content discovery and download.

I find it shocking that, two years after the iPhone launch, so many handset manufacturers still continue to waste the retail space of their handsets. If you turn on a regular handset today, regardless of the maker, the majority of the home screen retail space is unused. I don't necessarily blame just the carriers; I also blame the handset vendors. If the operators could convince handset manufacturers to improve the user experience and also improve the handset interface to make content discovery easier, then that would help.

In what way?

Content discovery for many consumers is still easiest when they can find content directly embedded on their handsets. Some carriers have done a good job here. Vodafone Group and a couple of others have worked to get embedded, pre-loaded content on handsets.

So, there is a role for mobile operators to play. But I don't think they have a role to play in building app stores and managing content directly. I think that they need to leave to others.

What revenue share models work? There is the Apple model, which cuts out the carrier, and then there is GetJar, where you sell content but don't monetize it – yet.

There are a lot of models. In the case of GetJar, we make money through our pay-per download systems. Basically, developers are paying us and the content is given free to consumers. A major project for us in the next 12 months is to launch payments. Do we keep the revenue? Or do we share with a carrier partner? Or can we give a 100-percent share back to developers and charge them for top-notch placement in our app store? In that scenario we clearly make a lot more money on merchandising and retailing apps than we will from the actual sale. So, the short answer to the question is: there are many different monetization models out there and it's going to take some time to play out in terms of which one is going to be successful.

Mobile in 2010 is INTERACTION: Mobile continues to gain traction as the way we access content and communicate with our friends, peers and wider social networks.

Despite a difficult economic climate and a declining handset market, the mobile content market got a much needed boost from the advance of smartphones with multimedia capabilities and the emergence of more open distribution channels known as app stores .**See Activation, page 12**.

Application stores from a vibrant mix of mobile operators, platform providers and handset manufacturers ignited the mobile content market in 2009. But will it be too much of a good thing in 2010? Data from Screen Digest's Mobile Intelligence Service, for example, shows revenues from applications other than voice and messaging on mobile are set to reach €100 billion by end-2013. However, Screen Digest warns the exploding number of app stores and corresponding development platforms may also create unnecessary market fragmentation – and headaches for content companies that seek to monetize their apps across a slew of app stores from Apple, Google, Nokia, Samsung, Microsoft, Vodafone and Orange, to name a few.

"Companies such as Apple and Google have brought a much needed breath of fresh air to the mobile content industry by opening up the ecosystem, providing flexibility to developers and content providers, driving innovation and increasing consumer awareness," Ronan de Renesse, Screen Digest Senior Analyst, said in a press statement. "While 2009 proved that there is strong demand for mobile content, 2010 will be much more about how to sustain usage."

Growing confidence

Meanwhile, the Business Confidence Index, a report compiled for the Mobile Entertainment Forum (MEF), the global trade association of the mobile media industry, shows a positive attitude toward the app opportunity among companies surveyed. Despite an economic downturn, the industry reported it expects an average growth of 33 percent for the coming year, 6 percent more than expected at the beginning of 2009. Overall, respondents reckon 14 percent of their revenues will come from app downloads.

Table: Mobile Social Network Users Worldwide, 2008-2014 (millions and % penetration)

	2008	2009	2010	2011	2012	2013	2014
Mobile social network users*	76.0	141.4	223.4	318.3	454.0	607.5	760.1
% of mobile phone subscribers	1.9%	3.1%	4.6%	6.1%	8.4%	10.8%	13.3%
% of Mobile Internet users	19.0%	28.0%	34.0%	37.0%	40.0%	43.0%	45.0%

Note: as of December for each year; *CAGR (2008-2014)=46.8%
Source: eMarketer, November 2009

As Rimma Perelmuter, MEF Executive Director, put it: "The 'iPhone effect' has changed the industry's perspective on mobile applications. As a result, handset manufacturers and operators have launched their own app stores. This interest and activity raises the issue of fragmentation. Companies must bear the cost and complexity of developing apps for a wide variety of platforms and devices, but they also benefit from the existence of a huge and targeted market for apps." **See Interview, page 33**.

Social call

But applications weren't the only hot item in 2009. Mobile social networking continued to break records and exceed expectations around the globe.

In the U.S. social networking dominated mobile Web usage, with access to social networking websites accounting for almost half of total usage. According to October 2009 Mobile Insights report, a report complied by mobile software applications and infrastructure provider Openwave Systems, four of the top 10 web domains accessed via users on their mobile phones were social networking sites.

In Europe marketing research company comScore says a third of European mobile social networkers access nothing else from their phones. ComScore estimates there were 12.1 million mobile social networkers in Western Europe (France, Germany, Italy, Spain, U.K.) in November 2009, a figure that is up 152 percent from November 2007. U.K.

Mobile social networks are also flourishing in Africa and Latin America, according to new figures from market research firm Frost & Sullivan. It estimates the market for mobile social networks in Latin America and Africa is set to increase ten-fold to 527 million users and $2.4 billion in revenue by 2015.

But the real scope of the social networking phenomenon comes through in a new global forecast by market research firm eMarketer. It predicts the number of mobile users accessing social networks from their mobile devices will reach 607.5 million worldwide by 2013, representing 43 percent of global Mobile Internet users. **See Table**

Despite the promising user base, eMarketer reminds us that mobile social networking companies and marketers have yet to develop effective monetization models.

Flirtomatic, a U.K.-based pioneer mobile flirting service and one of the most popular social mobile services used by young adults in the U.K., Germany, Australia and the U.S., has cracked the code. It reports a string of successful campaigns with consumer-focused brands and plans to expand its premium ad sales. As Mark Curtis, Flirtomatic CEO, explains: "There are several ways we use the real estate at the top of the page. We sell it to commercial advertisers. And we are seeing renewed growth now after what has frankly been a pretty flat year up until three months ago." **See Interview, page 36**.

Games people play

Social networking is also becoming an element of mobile games. Market research firm IDC observes a distinct trend to community-based gaming that harnesses mobile social networks and, in some cases, location to engage users. In Japan, for example, game-related virtual communities flourish, with some games counting over 11 million regular users.

The interplay of mobile and social also sits at the center of Foursquare, a cult hit location-based social mobile iPhone app that rewards players for visiting local venues regularly (checking-in) and interacting with friends. In January 2010 Foursquare reported it was averaging more than one check-in per second, or an astounding 86,000 check-ins in a 24-hour span. The company hasn't publicly stated how many users it has, but – judging from the rate of check-ins – mobile industry news site TechCruch concludes the Foursquare social gaming community is extremely active and engaged.

Little wonder that more games publishers make the decision to wrap social features around their games. Companies including Zynga, Playfish and Digital Chocolate don't just integrate social elements into their games. They generate serious revenues from selling in-game items and encouraging what Digital Chocolate CEO Trip Hawkins calls "virtual item economics" as a means to increase the lifetime value of the customer relationship.

Against this backdrop, analyst firm DFC Intelligence predicts the global mobile and portable games market will be worth $11.7 billion in 2014. Meanwhile, market research firm Pyramid Research is slightly more optimistic. The popularity of apps

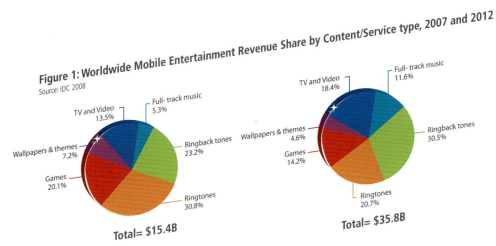

Figure 1: Worldwide Mobile Entertainment Revenue Share by Content/Service type, 2007 and 2012
Source: IDC 2008

and the uptake of social gaming will push the global mobile gaming market to $18 billion by 2014.

Full stream ahead

Another bright spot in 2009 was mobile music thanks to the popularity of music apps, the uptake of ringback tones, the success of bundled offers and subscriptions, and the excitement around music streaming.

Market research firm Juniper Research, which combines the revenues from all the categories of mobile music, pegged the market at just over $11 billion in 2008, a figure it predicts will rise to nearly $14.6 billion by 2013.

In its worldwide mobile entertainment forecast IDC reports mobile music continues to be the main driver of mobile entertainment services. Overall, it estimates total mobile entertainment spending will reach $35.8 billion in 2012, up from 15.4 billion in 2007. **See Figure**

The growth is fuelled by the continuing popularity of ringback tones (RBTs) in Asia/Pacific and a shift from more established categories of entertainment, such as ringtones, wallpapers and games, to full track music (FTM) downloads and mobile video. China, India, Japan and Korea together already represent some US$ 10 billion of forecasted 2010 mobile content revenues* for music, games, images, TV and video. (Source: Informa)

The impact of ad-supported streaming music services from Spotify and Deezer sparked an industry-wide debate about business models. Indeed, 2009 saw a string of companies jump on the streaming bandwagon. Dada Entertainment, a leading direct-to-consumer entertainment service, launched unlimited streaming for $10 a month, bundled with

* Please refer to the Country Data section in this Guide for the revenue forecasts for other countries.

five free DRM-free downloads; Skype founders unveiled a subscription-based streaming service called Rdio; and mobile operators such as Sweden's Telia and 3 UK join with Spotify to offer customers a premium version of the streaming music service.

Another milestone development that impacted the mobile music market at all levels was the decision by Vodafone to remove DRM from its music stores, adopting a strategy that first gave iTunes the edge.

Based on the unexpected flurry of activity in 2009, market research firm Juniper Research concludes that the freemium model (the basic service is offered for free, while charging a premium for advanced or special features) will become more widespread over the next five years.

The new variety of monetization models is good news to Sony Music Entertainment, which believes 2010 will be a banner year for music bundles and packages. As Ian Henderson, Vice President, Digital Business Development, Europe & Africa, Sony Music Entertainment, put it: "Until this year [2009], the subscription model wasn't happening in Europe. But that has changed and what changed it is companies such as Spotify and Deezer …showing that you can create a successful subscription service that lots of people will want to use. More importantly, get it right and there is a subset of customers willing to pay a premium price point for it. Vodafone also shows us that, if you've got the right kind of music tariff, that can add a lot of value for mobile operators." **See Interview, page 39.**

The increased popularity of bundles and the pivotal importance of social elements in a variety of mobile entertainment content are a clear sign that the barriers between content types and offers are blurring. Moving forward, mobile operators and service providers will need to be more flexible in how they create and charge for mobile content. It's a tall order but work invested in breaking down the silos that separate content to deliver customers discounted bundles will be richly rewarded. After all, customers who get what they want at a reduced price point will likely line up for more. And operators that can deliver such offers can count on additional volume for themselves and their content partners.

TAKING THE INITIATIVE

As the global trade association of the mobile media industry, Mobile Entertainment Forum (MEF) works on behalf of companies across the mobile entertainment value chain to drive mobile entertainment adoption, shape regulation and deliver competitive advantage to its members. In 2009, MEF continued its expansion, announcing new members and establishing a new chapter in Latin America. MEF also unveiled a number of industry initiatives including Content Sales Reporting, which addresses the need for accurate reporting, and Smart Pipe Enablers, aimed at devising a workable model for enabling services and accelerating their uptake. Rimma Perelmuter updates us on progress and discusses the current state of the content industry.

Let's start with the MEF initiatives. What have you achieved and why are these initiatives core to your mission?

An ongoing debate has focused on the role of the mobile operator and whether they will become 'dumb pipes', carrying – but not sharing in – the value of mobile entertainment, or 'smart pipes,' earning revenue by providing valuable services to the content industry. The global mobile entertainment industry is worth about $32 billion dollars, of which nearly half is generated by content sales and services uptake 'off-portal.' In other words, companies other than the operator are involved. These companies increasingly rely on operators to provide so-called 'enabling services – such as bulk SMS, premium billing capability and shortcode number rental – that 'enable' them to create, deliver and bill for their mobile content or service. To date many operator groups are working on defining and implementing a new generation of 'smart pipe' enabling services. However, the content industry had not been involved.

Our Smart Pipe Enablers initiative changes this, ensuring that media, content owners and retailers have a say in the functionalities and features included in these enabling services. The MEF initiative provides a forum for content owners and providers to discuss enabling services and communicate their requirements. To date we have held two educational webinars and are producing a

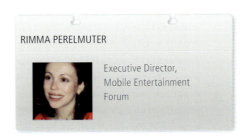

RIMMA PERELMUTER

Executive Director, Mobile Entertainment Forum

guide we plan to publish in Q2 2010. Input from the content industry is vital to ensuring that mobile operators produce enabling services which enhance the user experience and meet the needs of the content marketplace.

For 2010, MEF is forecasting that operator enabling services will start to be widely deployed, facilitating the growth of rich media content that is simpler, faster and offers a better user experience.

As you say, off-portal activity and sales are significant. But it's no longer limited to mobile downloadable content. What are the chief mobile commerce opportunities and what is the MEF doing to facilitate this?

The recession, advances in mobile banking and an increase in the number of NFC pilots and services are all raising interest in m-commerce. While mobile operators are still the main payment processors, we are also seeing third-party systems used to process payments, particularly micro-payments. The growth in micro-payments can be linked to an increased willingness of consumers to pay for things like car parking and theater tickets with their mobile phones.

The market is changing and demanding leadership in mobile commerce. To this end, MEF will explore the evolution of m-commerce in an online guide and handbook for Q2 2010. The aim is to help brands, content producers and retailers better understand how to leverage the mobile phone to drive customer acquisition, retention and create a high quality user experience.

MEF has also launched a Content Sales Reporting (CSR) initiative. Why the interest?

By surveying the industry, MEF identified that up to 10 percent of gross revenues are lost because of a lack of consistent and timely CSR. Our initiative addresses the need to establish best practices in reporting content sales regardless of region and mobile content type. We subsequently produced a generic template based which is now being used by the TM Forum, an industry association for service providers and their suppliers, to develop a working model for CSR. Working in collaboration, in 2010 MEF will hold a webinar and publish a guide showing how the issues of mobile content and advertising revenue management can be resolved.

In 2009, MEF's Third Business Confidence Index (BCI) found that members predicted an average revenue growth for the mobile entertainment industry of 33 percent, 6 percent more than expected at the beginning of 2009. What other surveys can you share that shed light on the state of the market?

The Business Confidence Index indicates that the industry is quite upbeat about the outlook for mobile entertainment but we also wanted insights into what consumers think. So, we conducted the global MEF Consumer and Convergence survey of 4,000 consumers in 19 countries with KPMG in March [2009]. It revealed that consumer satisfaction with mobile music downloads is fairly high, with almost a third [30 percent] of consumers having purchased songs on their mobile phones in the last year and 66 percent satisfied with their download experience. The top factors impacting respondents' choices for their next music download were clear pricing [84 percent] and cost [83 percent].

It also found that almost half of consumers [49 percent] would be willing to receive advertisements on their mobile phones for free music downloads. However, respondents revealed an unwillingness to receive advertisements on their mobiles without an incentive or without receiving free content in exchange. In addition, the study found that 38 percent of respondents had watched video clips on their mobile phones in the last year.

What are the growth opportunities in 2010 and beyond?
The 'iPhone effect' has changed the industry's perspective on mobile applications. As a result, handset manufacturers and operators have launched their own app stores. This interest and activity raises the issue of fragmentation. Companies must bear the cost and complexity of developing apps for a wide variety of platforms and devices, but they also benefit from the existence of a huge and targeted market for apps.

This development is a key trend in our top ten forecast for 2010. We predict fragmentation will continue to plague the industry. However, the growth of applications on the Android platform will close the gap on Apple's App Store. We also expect media publishers will start to experiment with micro-payments, subscription service models and alternative payment methods, challenging the operators' dominance, with Rupert Murdoch's decision to charge for online media content highlighting an already fierce debate.

The industry will need to also grapple with a number of issues. The growing consumer demand for data-heavy services will put greater pressure on networks, with flat rate data tariffs increasingly subjected to stringent download limits. The emerging risk of illicit charging by in-app billing will be met by firm regulatory action. The complexity, confusion and ambiguity in the application of rights to the mobile platform will also be addressed seriously in 2010.

At the same time, some exciting developments are underway for the consumer. We are forecasting the emergence of books as a new and popular content category for smartphones and widespread experimentation with 3-D mobile video viewers and augmented reality for mobile. Finally, 2010 will be the year of multiplatform dual-delivery of content including music, video and games, across mobile phones, TVs and PCs.

FLIRTING FOR FUN AND PROFIT

U.K.-based Flirtomatic is a pioneer mobile flirting service and one of the most popular social mobile services used by young adults in the U.K., Germany, Australia and the U.S. It counts over 1.7 million registered users and distribution partnerships with Vodafone, T-Mobile, Orange, ninemsn, ProSiebenSat1, and Samsung. But it's not just about flirting and fun; Flirtomatic has successfully monetized its traffic through virtual gifting and mobile advertising thanks to deals with ad networks such as AdMob and major brands including L'Oreal, o2 and Strongbow. Mark Curtis talks about the company's transformation from meeting place to marketplace.

Flirtomatic stands out as a cross-media mobile social network that is also highly regarded as a thriving mobile business. What has contributed to this success?

For that you have to look at the company history. At first we thought the supreme user experience would win out on the phone; and Java was the place to deliver that supreme user experience. However, it soon became clear to us that this assumption was wrong. Java proved to be flawed for what we wanted to do, which was deliver a complex, rich and ever-changing social experience as opposed to a one-off games download. We switched tactics to focus on the Mobile Internet, and we have never really looked back.

What is your strategy for apps?

Apple has convincingly demonstrated that supreme user experience does win out.

We will soon launch an Apple app and one for Android next year. This, of course, complicates the life of a company trying to innovate rapidly, because we will be working across four platforms. We're on the fixed Internet as well.

In my view, there is a high likelihood that things will swing back to a browser-based environment over the next two or three years. Good mobile browsers are already capable of doing quite a lot of things that you can do in an app, so the world will probably swing back to a browser experience because users won't be able to tell the difference.

How has your approach to monetization changed over the years and why?

We started with what I would call a pay-for-access model. We never went down the route of the automatically renewed subscriptions because we felt it was not customer friendly.

MARK CURTIS
CEO, Flirtomatic

We saw an enormous number of page views and that made us think that there's an advertising opportunity here. At around the same time AdMob appeared on the scene and we became one of AdMob's first publishers. From there, offering virtual goods as a means to generate additional revenues was a three-minute thought.

You offer virtual gifting, allowing users to buy each other witty items. But you also enable members to advertise themselves to the group. Where is the growth opportunity in advertising?
There are lots of rich answers here. You can sell advertising to a commercial advertiser and you can also make money with your customers. There are several ways we use the real estate at the top of the page. We sell it to commercial advertisers. And we are seeing renewed growth now after what has frankly been a pretty flat year up until three months ago.

I might add that we brought someone from Blyk [the world's first ad-funded MVNO] on board to sell premium ad sales and create new advertiser- based creative solutions for advertisers. She's been with us now for three months and that's also why the revenues are beginning to role in.

How do you see the overall outlook for mobile advertising?
We think mobile advertising is going to grow very strongly over the next few years. The market is still in its infancy and the Google-AdMob deal could be regarded in Churchillean tones as the 'end of the beginning.' Now we move into the next phase.
To go back to that Churchill quote, the end of the beginning was pretty early in the Second World War, and there's still a long way to go in mobile advertising. We haven't yet conquered the question: are banners the ultimate format? We're seeing some significant changes as a result of the iPhone. AdMob have done some interesting experimentation there and we'll see more on Android.

You are particularly bullish about premium ad sales side of your business. Please update us on your progress to date.
The premium ad side is about creating solutions with advertisers that integrate more deeply into our products. A classic example of this approach is the Strongbow campaign we did a little over a year ago. The company ran a campaign that allowed Flirtomatic users to send each other a virtual pint of Strongbow cider. The recipients then received a voucher on their mobile phones, which they could redeem at participating pubs. The campaign exceeded our expectations, with 365,000 pints sent by users to their friends.

You are expanding to new commercial areas, such as premium, and new regions, such as the U.S. How do you maintain the momentum?
The key to this is to move away from a belief that what one has created is a platform. Companies that offered a chat platform to operators weren't building a brand; they were delivering a platform through which people could talk to each other. Our strategy has been slightly different. We always wanted to have a voice with our users and decided at an early stage that Flirtomatic would be a service that would speak to its members and so users would be accustomed to hearing from us.
If you use Facebook, MySpace Twitter, you don't expect to hear that much from them. They're in the background and they offer a

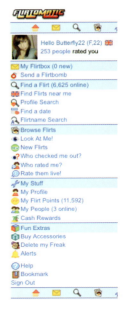

platform you use to communicate. We talk to our users quite a lot, so much so that we see ourselves as being more like a media owner than a platform provider. We have built our success – and continue to succeed – because of the mindset that we're a media owner.

Being a media owner gives us permission to say to users 'hey, we're going to have some fun here with Halloween'. This allows us to promote fun and offers, and this also gives us differentiation from dating sites that can't do promotions.

Can you provide examples?

We do something called 'bundle days,' when we give users access to a whole load of services at reduced prices. It's just like doing a two-for-one offer. And when we last did this we saw our revenue triple.

We do outbound communication, which is aimed to drive revenues and engagement with the customer the customer. But we also focus on the customer and responding to their needs. Investing in the team and taking the time to deal with customers has two great benefits: we're close to our customer base, and they trust us to give them live and instant feedback.

SUPER MODEL

Sony Music Entertainment (formerly Sony BMG Music Entertainment) – the number two recording business in the world behind Universal Music Group – turned up the volume in 2009, taking the wraps off an impressive line-up of digital and mobile music ventures. It began the year by sealing a deal with Kyte, an online and mobile video platform provider, allowing its artists and labels to engage directly with fans. For an encore the recording company joined with Vodafone, the first global operator to offer DRM-free music across mobile devices and PCs. Sony also unveiled plans to add music downloads to the PlayStation Network (PSN), expanding it into a full digital download store, offering music, books and mobile apps. Music video also got a boost when Sony teamed up with other labels and Google to launch Vevo, an online music video joint venture that, despite a few initial technical bugs, is expected to be a promising venture in 2010. Ian Henderson talks about the models are igniting interest in downloads and the future of music.

What are the projects and pricing models highest on your radar?
I'm excited about two developments. One is the advance of the freemium model with partners like Spotify, a proprietary peer-to-peer music streaming service that allows instant listening to specific tracks or albums, with virtually no buffering delay. Spotify's model is built on a free, ad-supported Web-based service and then, if users want, they can pay to access their music account on their iPhone, Android, Blackberry or Nokia smartphone. It's great that we in the industry have a dual-tier level of service where, at one level, the free service offer gets people away from illegal download sites and piracy. At the same time, we can offer a premium level of the service by leveraging the new and quickly developing smartphone application platforms to make some good money.

The second is the work we're doing with major operator groups like Vodafone to create subscription offerings. Vodafone has been particularly aggressive in not only trying out different subscription offerings, but also in rolling them out over many territories, including the U.K., Germany, Spain, Portugal, Greece and The Netherlands. For example, Vodafone is trying 'all-you-can-eat'

IAN HENDERSON

Vice President, Digital Business Development, Europe & Africa, Sony Music Entertainment

offers that resemble a music rental service. But they also offer limited MP3 bundles – so, ten MP3s a month for €5 or £5 – at half price iTunes would charge. We see that those MP3 bundles seem to be doing really well with customers and so we're naturally excited about that going into 2010.

Just a year ago the industry had its doubts about the subscription model for content. What happened to change this?

Yes, until this year [2009], the subscription model wasn't happening in Europe. But that has changed and what changed it is companies such as Spotify and Deezer, a free and legal French-based music streaming website, showing that you can create a successful subscription service that lots of people will want to use. More importantly, get it right and there is a subset of customers willing to pay a premium price point for it. Vodafone also shows us that, if you've got the right kind of music tariff, that can add a lot of value for mobile operators.

What has changed? One, record labels are more willing to try some new approaches. Obviously, to make Vodafone's ten MP3 per month subscription work we have to offer people music at a price point that's significantly lower than iTunes. But if we work together to attract and retain subscribers, then we're going to make more money over time. Downloads on iTunes are a one-time purchase. Vodafone is half-price, but it is a monthly subscription. We have partnerships with both companies. Second, the smartphone application platform allows a variety of music content and technology companies to monetize the users that might otherwise just be using free, pirated services.

And, finally, I think the key driver is the outstanding execution, especially by Spotify, and the creation of a great user experience. To be clear, Spotify wasn't the first to do free on-demand streaming. But it was the first to take the concept to the next level with features that let users easily and intuitively search and play music, and create a playlist with simple drag-and-drop. To top it off Spotify has done a lot of clever technical things to make using Spotify faster than using MP3s that are on your computers on hard drive.

As you point out, the freemium model is gaining traction. What other progress had been made to combat piracy?

Part of it is about offering services that can compete with illegal services. The other part is that, in 2009, we also saw European governments starting to agree with music companies and understanding that piracy impacts national economies. The Swedish government enforced some strict legislation and prosecuted the founders of Pirate Bay, a major illegal download site that has been called the most visible member of an anti-copyright movement. In France we saw the passage of a three-strike law that warns the users of illegal services and might eventually even disconnect their broadband. Spain is often cited as one of the biggest users of peer-to-peer sharing in the world. But now there is new enthusiasm there, among entrepreneurs and telecom companies, for freemium services and offers that lure people away from free illegal services.

What happened to the buzz about ad-supported content and models and the combination of music and mobile social networks?

In my view, a pure advertising model is

probably not going to make much money, and it's certainly not going to be profitable in the current global advertising environment. A hybrid model offers the basis for an interesting business model. If we go back to Spotify and Deezer, they have several revenue streams. One is advertising and the other is subscription. They are also able to sell MP3 à la carte. It's the combination of those three that lays the groundwork for what starts to look like an interesting and profitable business.

Once music services start getting integrated into social networks, it's going to take them to an entirely different level. You already see Vodafone pursuing such as strategy. In fact, you could argue that Vodafone 360, their new social network platform, is about the interplay between music and social networks. Vodafone is also focused on developing its own music services through a partnership with Real Networks. Moving forward, you're also going to see companies such as Deezer and Spotify try to integrate with platforms like Facebook.

Music content is a great fit with video and mobile TV. Smartphones and the iPhone have boosted interest in and usage of video content. Are you experimenting with new content types for these new platforms?

Actually, we have been working for a little over a year now on a project that does take advantage of this trend and Apple's increasing focus on video. To this end we have created a small but growing library of concert videos that we call 'long-form' videos. It's different from the typical MTV three- to four-minute videos in that it is a long-form video of an entire concert. As Apple becomes more focused on movie-type content, there's definitely a place for long-form content. As we productize more of these content types we're also finding that there's a number of platforms out there - like the on-demand platforms run by large telcos and cable operators in the U.S. – that want access to this content as well. It's a relatively new focus for us and one we think is going to be a growing product category.

CONVERSATION

MARKETING
ADVERTISING
COMMUNICA-
TION
CUSTOMER
CARE
CAMPAIGNS

Mobile in 2010 is CONVERSATION: consumers connect with brands they appreciate and brands talk back. The result is direct, anytime, anywhere, two-way exchanges between people and the companies that serve them.

Google's purchase of AdMob for $750 million in stock in November 2009 and the news that Apple had followed the search giant's lead in January 2010, snapping up mobile ad network Quattro Wireless for $270 million, was read as a much needed validation of mobile marketing and a confirmation of its true potential. As Paul Palmieri, CEO of Millennial Media, a mobile advertising network and solutions provider with largest mobile media audience in the U.S, put it in a press statement at the time: "Google validated what many companies including Millennial Media has known for years – that mobile is a different market with a huge potential for advertising, possibly a bigger opportunity than online media."

Together the two milestone acquisitions pushed the value of the mobile advertising industry passed the $1 billion mark, strengthening the business case for mobile and heralding a banner year for mobile advertising everywhere. "If there is any doubt that 2010 is the year of Mobile Advertising, Apple just cleared up any speculation," commented Paran Johar, CMO of JumpTap, provider of targeting and mobile advertising solutions. "For pessimists who thought the Google acquisition of AdMob was a fluke, this reinforces that mobile advertising is here to stay."

The majority of industry analysts reflected this new optimism in their mobile advertising and marketing forecasts, although many revised their numbers to account for the worldwide economic slowdown. Market research firm eMarketer, for example, reported that mobile ad spending, including messaging-based formats, will reach $416 million in 2009, compared with the nearly $24 billion that will be spent for online marketing. **See Figure 1**

However, eMarketer stressed spending on mobile advertising will gain momentum over the next five years, reaching $1.56 billion by 2013. Key drivers are the increase in smartphone penetration and the number of marketers and brands moving from experimentation to execution. "Mobile has an additive effect on other advertising and

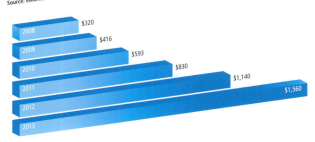

Figure 1: US Mobile advertising Spending, 2008-2013 (millions)
Note: includes display, search and messaging based advertising
Source: eMarketer, September 2009

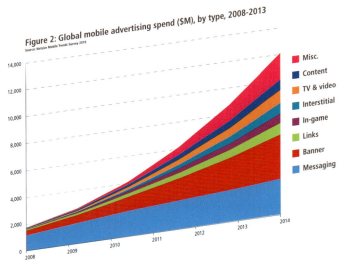

Figure 2: Global mobile advertising spend ($M), by type, 2008-2013
Source: Netsize Mobile Trends Survey 2010

marketing efforts, and can bridge the gap between digital and traditional campaigns," the report concludes. "It is also flexible, lending itself to both direct response and brand reinforcement and awareness campaigns."

In its 2009 report on Mobile Content and Mobile Advertising Revenues, Informa Telecoms & Media forecast that total annual adspend on mobile advertising – via channels including SMS, MMS, personal messaging, idle screen, mobile TV and in-app promotion – would exceed US$ 12 billion by 2013. However, it should be pointed out that this figure is equal to just 2.5 percent of total global ad spend. **See Figure 2**

A detailed breakdown of adspend by channel shows heightened interest and investment across all types of advertising, with fastest growth presented by in-game, interstitial, TV/video, and content ads, whilst messaging and banner advertising types remain the largest categories. It links this to increased realization among brands and

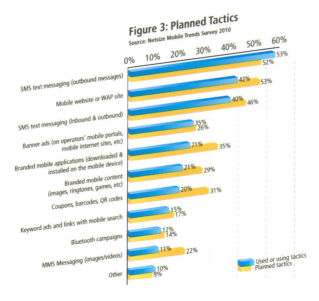

Figure 3: Planned Tactics
Source: Netsize Mobile Trends Survey 2010

marketers that mobile does indeed offer unparalleled opportunity for consumer engagement – provided the messages are personal, relevant and permission-based.

Getting personal

The pivotal importance of personalized messaging is echoed in Netsize Mobile Marketing Survey 2009: Can companies and brands rise to challenge and cash in on the mobile marketing opportunity? The report drawing from an online survey of 220+ professionals and practitioners conducted by Netsize to identify the chief drivers and obstacles impacting mobile marketing growth.

Specifically, the survey uncovered a decidedly positive attitude among respondents toward mobile marketing approaches and formats that build on the popularity and usability of text messaging and made-for-mobile destinations. A whopping 40% of respondents expect their messaging volume to increase significantly in the next six months (compared to the past 12 months). **See Figure 3**

When asked about their future plans and choice of communications channels, respondents expressed strong and continued interest in SMS messaging (inbound and outbound in order to create and continue customer dialogue) and WAP/websites (to present consumers exciting options and destinations after they click on a text link or a display banner). The Netsize survey also revealed that branded applications, branded content, mobile coupons and bar code campaigns were also at the top of the mobile marketing agenda.

Picture perfect

Sensing a business opportunity, a growing number of mobile operators, marketers and publishers are embracing 2D bar codes to enhance mobile marketing campaigns and engage with consumers via their camera phones. To date more than 70 percent of all mobile phones have a camera, a feature marketers are understandably anxious to harness to interact with consumers and bridge the physical and digital worlds. In this scenario, consumers can photograph or 'scan', bar codes printed on any media or packaging to launch a specific website or Web-based application, download content or a coupon, dial a phone number, compose an SMS/email, or receive a contact or calendar appointment.

Scanbuy, the leading provider of mobile marketing solutions that use a 2D bar code, believes 2010 marks the tipping point for this technology and a vast range of vertical business models. "In the long term barcodes enable a range of models around marketing, advertising and commerce. In the short term there will be pockets of activity that outstrip others. We're seeing big brands use barcodes to create interactivity with their printed materials, printed materials, in-store promotions and product packaging," states Jonathan Bulkeley, Scanbuy CEO. **See Interview page 89.**

Moving ahead, the most exciting opportunity is the new interactivity this technology can bring to standard one-dimensional bar codes already displayed on hundreds of millions of consumer items. In practice, Bulkeley says, marketers could use the Scanbuy platform to create a link between these 1D bar codes and their mobile websites, campaigns or offers.

Speak to me

Marketers are also urged to use the tools at their disposal to step up relationship marketing and loyalty programs. Indeed, the increasing importance of mobile in a range of schemes to secure brand loyalty, build customer relationships, encourage ongoing dialogue and create buzz about products and services comes across loud and clear in a series of commentaries published by market research firm eMarketer. It advises brands to rethink how they engage with the customer and build brand loyalty based on the communication of "more intangible, emotional values."

Figure 4: New Media user overwhelminlgy believe companies or brands should have a presence in the new media environment and interact with consumers
Source: Netsize Mobile Trends Survey 2010

Companies or brands should have a presence in new media and interact with consumers regularly — 36%

Companies or brands should have a presence in new media but only interact with consumers as needed or by request — 53%

Companies or brands should can have a presence in new media but should not interact with consumers — 7%

Companies or brands should not have a presence in new media — 5%

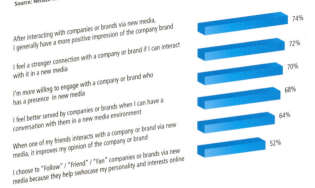

Figure 5: New media users think more highly of companies or brands when they or their friends can interact with them in a new media environment
Source: Netsize Mobile Trends Survey 2010

After interacting with companies or brands via new media, I generally have a more positive impression of the company brand — 74%

I feel a stronger connection with a company or brand if I can interact with it in a new media — 72%

I'm more willing to engage with a company or brand who has a presence in new media — 70%

I feel better served by companies or brands when I can have a conversation with them in a new media environment — 68%

When one of my friends interacts with a company or brand via new media, it improves my opinion of the company or brand — 64%

I choose to "Follow" / "Friend" / "Fan" companies or brands via new media because they help swhocase my personality and interests online — 52%

Ironically, creating an ongoing and meaningful dialogue with customers might only require companies to embrace tools and technologies such as social networks, microblogs, mobile devices or video-sharing sites – or all of the above. This is the view of Cone, a strategy and communications agency engaged in building brand trust. Its 2009 Cone Consumer Media Study, based on an online survey of 587 U.S. consumers aged 18 years and older, found that consumers develop "positive feelings" towards brands they felt they could interact with on new media channels. **See Figures 4 & 5**

"If companies are going to be a mainstay in new media, they're going to have to realize consumers expect more than a passive existence," concludes Mike Hollywood, Cone's Director of New Media. "New media are about experience, dialogue and immediacy. There was a time when just being in new media got you the gold star for effort. But consumers are continually refining their expectations and more and more are looking for specific interactions."

Genuinely useful

What do consumers really want from brands? It's a tough question, but the Global Web Index, a recent report from market research firm Lightspeed Research offers some important insights on the U.S. market.

It found that Americans want brands that provide utility. Among the responses: helping consumers keep up to date with relevant news and analysis was rated important. In addition, brands should be entertaining and become part of a daily routine.

For Rory Sutherland, Ogilvy UK Vice Chairman, the most successful brands may be the ones that combine their message with branded utilities and life-simplifying services. In an interview with MSearchGroove, a leading source of strategic mobile industry analysis, Sutherland advised marketers to make more use out of the direct feedback channel mobile provides in their campaigns and efforts to engage customers and build brand loyalty. "Advertising is talking and listening. Mobile is brilliant [because] you can do it in real-time."

Moving forward, Paul Berney, Managing Director Europe, Mobile Marketing Association, believes brands will harness mobile CRM tools such as reminders to increase the ongoing value and convenience they deliver their customers. "Appointment reminders, bank balance texts, paying for parking or congestion charges are all ways to interact with the customer via mobile. But they are also mobile CRM tools that make it possible for brands to engage with their audience on a deeper level. This communication represents a new opportunity for brands to embed themselves in the customer's daily routine."

Clearly, advertisers won't get far if they insist on using mobile to deliver a one-to-many pitch. It's about enabling a balanced exchange that respects our personal space and excites our individual passions.

CALL TO ACTION

The last 12 months have been transformational for the Mobile Marketing Association (MMA) and the mobile marketing ecosystem it represents. The global non-profit trade association made significant progress, clearing chief obstacles to market development and identifying best practices to support sustainable industry growth. To this end, the organization increased its presence through councils and partnerships in Brazil and Germany; launched the MMA Global Research Panel, the industry's first research capability to collect data via the mobile channel; and continued to ensure the adoption of industry standards by issuing the Mobile Ad Guidelines, the Code of Conduct and an updated definition of Mobile Marketing. Paul Berney talks about the growth opportunities and the positive outlook for mobile CRM.

Mobile marketing appears to be crossing the chasm. How does that change your work and your role in the industry?

With more than 700 members globally the MMA is now bigger and stronger than ever. We've opened regional branches in Latin America and Asia, and the EMEA branch has continued to grow apace with strong local councils in the U.K., Spain, France, Germany, Ireland and Austria with new councils launched this in year in South Africa and Turkey as well. Elsewhere we have added councils in the Philippines and India. Having achieved success with the mobile elements of the ecosystem, our focus is increasingly on working with brands and agencies, showing them how they can benefit from the mobile channel.

Your main focus is to educate and evangelize. Where does the certification program for mobile marketers fit in?

MMA Track, open to individuals and organizations involved in marketing at any skill level, is designed to educate them on industry terminology, budgeting and financial planning for mobile campaigns, regulatory requirements and industry best practices in mobile marketing. We see the program as benefiting the entire mobile marketing ecosystem by ensuring the highest industry standards and providing a seal of approval that brands, agencies and other employees

PAUL BERNEY

Managing Director Europe, Mobile Marketing Association

can use to identify the individuals and organizations best qualified to create and execute mobile marketing campaigns. It is a major part of the MMA's collaborative approach, and it is our aim to ensure that the qualification is used and recognized by the entire industry as the de facto standard for a mobile marketer.

This program is for companies across the mobile marketing ecosystem. How is the value chain shaping up?

The mobile value chain is the structure that allows mobile communications and interactivity to take place between brands, content owners and marketing agencies and mobile subscribers, or consumers. The ecosystem consists of four interconnecting strategic spheres: Product & Services, made up of brands, content owners and marketing agencies; Applications, which brings together application providers and mobile ASPs; Connection, which is where we find a variety of aggregators and mobile operators; and Media and Retail, which is the group that spans media properties, and 'bricks and mortar' and virtual retail stores. In order for mobile marketing to take off all the spheres have to work together. That's where the MMA comes in. We are the glue between all of the different players in the industry, educating and evangelizing the mobile channel for use by brands and content providers.

Moving forward, companies will group and emerge as the new power brokers in mobile marketing. One such group will be the brands. They will essentially fund the whole system. At their side the enablers, the players capable of getting the brands' message to consumers, will also have a role to play. The other group, or power block, will be made up of the companies that control the inventory. They will have power because the actual placing of the ads and programs into the content stream will play deciding major role in generating the ROI for the mobile campaign. In the end, it's all about ROI; it's what motivates brands to go mobile and it's what drives the system.

How does 2009 compare to 2008 in terms of mobile marketing interest and investment?

Despite the economic downturn and fears it would negatively impact the acceleration of the mobile market, we've actually seen brands begin to move away from more traditional media such as press and TV to focus on mobile. In fact, a recent MMA survey found that average mobile marketing budgets are likely to increase by 26 percent this year [2009] even as overall marketing expenditures decline by 7 percent. We project that mobile ad spend will grow from $1.7 billion this year to $2.16 billion in 2010. Another positive development was the heightened interest by major brands in mobile marketing. Nike, BMW, Lufthansa, Coca Cola, Unilever and Procter and Gamble are out there actively marketing on mobile, and they have made mobile a line item in their budgets.

What can be done to accelerate the adoption of mobile marketing and, at the same time, safeguard consumer interests?

There are some universal inhibitors to the growth of the mobile channel that the MMA has addressed in 2009 and will continue to focus on moving forward. Specifically, the industry needs more brand and agency education, meaningful measurement and metrics, and initiatives that create standards and clear specific barriers to growth.

It's crucial that we make consumers aware of all of the systems and policing mechanisms in place to ensure that their mobile marketing experience is a positive one. After all, the mobile is a highly personal device and consumers that accept marketing messages on their devices need to have confidence in marketers and what they will and will not do with the personal information consumers have shared out of trust.

In practice, marketers must manage and limit he messages they deliver to a reasonable number. More importantly they must make a commitment not to share consumer information with non-affiliated third-parties. To this end, the MMA has published a Global Code of Conduct and the Consumer Best Practices Guidelines in North America. These documents guide companies within the mobile ecosystem so they may effectively and responsibly leverage the mobile channel for marketing purposes, while always protecting the consumer experience.

The recent Netsize Mobile Marketing survey revealed a huge interest in mobile CRM. Is this the next growth opportunity?

Make no mistake about it: mobile CRM will be one of the growth areas of mobile and a major driver in obtaining consumer adoption of the channel. Operators, brands and digital agencies are all focusing on personalization, targeting, direct engagement and the quality of interaction in order to achieve a sustained dialogue with the customer. Of course, the ultimate measure is the lifetime value of a customer. And this is where mobile CRM comes in. It increases the value of the customer and boosts their brand loyalty. How? Appointment reminders, bank balance texts, paying for parking or congestion charges are all ways to interact with the customer via mobile. But they are also mobile CRM tools that make it possible for brands to engage with their audience on a deeper level. This communication represents a new opportunity for brands to embed themselves in the customer's daily routine. What better way to achieve differentiation and deepen personal contact?

LINKING MOBILE, INTERNET AND E-COMMERCE

Despite the economic downturn mobile appeared to be the bright spot in many industry reports. This was certainly true in the U.K., where the Internet Advertising Bureau (IAB), the trade association for digital advertising in the U.K., published the first-ever mobile ad spend figures. Among the key findings: GBP 28.6 million was spent on mobile in 2008, a figure almost double the previous year. Overall, investment in mobile advertising grew at a faster rate than predicted as more brands invested in the medium due to its exceptional targeting, immediacy and return on investment. Jon Mew looks at the campaigns and formats likely to take it to the next level.

Mobile advertising is about experimentation but it's also more about execution with more brands and agencies getting involved. How has this impacted the IAB and your mission?

Over the last two years we have seen a quick evolution of mobile advertising: Looking back at 2008, there was a 100 percent increase in mobile advertising spend. While we don't have official figures for 2009, we've certainly seen that spend is still on the up.

Our mission has evolved with the market trend. In 2009 our focus was very much on delivering the fundamentals. It was all about showing the effectiveness of mobile, educating the market and helping companies understand who's doing what on mobile.

That's still going to be a focus for us moving forward. However, our mission is also expanding. It's still about helping companies understand the basics in mobile; but it's also about looking at how mobile integrates with other media. It's also about looking at the connection with mobile commerce and how that is changing.

Mobile allows a two-way conversation with consumers, so there is an opportunity to encourage real commerce. However, the feedback channel mobile offers could be harnessed to improve Customer Relationship Management (CRM) as well. Where to you see the growth opportunity?

I think they will both become a lot more important. To be honest, mobile commerce has been centered on mobile content. But the iPhone and the App Store have gone a long

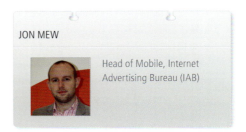

JON MEW

Head of Mobile, Internet Advertising Bureau (IAB)

way to prove that, when you get them the model right, people are quite happy buying stuff on their phones.

If we draw a parallel to the Internet, advertising and marketing took off when e-commerce took off. That was the point when brands realized they could go the whole journey, from getting people to interact with the brand to engaging them through to the final purchase. As far as mobile CRM goes, it will definitely increase, just as we have seen it increase online. After all, marketing via mobile is changing. It's more about engaging customers and building a dialogue, than making a pitch.

Who "gets" mobile, in your opinion? What are examples of campaigns that set the bar?

Nike has done some fantastic stuff. They have thought about the context in which consumers use mobile and built solutions that work better on mobile than on any other media. Take Nike Bootcamp, an award-winning campaign centered on teaching and training consumers. It included a free-to-download app complete with a range of training aids, allowing users to improve tempo, speed and performance. It also let users record test scores and results and receive daily and weekly training reminders.

Other good campaigns emphasize engaging with customer. Walkers [a U.K.-based maker of snack foods] have also done some fantastic campaigns. One that stands out asked consumers to suggest names for a new flavor of potato chips, using mobile and online as a response mechanism. The brand also got customers to vote for the flavor they wanted most. When you interact with your customers in this way, as this brand did, it's also a clever way of thinking because you're encouraging people to select what they would pay for. It's valuable input from the customers that confirms you are launching a product that's likely to do very well.

Indeed, there are many examples. But there is also a set of common characteristics that distinguish a good mobile campaign. They tend to be personalized, innovative and useful.

Where does that leave text messaging? It's the most popular format now. How will that be moving forward?

Text messaging is still really important because it's what everyone can do with their phones. The stuff that tends to excite brands more is the new stuff and cool new technologies such as AR [Augmented Reality]. But the reality is text is still what is most valuable and useful to consumers. There is also a lot of potential in mobile vouchers and coupons, particularly for FMCG [Fast Moving Consumer Goods] brands. It's still quite early days – at least in the U.K. – for QR codes and 2-D barcode campaigns.

We've also asked our members about apps and companies have definitely gone app crazy. They are particularly excited about branded apps, so I think there will be massive growth in this in the next year or so. Personally, I'm not sure that will continue forever. Once the browsers get better on mobile devices, then you start to question why you'd want to put effort into building an app when you could build something for a browser that would be accessible on every handset.

Brands and agencies are more involved in mobile advertising. Are they noticing new or additional obstacles that were less obvious last year when many were just dipping their toe in the water?

Judging from the feedback we get and the research we do amongst our members, the number one barrier is lack of understanding. In the case of mobile advertising – and even more so with mobile commerce - brands just aren't aware of what's possible with mobile. Of course, there are other barriers, such as convincing companies to put in the effort to build a separate mobile strategy and a mobile Web presence. But the number one barrier is just getting companies to understand what they can do with mobile.

That's a particularly interesting observation because it dovetails well with the findings of the Netsize Mobile Marketing Survey. Respondents also reported lack of understanding was a barrier. How can companies close this skills gap?
I think there's an onus on everyone involved in the marketing and media industries to make an effort to better understand mobile. Mobile advertising and marketing is growing and, if people don't make the effort to understand and utilize it, then they'll be left behind.

Again, we have to look at the fixed Internet. Almost a decade ago we saw the emergence of online agencies because traditional media agencies weren't really including digital in what they were doing. The same is starting to happen in mobile and you're seeing more traditional agencies starting to partner with mobile companies and even acquiring companies for their mobile expertise.

PARLEZ-VOUS MOBILE INTERNET?

French-owned Havas is a leading global advertising and communications services group. In January 2009, the Group reorganized into two business units: HAVAS Worldwide and HAVAS Media, which is also the fastest growing global media network whose main clients include: BBC , Credit Suisse, Danone, Exxon Mobil, Air France-KLM, Reckitt Benckiser and Sears. Havas Digital is the umbrella holding company that manages all Havas Media's interactive companies worldwide. The company also expanded into new areas such as mobile analytics. Dimitri Dautel talks about mobile advertising opportunities and top trends in the French Mobile Internet market.

This year was packed with milestones for Havas. Let's start with a high-level view of your mobile activities.

We started doing mobile campaigns as far back as 2004. At that point is was mostly about advising brands on the databases they should use to SMS campaigns and display advertising. We have evolved that into a full-service offer. Questions from clients that we answer these days are more focused on how mobile could be relevant to their marketing objectives.

Importantly, companies are not focused on the technology. They are interested in a full-service offer and listen to advice on media planning and direct marketing campaigns. We are also there to help them develop content for mobile because many advertisers – and their agencies – lack the staff or tools to build and host a mobile site.

What is the role of mobile? What do you tell your clients?

There is no easy answer. Mobile is a channel connected to a single unique individual, which mean we can do a direct marketing campaign using their phone number, for example. But mobile is also a mass media because people use it to consume content, like video and music, and applications.

So, mobile is a form of mass media and channel to the individual consumer. And the idea is to understand not only what can be done but also what is relevant to the consumer. Branding, direct marketing, loyalty programs. They are all possible. What a company should do with mobile depends on its marketing objective.

DIMITRI DAUTEL

Director, Havas Digital Mobile

You are seeing interest in a wider range of mobile advertising approaches. How does that interest translate into spend and investment in mobile?

Of course, 2009 was an interesting year in mobile marketing because there was so much in the media about it. All that buzz triggered more interest among our clients in understanding what they can actually do with mobile.

But a shift came when major traditional print media publishers unveiled their mobile strategies. Before it was mainly the small- and medium-sized companies we know from the mobile industry that embraced mobile. But, when major newspapers such as Le Monde and Le Figaro got involved and offered advertising space on their mobile sites and applications, advertisers saw this as a serious opportunity to take their message to mobile.

But 2009 was also a crisis year. So, advertisers wanted to move to mobile, but they also had cold feet about introducing a new item line in the budget line. There's a big difference between the way companies in the French market look at mobile advertising, compared to how brands see it in the U.S. or the U.K. In those markets advertisers are interested in innovation as a way to stand out of the crowd. In France brands see the risk they take, not necessarily the reward if they innovate. To sum up: in 2009 we saw a lot more interest among companies in mobile advertising, but we also saw that not everybody wanted to take the plunge.

How do "sell" mobile to your clients? Does it compete in their mind head-on with other media such as print and online? Or do they see it as a complement?

We explain to our clients that mobile does not compete with other media such as press, radio and Internet. To make this point we encourage them to consider an average day in the customer's routine. They are exposed to the radio when they wake up and then to a newspaper during the commute, for example. During the work day they might be on the Internet and then it's a newspaper in the train or a radio in the car, followed by TV in the evening. If you have a campaign on any of these media then your interaction with the consumer is limited to specific times of the day.

In contrast, if you have a mobile element then you are "always-on" because the mobile is the one device that people always have with them. So, if we go back to the customer routine, we see that mobile has a huge potential to bring together the variety of cross-media campaigns. If I see a press advertisement when I am in the subway, I can use my mobile to text in to received a voucher that I might use later when I am surfing the Internet on my PC. This is much more effective that hoping that I will remember what I saw in the subway when I sit down at my PC.

We also tell advertisers that mobile is not about the future; it's happening **now**. We count 40 million in France using the Mobile Internet at least once a month. There is a lot of room for that figure to grow and that spells a huge opportunity for brands. So, it makes sense for brands to get involved and benefit from the positive halo effect that comes from being a leader and not a follower in mobile advertising.

Which industry sectors are leading?

Banking was one of the first businesses to go there. At first it was about checking the account balance and maybe making money transfers. But then it evolved as banks saw that the group to adopt the Mobile Internet in the largest numbers was youth, a target demographic for banks. Since then there have been a number of mobile campaigns aimed at customer acquisition from financial institutions including Crédit Agricole and Société Générale.

The automotive sector has also been active. In this case, mobile is a channel that enables communication and direct contact between customers and dealers. Mobile campaigns from Peugeot, for example, offered consumers the chance to sign up for a test drive that was advertised via a print using their mobile phones.

How has the value chain shifted and what has been the impact of players such as Google and Apple?

Before 2009 was mobile operators in France had walled gardens and dominated the value chain. That changed when Apple and Google came on the scene with an approach all about building bridges where everyone before had been building walls. You have to remember that the Mobile Internet in France was French. When Apple and Google arrived, all this changed. Users could download content from anywhere in the world. This content arrived on our phones and new ad networks appeared on our media plans. Before this we were only working on French sites, so we were only working with French ad networks. Now we are working with global advertising networks to take advantage of a global opportunity.

HIGH PERFORMANCE

Universal McCann, one of the top ten global media networks with 90 offices in 66 countries, stepped up efforts in 2009 to ensure a central position for mobile in the marketing mix. It established a global task force with regional digital directors to guide digital marketing. The company also partnered with AOL and Questus, an interactive marketing and research firm, to conduct an extensive multi-phase research project examining how smartphones are influencing American lifestyles and media consumption. The survey found that mobile works powerfully with other media and identified a strong trend to 'media meshing,' which is driving consumers to simultaneously consume multiple media in order to optimize productivity or enrich the content experience. Universal McCann orchestrated a string of cross-media marketing campaigns for clients including Coca-Cola, Microsoft and legendary whiskey brand Jack Daniel's. Valérie Itey talks about brand awareness of mobile and why it can no longer be treated as standalone media source but needs to be integrated in the media mix.

Let's begin with some of the key takeaways from Smart Phone Smart Marketing, your company's survey of 1,800 mobile phone users in the U.S. What did it reveal about media consumption among users and the role of mobile?

The study looked at a variety of topics, including the level of satisfaction among users with the quality of their Mobile Internet experience and the interplay between consumer media usage, lifestyle and purchase preferences. We found that one out of seven minutes of media consumption today [2009] is through a mobile device. In fact, mobile is a more than a medium of transmission; it's the tool for both social communication and daily life management. This creates an unprecedented opportunity for marketers to transition with consumers as they move from activity to activity throughout the day.

Over one-third (38 percent) of consumers report having taken action from a mobile ad. Of those who were prompted to take action, 53 percent clicked on an advertisement, 35 percent requested information or a coupon and 24 percent made a purchase using their smartphone.

Significantly, nearly one of four users has made a purchase of non-device related products or services from their phones, indicating

VALERIE ITEY

Director Mobile Marketing, Universal McCann

a growing comfort with the medium as a shopping tool. The growing reliance of consumers on mobile devices and the Mobile Internet is a signal to marketers that they need to have a presence on mobile touchpoints. Of course, mobile is not a standalone media source, so we advise brands to integrate mobile in a cross-media campaign. Media works powerfully with other media. For example, mobile drives consumers to other media, which also drives consumers back to mobile – generating a circuit of juxtaposed mediation.

There are indications that mobile marketing is crossing the chasm. What will make mobile marketing mainstream?

The industry is gradually making a stronger business case for mobile marketing. This means agencies and brands must share mobile marketing success stories and the results they achieved. Also mobile operators must participate more, and they have started to do so, recognizing that advertisers require breadth and targeting. Once operators have internalized this and understand the targeting parameters an advertiser requires, they should work to make buying inventory simple, in a manner that is consistent with the media and planning processes in place in the advertising world today. At the need of the day marketers require consistent and reliable metrics to measure ROI and demonstrate the value of mobile in the marketing mix.

This is where operators can also add important value by providing marketers with a deeper understanding of consumer preferences, customer insight that translated into richer and more targeted inventory that yields more targeted and effective mobile marketing campaigns. A raft of reports shows that consumers like convenience and receiving targeted ads that help them manage their daily lives is a benefit.

Mobile is part of the mix, but there are other components to a successful cross-media campaign. How do you 'sell' your clients on mobile?

Fortunately, our clients are ready for mobile. Their objective is to be present on the medium that consumers have with them at all times, that offers the best targeting and segmentation, and allows them to engage with consumers in a meaningful way. Mobile covers all the bases, allowing advertisers to achieve reach, relevancy and real-time interaction with their customers. Major brands are therefore experimenting more with mobile, but this heightened interest doesn't remove the need for brand education. In our view, the education of brands on the opportunities and challenges within the mobile channel and insights into how advertisers view consumer engagement via mobile advertising is a key step towards enhancing brand participation in this rapidly growing industry.

Please share examples of your more impressive campaigns and the results they delivered.

Our client Coca-Cola wanted to prompt people to try its Coca-Cola Zero or Coke Zero, a product marketed as having zero sugar. To this end we developed a unique and exceptional experience to overcome the products to product trial. We constructed the world's largest interactive vending machine. The 19-meter tall structure in the Madrid, Spain, offered passerby the opportunity to send in a text message in return for a free can of Coke Zero. It was a new kind of push/pull campaign and we relied on Netsize to generate the short codes and validate the SMS request. This was important since we had to provide consumers with a kind of receipt for their text, a number that they could use to get a free can of Zero Coke once the request had been validated. It was a ground-breaking campaign and one that resulted in thousands of consumers texting in for their free product and adding their details to the client's interactive database.

Another campaign in Spain that drove positive results and extensive media coverage was a campaign by Jack Daniel's targeting music fans via mobile as part of its larger Backstage Parties marketing campaign that used posters, Bluetooth and short code calls-to-action. We also developed an app to promote a series of rock concerts, showing them what was on where and how to get there. But it was more than getting users to the party. Mobile made them feel as if they were backstage before and after the gig, providing them a great souvenir of the great night out and inviting them to continue that interactivity with their favorite bands after the show. In addition, features and functionality in the app – which was available as a Java download and an iPhone application -- let users compose their own songs using guitar, bass, piano and drum sounds, and participate in music-related quizzes. The campaign lasted from March to May 2009, during which time users downloaded our app 180,000 times with iPhone users accounting for a total of 4,000 downloads. More than 5,000 people opted in for future mobile marketing and the concerts sold out. What's more, the fans gave the backstage app 5 out of 5, a powerful recommendation that allows the brand to build a deeper relationship with users. In fact, based on this phenomenal success, we are planning to launch a new Backstage Parties app for Jack Daniel's in January 2010.

Which mobile marketing trends are highest on your radar in 2010?

In 2010 brands will allocate larger portions of their digital media plan towards mobile to further capitalize on the most personal marketing medium out there. For brands it will be of vital importance to be present on the small screen, through the mobile web or through apps. Mobile commerce and mobile CRM are starting to happen and we'll see more campaigns and strategies that harness mobile to move these activities forward. After all, brands are growing their opt-in databases through these campaigns and mobile CRM is a must! The advance of mobile coupons will also boost mobile commerce and encourage users to pay for goods and services with their mobile phones. A development to watch is Augmented Reality, which we expect will have a significant impact. We will launch a big campaign with Microsoft shortly that uses Augmented Reality to present the new products of Microsoft. Finally, geo-localization with the mobile carriers holds much promise, whereas mobile search will continue to define itself and grow.

MAPPING THE FUTURE

NAVTEQ Media Solutions is the mobile advertising group at NAVTEQ, a world leader in high value digital map data and content. In December 2009, Nokia Interactive Advertising joined NAVTEQ Media Solutions to offer advertisers premium mobile advertising and location-aware advertising across a variety of top publishers including Sprint, Airtel, OVI, Fox, and Reuters, spanning mobile phones and personal navigation devices. Diana LaGattuta talks about the value of location and the impact on retail.

Let's start off with a high level view of the new company and the decision to combine the advertising activities.

This past December, Nokia and NAVTEQ made the decision to combine their advertising organizations. This expanded group, called NAVTEQ Media Solutions, is positioned to provide true location-based targeting for brands. We believe that the world's largest device manufacturer together with the leading provider of digital map, traffic, and location data are poised to create the leading location-aware advertising ecosystem.

The combined unit will sell Nokia Interactive's existing mobile advertising inventory, which includes Nokia services, Sprint, Airtel, and a variety of top tier publishers, such as Reuters and Fox, as well as NAVTEQ's location-enabled inventory, including Garmin and AAA. Ad units span all major brands of mobile phones and personal navigation devices and include interactive banner ads, map search listings, and virtual billboards in a navigation experience.

What is the value of location in mobile advertising and where is the opportunity?

Interactive media has proven to be a powerful and measurable marketing channel for brands. The additional layer of contextual information from our location-enabled network will further strengthen the performance and ROI of mobile as an advertising medium and make it an indispensable marketing tool for industry segments including retail, entertainment, food and beverage, and consumer products.

Location-aware advertising has the potential to help us measure advertising's impact on driving foot traffic and transactions at the point-of-sale. Retailers are spending hundreds of millions of dollars trying to get a larger share of consumers' wallets. The fact is: 94 percent of retail sales still happen in

DIANA LAGATTUTA

Global Marketing Director,
NAVTEQ Media Solutions

physical locations. However, 80 percent of those buyers are carrying a mobile device.

How does 2009 compare to 2008 in terms of interest and investment?
We are focused on 2010 and beyond. To date, the largest spenders on mobile are companies that are transacting within the mobile channel. For those segments, mobile has been the most effective channel for direct response advertising. Mobile advertising will not explode for traditional advertisers until we can prove that it lights up ROI for the biggest advertisers. Location-enablement and mobile wallet are two technologies that can transform mobile into a direct response channel for brick and mortar brands, not just for mobile content sellers.

Some industry authorities argue the value of mobile advertising is its usefulness to consumers. Based on this advertising should help us manage our lives. Does location- aware advertising achieve this?
We are placing our bets on contextually targeted mobile advertising. Advertising that is so relevant because of where a person is at a given time or what they are doing that it becomes a useful service rather than an intrusion.

Is it about driving foot traffic in the store? Or is it more about mobile CRM to clinch the sale and follow-up contacts?
Trials have demonstrated that location-based mobile ads have average CTRs [click-through rates] of 4 percent. That rate is astounding compared to the lower CTRs non-targeted mobile ads generate. We are offering location-aware advertising to get consumers in the door. Then we have a team dedicated to the development of 'clicks to bricks' solutions to drive transactions.

Deloitte's 24th Annual Holiday Survey of mobile shoppers [in the U.S.] provides some interesting insights into consumer behavior. Of the respondents, 55 percent said they will use their mobile device to find store locations, 45 percent to research prices, 40 percent to find product information, 32 percent to find discounts and coupons and 25 percent to make purchases. In addition, 90 percent of shoppers make unplanned purchases and 51 percent of those purchasing decisions happen in the aisle. After we get consumers in the door, we will help brands reach them when they are in the store aisles.

What are the top three trends on the horizon?
Location-awareness will literally put mobile advertising on the map. Second, changing business models will continue to drive acquisitions of mobile ad startups. Finally, we will see better measurement for campaigns.

Where do you see the most work to be done?
Agencies need to get up to speed on mobile, media buying and creating for the medium.

What excites you when you look to the future?
When I see my technology-averse friends and family with their faces buried in their smartphones -- surfing the web, posting pictures to Facebook, getting turn by turn directions on maps -- I am stunned by how rapidly people are embracing the mobile device for more than just voice and SMS.

(BEST) PRACTICE MAKES PERFECT

Germany's mobile advertising market is poised for impressive growth after the emergence of some even more encouraging trends. Indeed, a recent survey of brands, agencies and enablers revealed a whopping 88.4 percent of mobile advertisers that ran campaigns in 2007 came back for an encore in 2008. In 2008 a total of 136 brands had advertised on mobile, representing a 316.3 percent increase over the previous year. Another milestone was the decision by the Mobile Marketing Association (MMA) and the German Federal Association for the Digital Economy's mobile division, known as the BVDW Section Mobile, to formally launch MMA Germany, marking a new phase in the partnership between the two organizations. Mark (Mr. Mobile) Wächter discusses recent developments and campaigns that push the envelope.

How has your mission changed and what is your role now in partnership with the MMA?

The partnership with the MMA dates back to April 2007. However, it only officially became a local chapter in 2009, when the MMA shifted strategy to focus on local chapter initiatives and having more local input, adding countries including India, South Africa, Turkey and Germany.

The German partnership means that members of the Section Mobile in BVDW are also members of the MMA. It's a benefit to the members, but it's also a boost for the mobile advertising ecosystem in Germany because there is the opportunity to leverage information and best practices across organizations and borders.

Germany is regarded as a huge, untapped market. What is your view?

In terms of the maturity of mobile as a medium, Germany is one of the top-notch markets. But Germany is not a leading market when it comes to using mobile advertising and understanding what it can do. That's why our top priority is to educate the industry.

How do you plan to achieve this?

For the second year we in the Section Mobile have produced the Mobile Kompass, which is a compilation of essays and contributions from mobile advertising professionals, practitioners and experts, ranging from operators to agencies. It's great orientation

MARK WÄCHTER

Founder MWC.mobi,
Chairman,
MMA Germany & BVDW Section Mobile

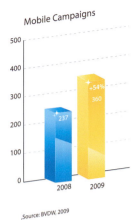
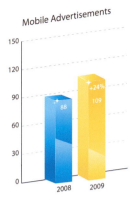

,Source: BVDW, 2009

for the mobile ecosystem, which is why we also call it a compass. In fact, other chapters of the MMA are looking at this publication as something they might duplicate in their own markets.

And we have made other contributions to educate the market. In Section Mobile we are some 60 companies representing the complete ecosystem – including major brands and operators - divided into work group and committed to meeting a minimum eight times a year. We are also charged with examining areas of mobile including mobile entertainment, Mobile Internet and mobile marketing and advertising. The aim is to provide the market a toolbox for going into mobile and understanding the complexity of mobile.

How active are German brands in mobile advertising?

The major brands have been quick to embrace mobile. German airline Lufthansa was one of the first brands to 'get" mobile. It made mobile part of its strategy and integrated it into its complete value chain from mobile check-in to buying tickets.

Another example is German carmaker BMW, which is perceived as the 'rock star' of mobile marketing because of the innovation of the campaigns and the fantastic results they have achieved. They are doing everything first: first in pre-marketing campaigns for models like the Mini or the 7 series and first in after-sales campaigns. A good example is how BMW combined advertising and CRM to show customers images of snow tires on their model and color cars when it started snowing in Germany to encourage them to buy snow tires. It was an innovative MMS campaign that used this kind of targeting to achieve a 30 percent conversion rate

These are great examples. How do you encourage others to follow?

Admittedly, mobile accounts for less than one percent of ad spend. Of course, we can't say for sure because we are not able to even measure the media spend on mobile. So, we have to convince more brands, beyond the ones I just mentioned, to look at mobile. But it's not just the brands. We also have to educate the media companies.

Take media planners, for example. Do they have all a clue about mobile? Not really. Media planners are taught to focus on reach and, of course, mobile doesn't deliver that reach – yet. A big part of our work is educating the young guys just coming out of college. Sure, their university curriculum includes online and digital marketing, but it lacks a focus on mobile, which is why we are working on training program and talking with educational institutions and universities to roll this out.

Part of your work in the next year is to arrive at a way to measure the value of mobile. What progress can you share?

Mobile advertising campaigns for this group are going through the roof. We see a 600 percent increase this year over the previous year. Of course, it's an increase from a very low level. The numbers come from the Mobile Advertising Circle, called MAC, which is a project within the Section Mobile of BVDW. Basically, everybody who does more than €250,000 net revenue with mobile advertising per year can be a member. Currently, we have some 13 members, including most major German operators, and media companies and publishers including Yahoo, United Internet Media, Tomorrow Focus, and so on.

The purpose is to count the campaigns, count the inventory and put value behind the inventory in terms of media space and spend. We recently asked the members – companies that together represent 95 percent of the mobile advertising market - how many campaigns they ran on their portals in Q1 and Q2 of 2008 compared with the same period in 2009. There was an increase of 50 percent – and that despite the economic crisis.

A recent Netsize Mobile Marketing survey asked respondents about advertising formats. It found more interest in MMS and in-app advertising. Which formats excite you most?

The recent deal, Google buying AdMob, clearly shows where the journey goes. AdMob is strong in in-application advertising. If you open any of these free apps, whether it's on Android or iPhone, you'll see advertising. Right now it's limited to a handful of devices, but that is changing. As we see more smartphone penetration, in-app advertising will be as normal as, well, buying bread. Whatever app you download, you won't pay for it. Instead, you will accept advertising in it. Other approaches become interesting when you connect mobile advertising with QR codes [2-D barcodes] and NFC [Near Field Communications].

Where is the real opportunity? Is it mobile advertising and marketing, or is it mobile CRM?

Mobile enables a one-to-one relationship on a high level. It's what brands dream of. So, if the content and the advertising fit together, it creates a good environment for brands and a perfect opportunity to use mobile as a tool for CRM activities. I just wonder why mobile operators don't use mobile for CRM more often. They have all the customer data they need but they appear to be very careful. Beyond sending a birthday greeting via SMS, I haven't seen what I would consider an innovative CRM campaign, and I've been in the industry for more than a decade.

TRANSACTION

BROWSING
SHOPPING
BUYING
CUSTOMER
SERVICE
COMMERCE

Mobile in 2010 is TRANSACTION: browsing, shopping, buying, customer service. It is all about commerce, convenience and the convergence of bricks and clicks to create shopping experiences that blurs the boundaries between physical stores and digital worlds.

Up until now, mobile payments have mainly been focused on micropayments, purchases of mobile content downloads such as music and games, and general transactions with a value of less than €10. However, as the development of these services moves in the direction of more openness and interoperability with other telecoms and financial services networks, the stage is set for the emergence of new mobile payments business models and new competitive pressures.

All forms of mobile payments got a boost from the advance of smartphones and the popularity of the Mobile Internet. But the deciding factor in 2009 was a shift in consumer attitudes. As Jamie Wells, Director of Global Trade Marketing at Microsoft Mobile Advertising put it in a recent interview with Mobile Marketer: "Consumers are getting over the trust barriers associated with mobile commerce."

Encouraged by signs that 2010 would be a pivotal year for mobile payments and transactions Mobile Marketer – a leading destination covering mobile marketing and how the mobile channel can be used alone or in conjunction with other channels for branding and customer acquisition and retention purposes – launched Mobile Commerce Daily in December 2009. The new publication offers news, analysis and opinion on mobile commerce, an area Editor In Chief Mickey Alam Khan correctly calls "the next frontier of retail." In his view, it's all about how retailers and sellers of content, products and services can use mobile to acquire and retain customers by encouraging transactions on mobile phones as well as driving traffic to retails stores, catalogs, the Web or other channels.

Distinct opportunities

However, any discussion of the mobile commerce opportunity must begin with a discussion of what "mobile commerce" means. Each research firm defines and segments this market differently, with some identifying as many as five sub-markets. These sub-markets are further broken down into a myriad of segments based on defining

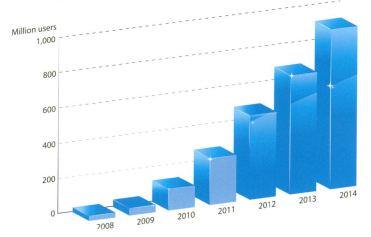

Figure 1: Active users of mobile banking and related financial services (Worldwide 2008-2014)
Source: Javelin strategy and Research

characteristics such as the nature of the goods or services purchases, the point of delivery and the mechanisms or technology used to complete the transaction or transfer of funds.

A straightforward approach comes from Edgar, Dunn & Company, a global strategy consulting firm specializing in payments and financial services. It breaks mobile commerce down into two categories: 1) mobile banking and 2) mobile payments and money transfers. Mobile banking refers to "situations where the mobile phone is used as an access channel to financial services." In contrast, mobile payments and money transfers refers to "situations where the mobile phone is used as a payment devices to affect the transfer of value from one party to another."

Mobile banking services continue to gain significant traction. In fact, market research firm Berg Insight anticipates that the number of active users of mobile banking and related financial services worldwide will rocket from 20 million in 2008 to 913 million in 2014. **See Figure 1**

Growth drivers include a rise in the number of customers responding positively to the ease and accessibility of services to check balances or transfer funds on their mobile phone and a marked increase in the number of financial institutions harnessing mobile to enhance functionality, portability and proactively deliver alerts and updates. According to a study by market research firm Javelin strategy and Research, mobile banking is "quickly moving from infancy to commonplace" in the U.S., where it estimates some 99 million adults will be carrying out mobile banking transactions at least once a year in 2014.

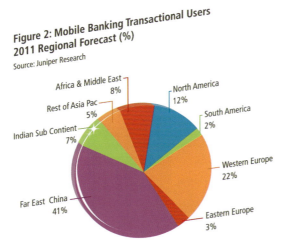

Figure 2: Mobile Banking Transactional Users 2011 Regional Forecast (%)
Source: Juniper Research

Figure 3: NFC applications in mobile phones
Source: NXP Semiconductors

However, Berg Insight reminds us there are stark differences between mobile banking for the banked population in the U.S. and Europe compared to the under-banked populations in Asia, Africa and Latin America. In developed markets, mobile banking is "seen as a convenience service that does not generate revenues, but more a service to build value-added applications upon." In emerging markets mobile banking is the only way to access banking services.

Market research firm Juniper Research is bullish about the outlook for mobile banking usage, particularly in under-banked regions. It predicts more than 150 million customers will have used mobile banking services by end-2011, more than triple the number of users in 2008. **See Figure 2**

The majority of these users will be in the Far East and China (41 percent).

Market breakthrough

Meanwhile, market research firm Informa, reports the real news is not the numbers. It's the market shift they represent.

Informa says the rise in mobile banking, mobile money transfers and mobile payments enabled by a variety of technologies including WAP billing and NFC (Near-Field Communications), will hit a landmark in 2013, generating 300 billion transactions worth more than $860 billion. In 2008 mobile digital content, such as ringtones, games and music, accounted for a third of the total value of the market or $71 billion. But by 2013, over 95 percent of mobile transactions will be for physical goods and services.

A huge boost will come from NFC enables handsets and new business models that get more mileage out of contactless payments. In 2013 Informa believes approximately 11 percent of all mobile handsets will be NFC-enabled. What's more over 178 million consumers will regularly use these mobile phones to purchase physical goods and services, such as tickets, at the point of sale. **See Figure 3**

Indeed, the application of NFC as a new kind of mobile retail tool marks a milestone in mobile payments. This is the view of Mobile Coupons & NFC Smart Posters: Strategies, Applications & Forecasts 2009-2014, a recent and timely report from market research firm Juniper Research. It forecasts that the fit between NFC-enabled devices and coupons, smart posters and ticketing schemes will jumpstart significant growth in NFC-enabled mobile payments and transactions. Specifically, the value of these transactions will generate a worldwide redemption value of nearly $6 billion.

More importantly, Juniper states, NFC is "poised to revolutionize the way people shop." Smart posters with embedded NFC tags will "bring to life static billboards, creating immediate interaction between potential customers and their prospective purchases."

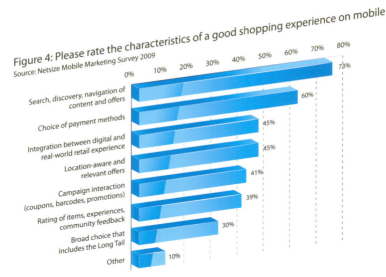

Figure 4: Please rate the characteristics of a good shopping experience on mobile
Source: Netsize Mobile Marketing Survey 2009

Big spender

The central role of mobile in commerce became clear at the close of 2009, when mobile companies and analyst firms came to the same conclusion: holiday consumers are using their mobile phones to shop and conduct a range of shopping related activities such as price comparison and store location.

According to eBay, the number of items bought via eBay mobile apps in 2009 was triple the previous year. In 2009, eBay buyers and sellers generated more than half a billion dollars of transactions via mobile. "Mobile is changing the way people shop this holiday season," Lorrie Norrington, President of eBay Marketplaces, said in an interview. "This holiday season has been a mobile commerce tipping point."

Francesco Rovetta, Director of Business Development, PayPal Mobile, the eBay-owned ecommerce business that enables payments and money transfers, likewise concludes that 2009 was a pivotal year for mobile commerce. "In addition to electronics and apparels, for example, a Lamborghini sold for more than $500,000 through mobile on eBay. It confirms that mobile commerce is not just a vision, but really becoming reality." **See Interview, page 92.**

Worlds combine

But it may be the ability of the mobile device to link the physical and digital worlds that trigger new – and lucrative – revenue opportunities. This realization prompted a number of companies to launch a host of new services allowing merchants to deliver discount vouchers and coupons to mobile phones, help consumers to compare prices and blur the boundaries between the physical and digital shopping experiences.

Sensing a business opportunity, Amazon announced a new addition to its mobile store that harnesses image recognition, allowing iPhone users to literally buy what they see. They simply capture an image with their camera phones and the Amazon system responds with a link to the closest match in its database and options to buy the item at once or put it in a shopping basket for later purchase on a PC.

Moving forward, the ability of mobile to deliver an enhanced and holistic retail experience may become its most important selling point. The Mobile Trends Survey 2010 conducted by Netsize asked respondent to rate the ingredients of a good mobile shopping experience. Interestingly, respondents viewed the ability of mobile to combine bricks and clicks as a real boost. **See Figure 4**

The ability of mobile to provide location awareness and interaction through coupons, bar codes and other marketing methods that drive store traffic were also rated highly.

Mobile commerce reached a new threshold of acceptance in 2009, becoming a service – and convenience – consumers will come to expect from merchants. In view of this, analysts expect other verticals such as entertainment, publishing, media and travel will harness mobile in 2010, using the medium to offer simple, one-click transactions that enhance their real world offers and deliver real value.

THE SECOND WAVE OF MOBILE PAYMENTS

There has been a flurry of recent activity around mobile payments, with many companies launching pilots and live applications around the world. The race is on and the stakes are high because many companies at the intersection of mobile and commerce – including financial institutions, mobile operators and merchants – are all competing for the consumer.

Financial institutions are keen to take a lead role in mobile payments as a means to maintain control of consumers' accounts and related product offers such as loans. But there are other advantages. A lead role in mobile payments allows financial institutions to avoid further disintermediation, reduce cash and cost and effectively service under-banked geographies such as Africa.

Mobile network operators can use mobile payments as springboard to diversify into servicing other consumer needs and lifestyle requirements, thus reducing churn and boosting loyalty.

Merchants also benefit. For one, mobile payments speed up purchases at the point of sale (POS), allowing cashiers to move more consumer through the checkout more efficiently. And, because consumers carry their mobile phones with them throughout the store, merchants have an additional opportunity to deliver marketing and promotion messages to consumers in the store in real-time. Even better, if the merchant can match messaging to content and so encourage cross-sell, up-sell and the all-important impulse buy.

From the perspective of the end-consumer, mobile payments are fast becoming part of their mobile routines. After all, consumers have already become accustomed to using the mobile to do more than make telephone calls.

Where do mobile payments make business sense?

There are many mobile payments scenarios, but a few stand out because they have the best chances of success.

CHIEL LIEZENBERG

Founding partner, Innopay

First on the list is the purchase of non-physical goods, such as mobile downloadable content, or services, such as parking. These purchases would clearly benefit from payment solutions that link directly to existing financial instruments, such as current accounts and debit cards, allowing consumers to use these instruments without having to register using their mobile phone.

Contactless payments, specifically NFC (Near Field Communications) transactions, may have a tough time breaking into the POS market. The competition is stiff and the position and effectiveness of existing solutions such as debit and credit cards, and even cash, could make this an uphill battle. By way of background, NFC is a short-range wireless connectivity standard that allows communication between electronic devices when they are brought within four centimeters of one another, thus enabling payment or a secure transfer of information.

On paper, NFC does have its benefits, all based around its usability and seamless integration with the mobile device. However, merchants and consumers may need to be convinced. While providers may achieve temporary success with early-adopters or limited sectors such as transport and parking, the real traction will come when providers sharpen their focus on improving ease of use and bringing down costs.

Thus, public transport is likely to provide the highest volume potential for mobile payments. However it is not clear what advantages mobile payments offer over contactless payments.

Mobile payments are also a perfect fit with Remote Point of Sale and purchases consumers make using vending machines. But again, real success here depends on whether providers can keep the cost of these solutions low.

It's the consumer, stupid

But payment is not just about technology choices. It's about consumer comfort. Indeed, the actual payment process carries a high emotional weight, and both the consumer and merchant have similar concerns. Both want to minimize payment risk (risk that the payment is not executed or guaranteed), maximize usability and keep costs low. Thus, the design of a mobile payment solution must take these behavioral considerations into account.

Granted, service providers are well aware of the technology and business barriers to mobile payments adoption. These include costs such as activation fees, learning costs and obsolescence fees. But service providers frequently forget the psychological barriers associated with changing consumer behavior to embrace mobile payments. In many cases, consumers must be convinced that they are receiving real benefit. People tend to stick to methods that they know and trust. Therefore, the smaller the consumer's change in behavior needs to be, the greater the chances of success are.

Technologies

The choice of technology has significant impact on the adoption and potential success of a mobile payment service. The table below summarizes the advantages and disadvantages, as well as use contexts related to four mobile payment technologies. To date SMS and NFC are the methods most frequently used to complete payment, although the number of initiatives using WAP/internet is on the rise. Many mobile payment initiatives are still in a pilot stage, with a few notable exceptions that have been commercially launched on a large scale. Examples of widely used, commercially available services are: Paybox in Austria, G-Cash in the Philippines, NTT DoCoMo's Osaifu-Keitai in Japan and M-PESA in Kenya.

TECHNOLOGY	ADVANTAGE	DISADVANTAGE	USE CONTEXT	EXAMPLES
NFC	Quick and easy	Lack of availability of NFC-enabled phones	Point of Sale (POS) only	Osaifu Keitai (Japan), Visa PayWave (Guatemala)
SMS	Widely available and every mobile user understands it	Relatively expensive, recipient not always available	Banking, Remittance	Rabo SMS betalen (Netherlands)
USSD	Available to every mobile user	Lacks user-friendly interface	POS, Banking	mPay (Poland), MobiPay (Spain)
(Mobile) Internet & WAP	Connects to user experience	Most mobile users are not accustomed to using it	Banking, POS (if real-time), Remittance	

Regional differences in mobile payments

When analyzing the mobile payment initiatives, we see that the type of initiative differs substantially depending on the region and the transaction context.

In the U.S. 'mobile payment' typically refers to mobile banking and – more specifically – Internet banking using a mobile phone, an activity that appears to be taking off. In this context mobile offers convenience and consumers use their mobile phones to access their bank account and perform basic functions such as checking the bank balance. In contrast, the mobile phone is less widely used to make an actual bank transfer.

In Europe, mobile payment refers to transactions – in part because bank card and inter-bank payment infrastructures are well organized to support this. Similar to the situation in Asia, mobile payment in Europe is about consumers conducting contactless Point of Sale (POS) payment via an NFC-enabled mobile phone. According to our definition, this is a true form of 'mobile payment'. In Asia this method is already quite successful. However, the underlying industry structure – specifically the role of both the mobile network operators and banks – in Asia is completely different from what we find in Europe and the U.S.

Additionally, NFC-based payment is typically successful in densely populated areas, where people are on the move and commute using public transport. These conditions create a variety of transaction contexts where micropayments make the most sense. But it doesn't automatically follow that the U.S. and Europe – regions home to large sprawling urban areas and mega-cities – are going the way of NFC-enabled payment schemes. The existing (card) infrastructure in the U.S. and Europe is well established, making it more of a challenge to prove the business case for NFC-based mobile payment. Thus, local-focused mobile payment solutions for public transport and parking have the best chances to become successful in the U.S. and Europe, but always in combination with card payment.

The picture is different in developing nations, where mobile is a delivery channel for a variety of financial services, including payments. This is because mobile is the only viable channel for financial services; online banking and payments via a computer in the home is not an option is areas where mobile phone penetration far outpaces PC penetration.

In these countries 'mobile payment' is about local money transfer and/or a remittance. Using technologies available in all mobile phones, such as SMS, operators and banks alike are piloting and introducing new payment services aimed primarily at providing banking services for the under-banked. The advance of these services is met by impressive success. However, there are concerns that the rapid spread of these mobile payment services may outpace the ability of governments and market bodies to introduce services regulation and ensure their security.

- Primarily NFC-based initiatives
- Primarily Mobile Internet-based initiatives
- Primarily SMS-based initiatives

The future is networked, and mobile

It is our vision that globalization leads to a network economy, and electronic infrastructures increasingly enable industries to cooperate in networks, in real time. As the (mobile) Internet develops into a true transaction channel, new transaction contexts are created that – in turn – encourage demand for new transaction services.

But progress has its price. The development of these new transaction services – one that harness mobile devices to perform the payment services consumers and conditions in each region require - is a complex and costly task. More importantly, it requires specialist expertise and a specific approach.

A priority on the agenda moving forward is to focus on remittances. We believe the industry would benefit from a more collaborative, networked approach to remittances, and we hope to see more initiatives and achievements around stakeholder collaboration in Europe and across other regions.

In a networked, mobile world, security and trust must be ensured. The responsibility lies with service providers and regulators to actively work together and seek solutions to get mobile payment 'right the first time.'

This viewpoint is excerpted from Mobile payments 2010, Market analysis and overview, a mobile payments report published by Innopay and available for download at **www.innopay.com**

LET US ENTERTAIN YOU

From buying tickets and accessing nearby movie times to downloading related content and trailers, mobile plays an increasingly central role in the cinema experience. Sensing a business opportunity French-owned UGC S.A., Europe's number one owner and operator of cinema theaters across Europe, has integrated mobile into a wider strategy to help customers organize and enjoy their moviegoing experience. But it's not just about boosting customer satisfaction; mobile is also paving the way for marketers to seamlessly integrate their brands into the experience and help forge stronger connection to their customers. Elisabeth Trochet tells us about the ways mobile can extend the movie going experience past the lobby and into our everyday lives.

As a leading owner of a chain of cinemas UGC has been involved in a number of projects and services to improve the moviegoing experience. Please outline the milestones.

UGC has been at the forefront, developing a variety of services and offers to enhance the customer experience. These include the Unlimited Card, allowing customers to enjoy unlimited cinema for an annual subscription, and an advance reservation service called UGC Prompto. With the advance of mobile and the boom in smartphones, we have also created services and projects to harness the Mobile Internet beyond just having a mobile website. UGC is gearing up to launch an iPhone app that allows users to access UGC cinemas and show times, and book their seat in the theater.

What is the role of mobile in your business? Is it central to customer acquisition? Retention? CRM? Something else? Please explain.

For UGC, the purpose of mobile is to provide customers assistance they value so they may manage their daily lives. This means helping people to access the right information – quickly and when they need it most. It starts with reading film synopses on their mobile phones and extends to a variety of services around the moviegoing experience: watching the trailer, finding the closest cinema nearby, booking their seats in advance, and even pre-registering for services by inputting their UGC card details into their mobile phone.

Focusing on developing applications and services that are utilities – that is, services

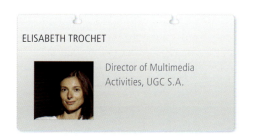

ELISABETH TROCHET

Director of Multimedia Activities, UGC S.A.

customers will find practical and easy to use – is the best way for UGC to become an integral part of their routines. And, by making it a habit for customers to use our service – to research the movie, to reserve the seat, and so on – they will naturally associate our offer with valuable advice. What better way to retain customers?

Last year, a main takeaway of the Netsize Guide was the pivotal and increasing role of mobile in a wide variety of businesses and business strategies. Some called it the "remote control of our lives." Others saw the future in bringing together physical and digital marketing and promotion. What is your view?

Mobile is about services and providing utility. Therefore, it is important for UGC to develop and launch services on mobile that have purpose and allow us to be as close as possible to our customers. With this in mind, and before we develop any service, we ask ourselves: what is the benefit to the customer? Location offers a clear benefit and value to our customers. By harnessing the location capabilities of mobile we can help our customers to find the local UGC theater or find out what's playing nearby.

You mention value to the customer. What is the value of apps and how should they be monetized?

What is free has no value. An application that provides added-value or content to our customers should be monetized.

A movie can bring a variety of players and brands together, including sponsors, actors and companies that have paid placement in the film. Some analysts suggest this interplay could also provide the basis of an "after-market"

for branded content and information related to the film. What are your views and would you pursue a strategy to forge relationships between movie brands and movie goers?

Our business is to create the best conditions for customers to locate and enjoy a wide range of movies from blockbusters to more niche films. To achieve this we develop a wide range of services to optimize the customers experience at our cinemas. However, we want to stick to our core business.

Amazon, Apple and other companies have success with models that are online-focused and rely on credit cards. What are your payment methods for your offer and what is the role of mobile now and moving forward?

From our website and our WAP site in the Mobile Internet our customers can book in advance and pay for their tickets. They can pay by credit card or with a variety of UGC cards. These include the Unlimited card I already mentioned, as well as the Cartes 5/7, a kind of pre-paid cinema card that is valid for 5 tickets.

We also offer our customers the possibility to pre-register their UGC card number so that they do not have to enter the number each time they reserve and pay with them. It is then quicker for them to make a reservation using their mobile phones. Once the reservation in confirmed, customers can complete the transaction with the cashier at the UGC cinema or by inputting their UGC card into a kiosk located on the premises. We do see a future in contactless payments using mobile, but we do not consider it a priority to develop such a service at this time.

SHOP YOUR WAY

Expansion into new markets and new marketing methods was a top item on the agenda for Marks & Spencer (M&S) in 2009. The company, one of the leading retailers in the U.K. with over 21 million people visiting its stores, marked its 125th anniversary with a series of Web and store special offers. But it also used the occasion to upgrade the company website's core functionality and design in a bid to support future growth and improve the customer shopping experience. M&S also sharpened its focus on mobile, launching a series of innovative mobile marketing campaigns, including a nationwide trial of 2D barcodes. Sienne Veit talks about the role of mobile and the company's wider strategy to improve the customer journey from browsing to basket.

What is the purpose of mobile in what you do?

We use mobile in a number of ways. In our innovative Back to School Campaign, where we created a mobile version of our school wear brochure, the objective was acquisition. We used mobile as a channel to cut through the enormous amount of marketing that happens in the run up to the start of the new school year. However, because we were also able to display products, include a voucher code and push people through to our call center through click-to-call, there was also a conversion element.

Where does mobile CRM fit in?

CRM is at the core of our mobile engagement. We include a call to action to sign up for mobile alerts, promotions and offers in all our loyalty direct mailings. The ability to message our most loyal customers at short notice and tell them about upcoming offers is very powerful, and mobile is the perfect channel to do this.

We have trialed integrating loyalty points into SMS campaigns and this has also worked well. For retailers, mobile provides the potential for cost savings over printed vouchers. For customers, they are useful in that they are portable and it is easier to remember to redeem them.

Where do you see the growth opportunity?

We have used mobile Web campaign sites to support school wear, our Dine in for £10 promotions and also our freshly squeezed fruit juices. As customers become more accustomed to connecting to the mobile

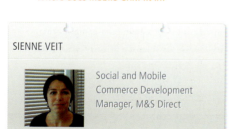

SIENNE VEIT

Social and Mobile Commerce Development Manager, M&S Direct

Web, the benefits of having content that is accessible via the mobile phone to support a product or service are very compelling.

For Marks & Spencer the growth opportunity is most definitely in providing transactional capability - whether through mobile commerce functionality via the Web or through contactless payments. However, as a channel, mobile is also good at engaging customers and deepening existing relationships with them, especially when linked into existing CRM activities,

What are the factors that limit your effective deployment of mobile marketing?

Currently, some of the technology we require is not yet available to all customers. In the case of mobile payments and voucher redemption, the technology is still in development and an industry standard has yet to be agreed upon.

There is an enormous cost to adopting new technologies, especially where hardware is involved, so we need to be sure that the technology we decide on is the market leader and will be available to the majority of our customers at no additional cost to them.

Which mobile marketing methods have you used or plan to use? And what are your plans in the next year?

We use SMS most often and broadcast relevant offers and promotions to over 100,000 customers every two weeks. We have just completed a campaign using the popular animated characters Wallace & Gromit, which included the ability to profile yourself or a friend on a mobile Website and then send that profile to yourself or your friend as an MMS. We have seen very good results and would like to use MMS more, where this is relevant and where the costs make sense for the campaign. We also plan to broaden our mobile activity and create better integration of mobile into campaigns.

Should mobile marketing be opt-in for consumers? Please explain your views.

Absolutely. Customers should always explicitly opt in for mobile marketing. The unregulated early days of mobile and premium services have made consumers very wary of providing their details to brands, particularly their mobile details, either because there may be a charge or the costs of doing so are not communicated clearly to consumers. For this reason, M&S is working with the

Direct Marketing Association to establish MobileSafe, a consumer focused mark of trust for mobile marketing campaigns. It will give consumers a clear expectation of what kind of messages they will receive, how to opt-in or out and any costs associated with that campaign.

What marketing campaign have you deployed or observed that really stands out and why?

Our nationwide trial of 2D barcodes on our Freshly Squeezed juice bottles within our **Food to Go** range clearly stands out. We used data matrix codes on our juice packs to push people to a mobile Web campaign site, which included visually-rich information about the product, daily offers, jokes, and more. Instructions on how to scan the barcode were available on pack. And, if customers didn't have a barcode scanning application, they could easily download one by texting FRESH to 65006. We were able to detect their handset and direct them to download appropriate scanning software for their phone. We had far more people than we predicted access the site in this way.

Not many retailers would trial a store-wide, national on-pack barcode trial, but M&S did. As a result, we have learned an enormous amount, not just about the processes and skills needed to execute a barcode offer, but also about how our customers are prepared to navigate their way through technology in order to access content relevant to the product and the situation in which they use that product.

As we reduce our packaging more and more, we need to find innovative ways for people to access the rich information they seek about the products they buy - and mobile is a great way of doing this. More importantly, mobile is a key way for us to bridge the experience divide between stores and the web. It is the perfect medium to link our two estates together.

Will people use their phones to buy items? If so, what kinds of items? And what will you do to facilitate this?

We are already encouraging mobile commerce. For example, we sell nametapes for school clothes using premium SMS. Customers can text TAG followed by a space, their child's name, their house number and post code to 65006. We validate their names and addresses, bill them £5 using premium SMS and then send them 50 iron-on nametapes within 3 days.

As a company, Marks & Spencer can see an enormous advantage in m-commerce. However, we need the industry to become standardized and for mobile payments technology to advance to a point where we can roll it out to other areas of mobile. We can certainly see a time where customers would want to pay for their lunch or sub £30 items using their mobiles, or to use their mobiles for some or all of their purchase journey.

TOUR DE FRANCE

SFR is France's number two mobile operator behind France Telecom-owned Orange with close to 20 million users. But when it comes to offering entertainment services such as mobile music SFR is the market leading innovator thanks in part to its relationship with Vivendi, a French media conglomerate that has a controlling stake in SFR (56 percent) and a majority share in Universal Music group, the world's biggest music company. In 2009 SFR continued to focus on cutting-edge entertainment offers and also emerged the second provider in France to offer the Apple iPhone 3G. SFR, which acquired fixed-line operator Neuf Cegetel in 2008, also became the first in France to deploy femtocell technology in a bid to boost indoor 3G coverage and provide users enhanced broadband experience. Olivier Céchura talks about the role of the operator, the lure of the applications store and the key importance of operator billing.

It was a busy 12 months for SFR. Please update us on company milestones and applications that boosted your business in 2009.
In 2009 SFR developed a variety of applications, including the mobile music offer SFR Musique, the mobile TV offer SFR TV and SFR Wifi, which allows users to locate and use hotspots to surf the Mobile Internet on their mobile device. Our customers downloaded some 1.5 million of these apps, with SFR TV being our most successful app. It represented one-third of downloads and more than 45,000 users per day.
Another area that saw interest in 2009 was the operator billing that SFR enables within applications stores. The Nokia Ovi Store was the first store to benefit from SFR billing integration, sealing a deal to enable this in September 2009. The combined expertise each party – the store retailer and the mobile operator – brings to the table has obvious benefits.

It has been said that the company with the most developers wins. What is your view of this and what are you doing to attract developers?
Clearly, applications stores are now in competition to attract and retain developers. Stores are indeed a key way to improve platform attractiveness, product differentiation, and boost end-user satisfaction.
It's early days for applications stores and, so far, most analysts have developed a single metric to measure success or failure: the number of developers. I believe the winning companies will be the one with the best developers, not with the most. And we should also abandon our zero-sum

OLIVIER CECHURA

Director B2B Enablers, SFR

view of this market. Professional developers and software companies can develop for several stores and platforms. Therefore, it is not - and should not be - a winner-takes-all scheme with only one company really winning.

Netsize conducted an online survey of over 1,000 mobile professionals to find out more about the requirements of a successful applications store. Respondents said the four C's - Convenience, Compatibility, Choice, and Charging – were the key capabilities. What is your view?

We have identified three factors that boost performance and the chances of success. First, local content. Content consistency with a focus on local market needs is critical. In France, as in all countries, there are national brands, such as newspapers and magazines that hold tremendous value for mobile users. Naturally, mobile applications stores tend to be international, but the ones that adapt to local tastes, brands and user needs will be the most successful.

Second, store experience. The look-and feel should be consistent and offer the user a satisfactory shopping experience. Attention to detail, all the way down to the animation, design and the daily offers, can produce positive results.

Third, developer support. You have to provide advantages and guarantees that will attract and retain developers. A big part of this is ability to monetize their applications with minimum cost. It is not specifically a question of revenue share, but more a question of customer reach. We believe operator billing is a way developers can reach a larger audience. This is because there is no need for users to share personal banking credentials.

More importantly, users are spared the hassle of having to register to pay for content. In the same manner, developers will need CRM tools.

What is the value of apps and how should they be monetized?

During the first year of operation of the iPhone App Store, ad-supported, free content were the main attraction. But things changed when the media companies – press and TV - experienced financial losses on the Web. Then some content owners switched to selling their apps, but we know a non-recurrent income based on one-time download is hardly enough for developers and rights owners to earn a living.

More recently, the advance of freemium offers – where users download the content for free and pay for additional features – shows business potential. We have seen this in France with the iPhone app offered by the daily newspaper Libération.

Considering this evolution, it is clear that the best way to make money is to give developers the tools to monetize their content and applications themselves. Thus, mobile operators such as SFR will rise to play a major role, defining new monetization models. Of particular interest are operator billing mechanisms including micro-payment, allowing transactions of €10 and less, and nano-payment schemes, permitting purchases of much smaller amounts, as well as innovative subscription models and in-app purchase options.

Amazon, Apple and other companies have success with models that are online-focused and rely on credit cards. How can mobile operators compete?

Our major advantage is the trust-based relationships we have with our customers. They have always trusted us with their banking and personal information. Billing and dealing with customer care issues has been the core expertise of mobile operators for decades.

Is the operator-owned app store the new 'on-deck portal'?

There is no reason today to develop specific or dedicated operator-owned app stores on existing smartphone platforms. The mobile operator portals will continue to have a strong attraction and customer reach. After all, we should not expect that everyone will use a smartphone and purchase content and services from app stores.

Operators can also benefit from the app store trend by being developers and by providing B2B enablers. SFR, for example, has developed a range of applications including SFR Find and Go, a geolocation and navigation service, and SFR Visual voicemail, which adds a visual aspect to phone voicemail such as allowing users to view a list of audio voicemail entries or even read transcripts of these voicemails.

At the end of the day, app stores are also part of a global ecosystem, where mobile operators can and should play. To date SFR is a major player in distributing mobile games in Europe and can bring this retail know-how to a range of app stores. Applications stores target a specific segment of our customer base. With this in mind we will continue to offer content and services to the app stores users, and we will continue to serve the other segments that are not smartphone users and consequently less tech-savvy. There is still room for everyone.

What is the endgame for applications stores?

Peaceful coexistence!

CONVERTING READERS INTO SHOPPERS

Success in retail is all about helping consumers find and buy what they want most. NearbyNow, a U.S. - based provider of personal shopping services, has taken this experience a step further, providing mobile shopping applications for magazines, brands, and retailers so that their consumers can stay updated on the latest products, buy online, or even locate and put products on hold at a nearby store. In 2009 the company released a succession of iPhone applications for lifestyle publications such as GQ, Seventeen, Brides, Lucky, Runner's World and others, all based on their iPhone Platform. NearbyNow currently partners with more than 65,000 stores across the U.S. and continues to build mobile applications for leading lifestyle brands, retailers, and publications. Scott Dunlap talks about the future of shopping and the role of social interaction.

NearbyNow started out as a way for consumers to search all products and sales available at local shopping centers using the Internet or mobile phones. Now you build branded iPhone application to drive local purchasing. Please explain this shift.

Our original service allowed consumers to walk into a shopping mall and find any product they wanted in the size and color they wanted – even put it on hold – before they got to the mall to buy it. Over time we noticed that the same items were in demand over and over again.

We dug into the numbers and consumer behavior, and we found out that it's really six or seven magazines and a couple of TV shows that most influence consumer purchasing. The real fashion-conscious demographic – teens and women aged 25-to 35 – were using their mobile devices to look for products that they saw in the magazines. Most of them were looking nearby, so they could try them on or try them out.

To connect and measure this, we built iPhone applications for the magazines. Consumers can see all the products that are in the magazine in one place and type in their size to find the closest store that has it. We connect the user from inspiration to trial.

You have begun experimenting with new combinations of services around mobile shopping. What can you share?

We have over 1 million mobile shoppers now, and it has become clear that "mobile shopping" has unique patterns of user behavior in discovery, purchasing, and social networking.

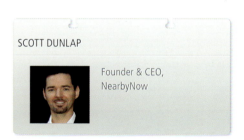

SCOTT DUNLAP

Founder & CEO, NearbyNow

Transaction _ Converting readers into shoppers

An example is the Brides Dressing Room, the first wedding and bridesmaid dress locator application on a mobile device. We found out that when looking at bridal gowns, most brides want feedback from a close set of friends, not everyone on Facebook. So we built a feature that allows a bride to send a picture of the dream dress to friends and family to get instant feedback via e-mail. It's a mini-social network capability designed specifically for interaction around a single purchase, albeit an important one.

We already have social networks such as Facebook, where we can post the purchases we are considering? Why create mini-networks?
The Bride example made sense because there was more social interaction prior to purchase than we had seen with any other item. We actually found that no one wanted to post the wedding gown they might buy on Facebook. It's just not a broad social network play. It's about communicating with a small group of folks involved in the wedding. There is a specific purpose to this network and we need a different kind of social network, not the tools that Facebook and MySpace provide.
Somewhere between the magazine and the in-store purchase is where all the action is happening. Capturing this on a mobile device says so much about purchasing behavior – who influences it, what products are considered, where they are considered, and more. It's just amazing!

Another thing that is amazing is the conversions on the mobile advertising. What are you seeing?
The conversion numbers are great, but the biggest impact is really about having information about purchasing that can be fed back to advertisers and retailers. Magazines are taking the data – which shows the number of consumers they reach and how much purchasing they incentivized – and handing that back to their advertisers, who can't get enough of it. Having a mobile app allows magazines to answer a lot of questions about conversion that they couldn't quantify before. In many cases, they can even show demand that was generated after the product had sold out, and how much business that represents. It's very powerful.
The overall conversion to purchase per use is about 6 percent. What's really fascinating is how that breaks down. Of the 6 percent, 5.5 percent are converting by finding a nearby store and purchasing there. The remaining one-half of one percent is purchasing the item directly from a mobile Web site.

Do you expect that to change going forward?

As the user base grows, we expect this to come down some. But I don't think the ratio of in-store to online purchasing will change that much. Offering both online and in-store alternatives really blurs the barriers between the physical and digital Internet world. It's important to note that mobile shoppers will always have a foot in both worlds, constantly evaluating between a product available now down the street, or cheaper online if you are willing to wait and pay for shipping. You can think of it as a "convenience curve" that trades off price for convenience and immediacy. The ultimate price is probably found online; the ultimate convenience is paying a premium to have the item brought to you wherever it is currently geo-located. In all of these scenarios the role of mobile is to be a connector device. It gives you that world of physical and digital options at all times.

Mobile commerce, mobile advertising, mobile social networking. Where do you see the growth opportunity in 2010?

There is a big opportunity for mobile to increase commerce for both online and physical stores, but the biggest opportunity will be innovation from mobile advertising. In the short term, companies like NearbyNow that host many apps on the same platform can give advertisers an opportunity to reach a wide range of people who are actively shopping. This solves the "reach" problem that holds back a lot of advertisers. NearbyNow will evolve into an ad network, but using ad "units" far more powerful than banner ads. We're talking engaging experiences, like how-to videos to get a celebrity look, a catalog of all the products in the video, and using the phone to make an appointment with a nearby stylist to help you purchase and try it on. These are things we are doing today. From here we will see a lot of innovation on mobile ads. How about a coupon that is only good for one hour to stop you from buying online? How about a similar ad targeted to people shopping at Nordstrom to get them to come to Macy's? Once the capabilities can reach millions, the whole game is going to change. That's the power of mobile shopping.

SEE IT, CLICK IT, GET IT

More than 70 percent of all mobile phones have a camera. Tapping into the hundreds of millions of consumers who carry these devices is the holy-grail for marketers and brands worldwide. Scanbuy is the leading global provider of mobile marketing solutions that use the camera phone as the link between the physical world and the digital world. Its technology enables consumers to interact with brands by using their camera phone to photograph, or 'scan', barcodes printed on any media or packaging. Thus, consumers can launch a specific website or Web-based application, download content or a coupon, dial a phone number, compose an SMS/email, or receive a contact or calendar appointment. To date Scanbuy's ScanLife mobile application and Code Management Platform have been deployed and supported by leading mobile providers and handset manufacturers in the U.S., Mexico, Italy, Spain, and Denmark. Jonathan Bulkeley talks about the growth opportunities in 2010 and beyond.

Scanbuy is rolling out its platform for four major global mobile operators. How are you progressing and what do you expect in 2010?
2009 has been a good year for us and for the industry. We're rolling our platform out to Vodafone, Telefonica, America Movil and Telenor. On the OEM [Original Equipment Manufacturer] side we've signed deals with six out of the top seven handset OEMs, and nine out of the top nine handset OEMs are preloading our software in at least one or two markets. In 2010 I expect we'll begin to see 2D barcodes become more ubiquitous, but it's going to take another 12-18 months.

What is the real value of 2D barcodes?
The value is the business model it enables. It allows operators to monetize an Internet business model so they get revenue per click just like Google, but from the physical world.

The value to the consumer is ease of navigation. Mobile devices aren't built to let consumers easily input URLs to access a destination and get relevant and specific content back on their phone. It's just clumsy. Barcodes are a simple and scalable way of fixing that issue. Consumers just point their devices and, with one click, they're transported to that destination.

And the third piece of this is the code publishers. Almost 10,000 companies and

JONATHAN BULKELEY

CEO, Scanbuy

individuals have signed up to create codes on our platform over the last 12 months, ranging from individuals, who create codes that link to their Facebook page, to some 1,400 companies. For these companies and marketers the technology allows them to create links quickly and easily that enable consumers to connect with them using their mobile phone.

Last year we saw publishers use Scanbuy's 2D barcode to link their physical books to the product page on Amazon.com. And we know an increasing number of marketers and brands use barcodes in mobile advertising campaigns. What are the business drivers and benefits?

In the long term barcodes enable a range of models around marketing, advertising and commerce. In the short term there will be pockets of activity that outstrip others. We're seeing big brands use barcodes to create interactivity with their printed materials, printed materials, in-store promotions and product packaging.

A second area of activity is retail. In this scenario retailers create interactivity in the store, allowing consumers to get information on a product or scan a code to make a purchase.

And then there's a whole new use case involving government authorities. In Santiago, Chile, for example, every bus stop has a barcode on it and, with one click, people can get the schedule or find out when the bus will arrive at that stop.

So, I think those three areas – public use, big brands, and retail – are going to lead the charge over the next 12-18 months.

As you said, we will see an explosion in the use of 2D barcodes in the net 12-18 months. How is the business ecosystem shaping up?

In Spain, Mexico, France and the U.S. we see that ecosystem is evolving. There are several differences between each of the markets at this point. In Spain Telefónica, Orange and Vodafone are all working on a common platform, which is run by us. So, each of the operators has what's called a code management platform, allowing them to sell codes in the marketplace or assign re-sellers to sell codes for them. The system is completely interoperable. In our role we run the platforms for each of the operators and – through our deals with OEMs – we have the barcode scanning software on the phones.

Spain is a good example because the whole market is participating. All the operator handsets will come preloaded with our software and, in the next couple of years, there'll be 53 million phones. As a result, marketers, individuals and public authorities will all be able to go to the platform, create their codes and know they'll be interoperable across all the operators.

That is impressive, but we're still not seeing the mainstream use we see in countries such as Japan and Korea. What are the obstacles?

It's the proverbial chicken and egg problem. Operators will say, 'we'd like to see the brands participating.' But the brands aren't going to participate until the software is on enough handsets. In Spain we have solved that problem because the software is on the handsets. Telefónica has pre-loaded the software on some 60 handsets already. By the end of next year [2010] we'll probably have 50 million devices with the software. When that happens, then advertisers, marketers and public authorities will begin to take it seriously and barcodes will become ubiquitous very quickly.

To be clear, how many handsets do you expect will come with your software pre-loaded by end-2010?

The software would be on a least 75-100 million phones. In 2011, you're looking at 200-300 million phones. They're will concentrations by market. It will be Spain, the U.S., Latin America, Mexico, Canada, Italy and Denmark, with some other European countries kicking in sometime soon.

We talk about advertising, but this year's Netsize Guide also highlights the opportunities across verticals such as healthcare. What are the exciting verticals on your radar?

The opportunities are unlimited. We see government use, B2B applications, consumer applications, social media – everything! In Japan codes even appear on gravestones so you can scan the code and see the profile of the person who died.

In healthcare we're working with a company that does medical cards. Each card has the person's picture, their personal information and a code. This allows us to update the information the code links to on the server, making sure that, when the doctor scans it they see the most recent medical information.

And that's just the first wave of use. As the mobile devices get better in terms of screen quality, services and content, it only gets better all around.

Whether it's a barcode or some other trigger mechanism, I can scan an ad on 39th Street in New York for Gucci and I'll be able to see immediately which retailers sell Gucci within a five block radius and what they have in stock. That's pretty powerful. The next five years will be revolutionary.

ALL SYSTEMS GO!

PayPal, the eBay-owned ecommerce business that enables payments and money transfers, is on a roll in mobile. The company integrated PayPal payments in to the eBay iPhone app, launched an Android app that lets people send payments to friends from their contact list and announced its decision to open its PayPal X global platform to developers, allowing them to embed payment directly into their existing website or choice of mobile platform. But the real coup was the move by Research in Motion to rely only on PayPal mobile for checkout capabilities in its own BlackBerry App World applications store. Franceso Rovetta talks about the evolution of a new mobile commerce ecosystems and traction for its own service.

PayPal has launched a mobile website, an app for Android and the SendMoney app for the iPhone. What are you seeing in terms of downloads and purchases?

As you point out, a lot has happened in mobile. The iPhone application now accounts for approximately $2 million worldwide. And we see a pretty significant amount of activity on a weekly basis.

In addition to that, we have power mobile commerce solutions. Our integration with RIM's BlackBerry app store positions us as the sole payment option for users who want to purchase digital applications in that marketplace. We are present in 13 countries across the globe. Unfortunately, I am not able to share a lot of data on the transactions.

We also power the mobile website for eBay, where we are seeing impressive numbers. Since the start of the year [2009] sales generated from mobile total around $400 million, which is staggering.

Is mobile commerce limited to content and apps, or does it extend to big-ticket items?

The good news is it's both. In fact, a Lamborghini sold for more than $500,000 through mobile on eBay. It confirms that mobile commerce is not just a vision, but really becoming reality.

What happened in the marketplace to increase consumer acceptance of mobile payments? What are the drivers?

It's a combination of factors. On one hand, devices have become much better, so you have great devices in the U.S., Europe and in

FRANCESCO ROVETTA

Director of Business Development, PayPal Mobile

Asia that really allow and encourage mobile payments. It's a better user experience, and new pricing models mean consumers aren't so concerned about how much they are spending to view a web page or download content they have purchased on their phone.

At the same time, consumers are getting more comfortable with the mobile medium. They are therefore more incentivized to see the mobile experience as a true extension of their online experience.

I expect commerce will become a mainstream activity on mobile. If you examine the figures for e-commerce penetration 1999/2000, you see that user preference for e-commerce shopping was near the bottom of the list. Since then e-commerce has grown dramatically. It will be the same growth trajectory for mobile commerce, which is currently at the same level e-commerce was some 10 years ago before it saw explosive growth.

What are the requirements for a good mobile experience?

The user experience is key in determining the success of a solution or an application. We work to make sure it's not only intuitive: it has to be immediate because the attention span of mobile users can be short. Having said that, we also need to pay attention to security, which is one of the key values at PayPal.

An immediate payment, a click-less payment, experience would be ideal. On the other hand, and particularly as the average value of an item bought via mobile rises, we want to ensure that the user is comfortable with making a transaction and has all the security layers in place to perform that transaction. We strive to enable the most immediate check-out experience, as we call it, without compromising in security. To this end we employ the same sophisticated risk management, loss prevention and fraud prevention tools that we use online. They are invisible to the mobile user and make the experience safer.

Mobile payments have evolved and so has the value chain. Please describe the business ecosystem and your position in it.

The iPhone phenomenon has started some discussions and changed the industry. Collaboration across the value chain is the result, and it's happening at a number of levels and layers, involving device manufactures, mobile operators, platform and operating systems provider, and enablers like PayPal.

Overall, the players in the value chain realize that the mobile commerce and payments opportunity is too big to be encapsulated into the traditional value chain. New models need to be built, and that's where PayPal, in particular, can play a role

U.S. regulations do not permit operators there to use their billing capabilities to enable transactions that are not related to telecoms. And, even in the case of digital content and applications, there is a limit to the amount operators can bill. So, there is a need for companies to implement alternative methods of payments and that's where players like PayPal can be a great help. We have experience, we have eBay and we have the large number of merchants we work with across the globe. This experience feeds into the mobile experience we are creating.

We are also seeing the advance of technologies, such as 2D barcodes, Augmented Reality and NFC that enable or enhance commerce on our mobile phones. What is your view of these methods and where do you see the growth opportunities?

NFC is fascinating because it converges the online and mobile – the physical and the digital worlds – at the point of sale. Having said that, there are many moving pieces and issues, such as the business models and the security on the device, which all the players want to and must solve.

Barcodes also hold great potential and we are working with Big in Japan, the developers of mobile application ShopSavvy. Integration with PayPal's APIs allow consumers to immediately buy items through their PayPal account after they scan the product barcode with the camera in their mobile phone. The check-out mechanism for the merchant that appears is PayPal. It's exactly these new technologies that allow the shopping experience to be very topical, very successful and very effective for the user.

ShopSavvy is just one application using your new Adaptive Payments API. What have you achieved by holding your first developer conference and what are your goals?

PayPal held its first conference in November 2009 to reach out to the developer community and answer their need to monetize their content and applications through what is truly an open platform combining what can be done online and in the mobile environment. Now a check-out solution or a payment solution powered by PayPal can be embedded in any mobile service or online website.

Our penetration in the U.S. and Europe is strong, and we are growing in Asia and in emerging markets. Of course, there is still a long way to go in all these markets. We want to capitalize on our brand and our reputation among the merchants - and now the publishers, the content providers, the developers - who trust our technology.

TRANSFORM-
ATION

AUGMENTED
REALITY
FUTURE
EDUCATION
HEALTH

> The biggest significance of mobile phones as media is that they have increased our closeness to virtual reality."

Toshinao Sasaki, Japanese writer and net culture guru, 2009.

Mobile in 2010 is TRANSFORMATION: the barriers between the physical and virtual worlds blurs – and both become actionable. The mobile phone becomes the remote control of our lives and an extension of our "selves".

As the previous chapters illustrate, 2009 saw a subtle yet seismic shift in the role of mobile in our everyday lives. The rise of the application stores, the advance of smartphones and the emergence of a new era of user experience prompted by the emergence of augmented reality services and browsers combined – even collided – to take mobile to a new level.

We no longer think of mobile as a device. It is the device that connects our communications, our experiences and allows us to manage both according to our real-time requirements, personal preferences and current location. It is the device that accepts advertising, conducts commerce and enables a variety of exciting business models we have yet to develop or even dream of. And, of course, mobile is a state of being and a way of life.

What is the future of mobile?

The Netsize Mobile Trends Survey 2010 reached out to professionals and practitioners for their insights and ideas. Granted, the vast majority of respondents perceive mobile as a communications device first and foremost. However, a significant percentage recognizes that mobile is becoming much, much more.

Mobile enables us to capture and consume content; it impacts how, when and where we connect with friends and family; and it links our physical and digital worlds. The result is the emergence of more immersive experiences and more holistic business models, future scenarios we will explore more in this chapter. **See Figure**

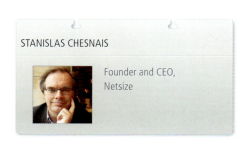

STANISLAS CHESNAIS

Founder and CEO, Netsize

Netsize also asked respondents to offer their vision of mobile and its role in our

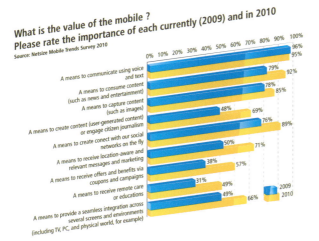

lives three years from now. Many answers focused on the services we will likely see cross the chasm (finally!) now that industry conditions and consumer acceptance are more aligned.

Mobile payments will take off, location services will deliver, mobile coupons and bar code schemes will become commonplace, mobile search will unleash the real potential of the Mobile Internet and other industry verticals, such as retail, healthcare and education, will embrace mobile to enhance services and improve our lives.

These are just a few of the trends that top the radar of our survey respondents.
However, respondents to the survey also shared visions that speak volumes about the exciting times ahead.
- "The consumer will be the boss, with communication services and information delivered on-demand and according to real-time requirements."
- "Mobile will become a means to provide seamless integration across several screens and environments, including TV, PC and the physical world, for example."
- "Mobile will be our personal link to EVERYTHING!"
- "Mobile is now an identity. My prediction is: mobile will … become more critical to everyday life."

And my personal favorite:
- "My mobile device becomes ME, customized to who I am, what I'm into and what I need to do."

Is mobile a bit like a trusted butler that faithfully delivers what you want – the way you want it –without you really having to ask for it? Or is mobile an extension of our "selves," allowing us to interface with the world(s) around us?

(R)evolution

There are no easy answers, but the observations of Mark Curtis, CEO of Flirtomatic, a pioneer mobile flirting service and one of the most popular social mobile services worldwide, provide us with a fresh perspective. **See interview, page 36**

During the interview with our author Peggy Anne Salz, Mark developed a thought-provoking analogy between the role of mobile in our everyday lives and the relationship between "daemons" and characters in the fantasy trilogy known as the His Dark Materials series written by English novelist Philip Pullman.

In the first book, The Golden Compass, the characters live in a parallel world to ours where all human souls take the form of animal companions called daemons. These small, often-changing animals are lifelong companions. Every person in this fantasy world has a daemon. What's more, daemons can change form to reflect moods or inner feelings of their owners. The bold and adventurous Lord Asriel, for example, has a snow leopard for a daemon. Severing a character from their daemon is like separating someone from their soul. The bond between the characters and their daemons is a close relationship that can never be broken.

In many ways, Curtis says, this was the role of mobile in phase one in the evolution of our personal mobility. In the last decade, mobile devices, like our daemons, became extensions of our "selves." We personalized them with ringtones, images and wallpapers. And a raft of reports detailed the feelings of isolation and even depression we felt when we were separated from our mobile devices, unable to receive text messages or connect with our social networks. Based on a series of surveys, interviews and focus groups, market research firm Solutions Research Group concluded that 27 percent of respondents suffered increased levels of anxiety when separated from their mobile phones or the Internet. A further 41 percent suffered occasional anxiety due to communications blackout.

Clearly, our lives and our devices have become inextricably intertwined.

Transformation_

Reality trip

What is the future of mobile in our lives?

Curtis draws from The Subtle Knife, the second book of the series, to offer us an answer. In this novel the "subtle" knife has two sides: one can cut through any known matter and the other can cut into different worlds. Put another way, this knife can cut through the fabric of space-time and open windows between worlds.

In phase two of the evolution of our personal mobility, a phase that begins with 2010, mobile is becoming our multi-functional subtle knife.

We use it to create and enter parallel places, and link between the physical and virtual worlds. With our mobile phones we can step away from the stress of our daily commute to enter personalized social networks, spaces where representations of us (images and avatars) connect with friends and family. Even better if this exchange is geo-tagged, providing us with the necessary bread crumb trail to follow if we want to meet our peers in real-life, visit the places we discuss or just check out the restaurant our communities currently say is all the rage.

And it doesn't stop there. The advance of smartphones – equipped with GPS, compass, video and accelerometers that allow devices to detect and respond to motion – pave the way for an avalanche of Augmented Reality (AR) applications. These applications harness the features and functionalities of advancements in mobile phone technology to merge the physical world around us with information compiled about people and places on the Internet.

It's a brave new world that we can see with new eyes thanks to the range of AR applications in development and on the market. The following interviews with GeoVector and Layar, two leading AR companies, describe the business models and industry drivers that could make augmented reality an integral part of our everyday lives.

As John Ellenby, CEO of GeoVector, a company providing "advanced pointing search" and augmented reality capabilities for location applications, put it: "[Mobile usage is no longer just about checking the weather or retrieving information about your bid on eBay. Now it's about discovery and ways to use my phone to find out what's interesting or what has changed." **See interview, page 113.**

New territory

But the future of mobile is not only about expansion into new dimensions that link our worlds together. It is also about the ways emerging regions will harness personal mobility to bridge the "digital divide" and overcome the disparity of access to information and communications technologies that exists between developed and developing nations.

Indeed, the benefits communication can bring to development are overwhelming and encouraging. A recent study by the London School of Business revealed that an increase of 10 mobile phones per 100 people translates into a 0.6 percent percentage point rise in GDP. However, this figure represents only the direct impact. The GSM Association (GSMA), a professional organization that represents the interests of the worldwide mobile communications industry, found that the indirect impact is at least three times as great.

Mobile is also at the heart of work underway at the Massachusetts Institute of Technology (MIT), where researchers within the Media Lab's Next Billion Network are exploring ways mobile can be used to improve life and eradicate poverty. New applications revolve around ways to facilitate mobile banking, improve healthcare and increase literacy rates.

In the following section, Susan Dray, President, Dray & Associates, Inc., walks us through some of the ways emerging markets are using mobile to achieve socioeconomic development goals. In her view, mobile innovation can close the gap between the information "haves" and "have nots" that exists everywhere, not only in Africa, Asia and Latin America.

As she puts it: "The success of mobile in the developing world is linked to the commitment of companies to understand local needs, and translate it into usable and affordable product. The impact of these innovations will be global, providing benefit to all people." **See interview, page 104.**

Vertical shift

Finally, mobile also opens up a new world of new possibilities for a range of vertical industry segments. An obvious success story is mobile marketing; where mobile is reinventing how customers interact with brands and products at store level.

Location search services, targeted and relevant advertising messages and 2D bar code campaigns are just a few of innovations that are turning mobile marketing into mobile shopping.

As James Crawford, Executive Director of the Global Retail Executive Council (GREC) said in a recent interview with Mobile Marketing Magazine: "Mobile retail applications offer retailers of any size solutions that significantly boost operational efficiencies, loyalty and sales. By offering interactivity and immediacy, from communicating shelf talkers to multimedia end cap promotions, the business of in-store, point-of-sale advertising is about to undergo a transformation that will have to be seen to be believed."

Mobile is also transforming healthcare. According to market research firm Informa, activity in the mobile healthcare sector grew considerably in 2009, driven by interest and investment in services such as tracking, tagging and remote patient monitoring. Notably, the European Union is investing more public funds into remote monitoring and the development of "intelligent environments" using wireless sensor networks.

Another driver comes from the combined efforts of the Rockefeller Foundation, the United Nations Foundation and The Vodafone Foundation, which joined forces at the GSMA's Mobile World Congress in 2009 to form the Mobile Health (mHealth) Alliance, a partnership that will work to maximize the impact of mobile health, especially in the developing world.

Terry Kramer, Vodafone Foundation Trustee, said in a press statement: "When you consider that there are 2.2 billion mobile phones in the developing world, 305 million computers but only 11 million hospital beds you can instantly see how mobiles can create effective solutions to address healthcare challenges. Mobile technology is providing new hope in the provision and promotion of quality healthcare in a number of ways, such as accelerating the collection and storage of patient data, training rural professionals and personalizing the way patients receive medical treatment."

The following section illustrates how the combination of mobile and healthcare can deliver tremendous benefits, such as cost savings for healthcare providers as well as convenience and improved quality of life for patients. We speak with James E. (Jim) Nalley, Co-Founder and CEO of EmFinders, a U.S.-based technology firm that has harnessed mobile to provide new support to caregivers and new freedom to a growing population of patients. **See interview, page 110.**

Enter the "Intersection"

I began this chapter with a discussion of the future of mobile, drawing from a selection of scenarios and use cases I believe provide valuable insight into the many ways mobile will impact our lives and our society.

Indeed, our worlds are combining and colliding, dynamics that will have a profound impact on our collective future.

What can we expect?

I would like to think that we are on the cusp of a modern-day Renaissance.

Frans Johansson, author of the business book, The Medici Effect: Breakthrough Insights at the Intersection of Ideas, Concepts & Culture, argues that breakthrough ideas are found at the intersection of different cultures, occupations, ways of thinking and points of view. Put another way, the Intersection is where we will find an explosion of extraordinary creativity and thought.

In fact, the book takes its name from the intersection that gave us the Renaissance and the remarkable burst of creativity that accompanied it. In the 15th century, the Medici family, a banking family in Florence, funded creators from a wide variety of disciplines. As a result, sculptors, scientists, poets, philosophers, financiers and architects converged upon the city of Florence. Together they forged a new world based on "intersectional ideas," ideas that emerge at the intersection of cultures, expertise and mindsets.

The good news is that intersections tend to yield an exponential increase in ideas and concepts. The better news: this explosion of ideas is percolating at a place within everyone's reach. In Johansson's view, "the movement of people, the convergence of scientific disciplines and the leap in computational power are increasing the number and types of intersections we can access."

I would add that for this modern-day Renaissance mobile is the critical factor.

Mobile allows us to collaborate, communicate, and connect with diverse networks of people, breaking down the walls between cultures, professions and fields of knowledge.

Moving forward, mobile is much more than a medium that we can use to link worlds and explore new possibilities. It is the door that opens a multitude of Intersections, where we will find new opportunities, surmount new challenges and gain new insights.

MIND THE GAP

The mobile revolution has been hailed as the enabling force for emerging markets and developing countries to become more active participants in the global economy. Given the right tools and environment, people can harness mobile technology to leapfrog more developed countries, creating localized content and services that address local problems and issues, and ultimately close the digital divide. Susan Dray has worked as both an internal and external consultant, combining her expertise in interface evaluation, usability evaluation and ethnographic research to help develop solutions that increase benefits to people in emerging markets and the service providers that operate there. She talks about the positive impact of mobile and the ways in which local communities are using mobile tools to achieve socioeconomic development goals.

What is user-centered design (UCD) and what are the benefits, particularly in emerging countries and markets?

Much of the motivation guiding design and development of mobile technology today is 'techno-centric.' User-centered design (UCD) begins from a very different premise. If companies are to design products and services that will truly meet users' needs, they have to start by gaining deep understanding of who their users are, and, most importantly, how the new product or service will fit into the cultural, social, technical, and physical contexts of the intended users' lives. Localization – or fitting a product to the users and context of another country – is not simply a matter of translation, adapting the interface to fit local information display conventions, or visual design preferences that are different from those we are used to. We also need to understand how people work and live in other places, so that the localized product will fit into their lives. When we learn about this, we may decide that the very product concept has to change for localization to even be possible. It is very common that early user research in a variety of international markets results in new product concepts. This is equally true for mobiles as it is for PC-based applications.

How has the market changed over the years?

In 2009 we saw a proliferation of people

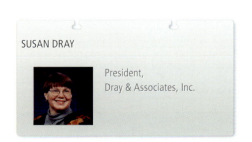

SUSAN DRAY

President,
Dray & Associates, Inc.

developing mobile phone content and services that fit their context because they finally have the tools to do it. Some of this driven by the advance of voice-activated services which are becoming ubiquitous and extend mobility to the functionally-illiterate in these regions.

But there is also a new wave of interest and excitement in SMS as more people design more applications that make use of text. Indeed, there is a groundswell of grassroots efforts around the globe to meet local needs with text services that are relevant to the lives of people and improve life in the community, particularly in areas where village residents share a mobile phone.

On one hand, it's about education, healthcare and using mobile to help bring socio-economic stability and sustainability. On the other hand, it's about progress and services such as mobile banking, where Africa leads the world because its people are under-banked and under-served. At both ends of the spectrum, it's fascinating how incredibly creative scarcity can make people.

From healthcare to banking, the mobile phone is at the center of this innovation. Can you provide some concrete examples?

Take Ushahidi, which means "testimony" in Swahili, a website that was initially developed to map reports of violence in Kenya after the post-election fallout at the beginning of 2008. Ushahidi's roots are in the collaboration of Kenyan citizen journalists using their mobile phones to capture and report incidents during a time of crisis. This initial deployment was the catalyst for realizing there was a need for a platform based on it, which could be use by others around the world. It has since been used in the DR Congo and South Africa. In fact, I was in South Africa during the xenophobic riots where Ushahidi was used to map the incidents of violence. It's an exciting project with obvious benefits that continues to grow in scope and impact.

Another example is Souktel, an SMS service based in the Middle East and East Africa, which uses text to connect users to everything from jobs and internships to humanitarian aid and youth leadership programs. Job seekers can register via SMS with Souktel, and then, through a series of text messages, enter details about themselves into the system. Whenever the job seeker is looking for a job, they can text 'match me' to Souktel to receive an instant list of jobs that matches the resume stored in the system. The service also helps connect humanitarian agencies with people who are looking for aid.

And let's not forget how mobile is improving healthcare awareness and treatment. In India IFFCO, a service provided by a fertilizer cooperative with over one million members, provides rural Indian farmers voice messages and regular updates about crop and veterinary information and empower them through technology. The voice messages are in local languages, so they are accessible even to illiterate farmers or those who don't speak English and who can't read text messages. In South Africa an impressive project is Cell-Life, which uses mobile phones in the hands of rural HIV/AIDS workers to monitor patient health and reactions to AVRs. The HIV Aids rate in South Africa is over 30 percent of the population, so services that allow healthcare workers to collect symptoms from patients and text those back to the doctor or pharmacist ensure that the right treatment and dosage is given. And in

Malawi, UNICEF has been using cell phones to monitor children for signs of malnutrition using the RapidSMS system that allows UNICEF can rapidly move into areas where malnutrition appears to be imminent.

These are some amazing success stories. What will ensure that there are more to come?

I am optimistic because I see signs that companies understand they can not just export their ideas to an emerging market or country. It's about understanding the people and their environment, and the more companies internalize this the more they are going to be able to mail it with an application that, like Cell-Life, is ethnographically-driven at its core.

What are some key learnings or lessons you can offer?

Mobile companies have to think locally and tailor services to the local environment. So, developing a basic toolkit and being able to tweak it is important. We also need to do more to educate people in different parts of the world so they can take these basic ideas and services and make them their own, using them to design new technology, new applications and spread brilliant ideas like m-banking. Mobile banking came out of nowhere and now it is everywhere [in the developing world] because it fits the local environment and understands the needs of local people.

The success of mobile in the developing world is linked to the commitment of companies to understand local needs, and translate it into usable and affordable product. The impact of these innovations will be global, providing benefit to all people. Some companies are retrenching due to the recession, but I am hopeful that these companies will soon realize that – if they really want to have impact – they must have a grasp of the local situation. Nokia and Intel, for example, are companies that understand the importance of local perspective in the creation of mobile technology and services. They also understand that the central position of mobile – the only screen for users in these regions – influences the kind of chipsets and services we will likely need for all mobile phones, in these regions and – ultimately – around the world.

BROWSE THE WORLD

Advancements in mobile phone technology have cleared the way for a flood of Augmented Reality (AR) applications that merge the physical world with information compiled about people and places on the Internet. One company riding that wave is Dutch-owned Layar. In 2009 it released its reality browser application Layar, this mobile browser shows people what is around them by displaying real-time digital information on top of reality they view through the device camera. On top of the camera image Layar adds content 'layers,' which are the equivalent of Web pages in normal browsers. The platform allows customers, such as businesses, the ability to offer a range of layers, allowing consumers to see houses for sale, popular bars and shops, jobs on offer in the area, and a list of local doctors and ATMs by scanning the landscape. Maarten Lens-FitzGerald discusses the ways AR enhances reality and paves the way for real business models.

Augmented Reality has been around for almost 20 years, but mobile AR exploded last year, when penetration of smartphones equipped with GPS systems, compasses and accelerometers increased. What level of interest are you seeing?

In the week that we launched the iPhone app we had over 100,000 downloads and we served over a million augmented views to the world. Currently, there are over 1,500 developers and over 300 layers have been published.

How do you make money on Layar?

It's free for the user and it's free for the content provider or developer. Where we make money is placement. To understand this we have to understand the user experience. Starting up the Layar application automatically activates the camera. The embedded GPS automatically knows the location of the phone and the compass determines in which direction the phone is facing. Each partner provides a set of location coordinates with relevant information which forms a digital layer.

There will be lots of layers, just as there are Web pages. The problem will be discovery. We address this by allowing companies to participate in our Pay for Prominence program. When users start Layar, it starts up in

MAARTEN LENS-FITZGERALD

Co-founder & VP of Distribution and Marketing, Layar

the Favorites list, which is like Bookmarks on your Web browser. Those positions are for sale. The same goes for the Featured section, a section where companies can pay for placement to reach the more advanced users who come back.

How do you make these layers relevant to me and my context?

What we serve in the Favorite and Featured sections is all based on your region. If you're in the U.S. you won't see the Dutch layers, for example. So, based on where you are, you select a layer and we send the request through our server to give you the relevant content. If you open up the Trulia layer to find homes for sale, you will be shown houses around your location.

How do you see your pay for placement model evolving? Will you harness personalization or targeting?

That is how it will develop. What we do now is help content owners get on top of the stack of layers, much in the same way that Google has AdWords. We will have premium layers where companies can pay to add something to a layer relevant to their offer.

In the future, the browser will know who you are, and that you're ready to go out, for example. Based on this the top layers you see will be layers about places to go, a lot like restaurant review guides. Some of these listings will be paid for by the restaurant owners or businesses who want to appear in the layer, the same way they advertise on Web pages, for example.

You focus on advertising in this example. Is that the big growth opportunity?

It's for the businesses that need to provide to their customers information right here, right now. I'm looking for a house for sale, so show me one. But it's not just about real estate; it's about goods and services nearby in the real world. Where is the bus station? Where can I get a taxi? Where can I get a bite to eat? Any business that has to get this information out to us can benefit from AR. And to enhance this we have added the ability for businesses to provide AR experiences complete with 3-D objects and interactivity.

AR is a nascent industry. What is the value chain and how do you work with other players in your ecosystem, such as operators and brands?

We're in for great ride and, as an industry, we'll see come change and consolidation. In the end there will only be one or two companies that have the browser and the platform, and will grow from there. I see that happening and within the next six months.

How the value chain is shaping up? Actually, it's not a chain; it's a web and it's all connected. On one hand, we have the users and we're working on a better user interface to satisfy them. An example of this is our 3-D release, for which we also need new 3-D content and the content developers.

On the other hand, we have the device manufacturers that we talk to in order to get pre-installation deals and also ensure their devices work well with our software, and vice versa. Then we also talk with the carriers about where we can get pre-installed and have a unique offering with Layar.

What is your vision for what AR can enable and how that will impact our lives moving forward?
An experience that is very core to AR is the ability to walk around and experience other worlds and walk around in a city the way it was a century ago, for example. That kind of storytelling will enable the creation of immersive experiences. It's easy to imagine the benefit to education. It will be like being able to not just read a book, but actually visualize it. This is why we added 3-D and interactivity.

AR will also be a boost to vendor relationship management, putting the individual in control of the information they will accept based on their needs. Put another way, AR will allow people to issue a 'Request For Proposal,' which businesses can answer.

Let's say you're looking for a table for four in a Mexican restaurant. You put that information out and people are only then allowed to see your profile and to reply to you using AR. So, a restaurant owner might pop up in front of you, saying, 'hey, I've got a table and we have good food – so take a look at the reviews here on the Web and then come on over.' If you end up going to that restaurant, then we might get a percentage of that deal. That's a model we're looking at.

We're also looking at ways to benefit organizations such as the Heart Foundation in Holland. In time for Valentine's Day we will make it possible for people to buy and display a 3-D heart in front of the house where their loved one lives, for example. The money will go to charity and people who walk around the city will see all these hearts placed by people who are expressing their love.

FINDING NOT TRACKING

Mobile is at the core of an increasing number of healthcare services and solutions, allowing hospitals and doctors to monitor patients at a distance. EmFinders has taken a different approach. The U.S.-based technology firm has harnessed mobile to provide new support to caregivers and new freedom to a growing population of individuals with Alzheimer's disease, autism, and a range of cognitive and developmental disabilities. The aim is to facilitate the rapid location and recovery of wandering or missing adults and children. EmFinders achieves this through EmSeeQ, which combines a small, watch-like, wireless device without buttons or a screen, and a location service that uses triangulation through the cellular network – and with 9-1-1 emergency response systems - to accurately determine a person's location. James E. (Jim) Nalley talks about the central role of mobile in tomorrow's medical and emergency services.

What does your service deliver and what is the response so far?

We are seeing a tremendous amount of interest from law enforcement, and the main attraction is the service saves lives and a great deal of money, time and effort in the process. As our population ages, Alzheimer's disease is going to strike a large percentage of that population. There are roughly 5.3 million diagnosed cases in the United States right now. Add children who have autism – that's one in 110 -- and individuals with Down syndrome, all people that have cognitive and developmental disabilities, and we're talking about an impaired community of around 10 million individuals.

Many of these folks really can't use a mobile phone, but we need to give them something like a mobile device that gives them some freedom. It's also important that these devices give some peace of mind to the caregivers and their families to ensure that – if the impaired person wanders off – then we can recover them quickly. Our goal since we started has been to take the search out of search and rescue missions. The company is getting some great traction and we're in discussions with some major hospitals and long-term care facilities that are looking to buy multiple units.

What is your main selling point?

It's around delivering peace-of-mind, safety,

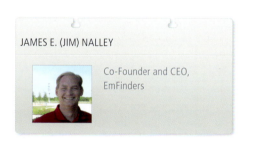

JAMES E. (JIM) NALLEY

Co-Founder and CEO, EmFinders

Transformation_ Finding not tracking

and convenience to our end-customers, the impaired individuals and their caregivers, and improving cost savings for everyone else. There are many ways mobile technology can be used to help save real dollars. A typical search and rescue operation can cost a local municipality anywhere from $15,000 to $25,000. You have to remember you may have helicopters in the air and multiple squad cars and K9 units looking for these individuals on the ground.

But if the individual has an EmFinders unit on their body, that recovery process takes one police officer driving to that location to pick them up and take them home. There's no additional cost to the police department, so we're helping save hundreds of millions of dollars in that process alone.

What is the benefit to your end-customers?
It's about personal mobility and giving these impaired people and their families the freedom they haven't had before. We're hearing back from our customers that we're making it possible for them to go on vacation for the first time in years because now they don't have to be worried that their mom or dad or child is going to wander off and not be able to be found again.

We also integrate directly into the 9-1-1 system. We're the only unit out there that does that and this allows the police departments and dispatchers to control the recovery process, taking the responsibility to track and act as a middle person off of the caregiver. Location information is delivered directly to 9-1-1 operators and doesn't float over the Internet, which we know is not the most secure place for data.

The experience for the user and the caregiver is positive because the device is a water-resistant, durable lightweight product that the impaired individual can wear all the time. And our charge cycle is seven days, so our device lasts longer than others out there that require people to recharge every day or every other day. We also send automatic alerts when the battery is low.

You are sending alerts, but you could use text to encourage a two-way conversation with caregivers or even pursue a more mobile CRM strategy. Are you exploring these options?
CRM is a growth opportunity. But first we're trying to gauge what the conversation should be with caregivers. Right now, we focus on low battery alerts and we send periodic emails to ask caregivers to update their loved ones' information. As the child who has autism child ages, for example, their description is going to change. We ask the caregiver to provide information, so we can

provide support.

We can also gather and share information about the individual and communicate that to the caregiver with permission and to law enforcement and emergency workers in the event of a search and rescue. This information can be medical information like whether the potential wanderer has diabetes or is on medication. This information can also be set up at the level the caregiver wants and updated as needed. I see that we will evolve as we learn more about what information and level of interaction the caregiver wants.

But we are also looking at other opportunities. If we could move this technology into other arenas to prevent kidnapping, for example, then you start to understand where all this can go. We don't track people, we find people. That's the big difference. I don't need to know where they are all the time. When something or someone is missing, then we want to recover them. We are not tracking the individual all the time, just when we are needed. It's not Big Brother watching, it's not an invasion of privacy.

Are you planning to expand into other areas and countries?

It's possible and we are looking at becoming more international. Of course, there are some network enhancements that probably need to be made to provide better accuracy at the network level to transport that location information. That's one reason why we chose GSM versus CDMA technologies. GSM is an international system, so there is some real opportunity to expand our offer. After all, there are some 150 million people with Alzheimer's in the world today. It's a big number and it's only going to get bigger.

Tracking technology is nothing new. Why the new interest in using mobile to deliver healthcare services?

We're just starting as an industry to understand what mHealth is and the services we should offer. A lot of companies have gone out and tried to build the best mouse trap, building better technology without ever asking the caregivers if it's what they really want or need. A lot of this innovation has missed the mark.

Many in the mobile industry had a 'build it, they'll buy it' mentality, which isn't the case anymore because this isn't a mobile phone. These devices are single-purpose-driven devices that provide a service to a certain group, such as the population of individuals with Alzheimer's disease. This is the trend we are seeing in the marketplace and I think this trend is going to continue and that we'll see more mobile devices being made to serve a specific purpose.

POINTING TO PROFITS

GeoVector, an industry pioneer headquartered in San Francisco, has been inventing, developing and fielding innovative pointing and Augmented Reality (AR) capabilities for mobile devices since 1991. Since then the company has experienced much success in Japan, where it launched the first commercial AR offering on the KDDI network with the help of local partners. In 2009 GeoVector released its first application for the iPhone and Android platforms aimed at the U.S. and European markets. The World Surfer application does more than hyperlink the real world; it also provides an attractive vehicle for marketers to connect with consumers on the go. John Ellenby talks about the company roadmap and the future outlook for more immersive mobile marketing.

GeoVector has a long track record in directional searching and AR.
Please walk me through some of the milestones and key learnings you can share.

We provided a commercial service in Japan beginning in 2006. As you know, this is a technology-savvy market. But it's also a market where users are concerned about user-friendliness and personal privacy. They want to have a service that's 24/7. More importantly, it should be easy to use and useful. The Japanese will also not put up with spam. So, if the phone grunts out or delivers some message like 'lovely lattes here' when you pass a coffee shop, that's a service that they will kill immediately – and with good reason.
What we have learnt from Japan is that there is a requirement for carrier-grade services, offering up-time, privacy and security. Our operations in the U.S. and Europe, where we have launched World Surfer, leverage our experience in Japan.

The World Surfer is a product that brings local search applications together with pointing and Augmented Reality to a variety of handsets, not just top-of-the-line smartphones. We're interested in reaching the middle-grade phones, if you like, and so are businesses and brands. So, we're trying to position ourselves as a highly-reliable service provider with an imaginative, easy-to-use and secure product that can be provisioned and be made available on a large variety and volume of phones.

JOHN ELLENBY

CEO, GeoVector

How does combining pointing and Augmented Reality add value to the service? And what is the end-user experience?

Accurate pointing underpins the service. It knows which way the user is pointing the phone and delivers the user information along the vector that the phone is pointing, hence the company name GeoVector. That information can be visualized in a variety of ways. We can visualize it as lists. We can visualize it on a compass. And we can show the things that at in that direction as well as the things that meet your criteria.

So, we can display this as a list. But it can also be shown in graphics, which is what World Surfer does. In addition, we have the ability to visualize information in other ways that are covered by our patents that harness various kinds of Augmented Reality. In fact, Release 2 of our World Surfer will have augmented reality as a part of that visualization, allowing users to retrieve information in camera view. This will also make entertainment content very engaging.

Can you provide an example of how entertainment fits in?

Let's take the example of a billboard advertisement for a movie. You point the phone at the billboard to receive some related content on your phone, as well as the times the movie is playing at a nearby theater. It's also easy to imagine that one of the leading characters in the movie joins you on the device screen and guides you – and you are in the form of an avatar on the screen – to the theater. As you know, one of our co-founders is from Pixar, so our company has a strong connection to animated entertainment and the scenario I described is not too far away.

What are the key business drivers?

I think the timing is right because the devices are available. Another driver is the strong interest we are beginning to see from advertisers. They are beginning to produce more imaginative content and campaigns for mobile. I'm excited about this development because these advertisers are going to bring considerable creativity and imagination to this space and produce some very engaging content.

A third factor is the willingness of people to use data services. But usage is no longer just about checking the weather or retrieving information about your bid on eBay.

Now it's about discovery and ways to use my phone to find out what's interesting or what has changed.

We've had positive feedback from users of World Surfer and people say it's actually rekindled their interest in the world around them. They use it to find out more about the area they're in, and this also represents an extraordinary opportunity to the merchandiser, the advertiser or the enterprise that wishes to serve them at that place and meet their needs. Moving forward, more of these services will be triggered through pointing and they will be personalized services available to you if you're willing to identify yourself to them. That's where the offer and the infrastructure that we've created in Japan comes in to provide people privacy and security, making them feel comfortable about identifying themselves to companies that want to reach out to them.

What kinds of services do you support now and what services do you envision?

In the U.S. Papa John's [pizza] and Starbucks are featured on our World Surfer application on the iPhone and Android platforms. Users can click the Papa John's or Starbucks channel and interact with the brands on several levels, including obtaining a guide to the nearest location and coupons. In the case of Starbucks this could facilitate the ordering and paying process, which beats lining up for service.

So, instead of standing in line and having to say, 'I want a double latte with a cinnamon twist and a cinnamon bun,' you pre-order it by pointing at the location of the coffee house. As you come closer it's ready for you. This is what is happening now and what we'll see more of in the future. Consumers will be able to do more than ever – order things they way they like them, access information they need and even buy books from Amazon related to the landmark where they're standing – all this and all at the point of action.

What do you expect in 2010 and beyond?

I expect the industry to experience massive growth. There will be more money invested to promote and provision these pointing and Augmented Reality services, and we'll see major carriers and portals offering them as well. This will happen because of the obvious value they offer to advertisers, enterprises and the venture capital companies the industry needs to get this started.

For GeoVector it will be an exciting year. We already partner with NEC and Mapion in Japan and we're interested in partnering with other companies on a revenue share basis. Advertising will be another focus. I am excited by the number of advertising agencies that are speaking with us because, to me, that's a sign that we have a real winner here.

READ MY MIND

Many companies offer tools and technology that will allow people to capture and share experiences with their mobile phones. However, U.S.-based Evernote has something much more ambitious in mind. It has developed a mix of technology and services to help users create and maintain an external brain. Put simply, Evernote's technology allows consumers to capture information in any environment using whatever device or platform they find most convenient. More importantly, Evernote makes this information accessible and searchable at any time, from anywhere. Since its launch in June, 2008, Evernote has released native versions of its software for Windows, Mac, Web, iPhone, Android, BlackBerry, Palm Pre, and Windows Mobile. Phil Libin talks about the role of mobile and what can happen when people have instant access to all their memories.

Evernote's stated ambition is to help us create and maintain an external brain. What does this mean and how do you facilitate this?

The 'Ever' in Evernote is all about everywhere and forever. We offer a lifestyle application for our customers to use forever, without worrying about the device, synchronization, copying, migrating and things like that. They also don't have to worry about remembering stuff because Evernote gives them a perfect memory.

We figure that everything that happens to you in your life can be broken down into two parts: the stuff that happens to you while you're sitting in front of a computer screen and the stuff that happens when you're elsewhere. When you're on your PC we make it simple for you to highlight whatever it is you want to remember – a section of a web page, a document, an email or anything else – and then hit one button to capture it. You can think of it as a universal clipping service. It captures the text, the images, the links, and sends them off to your Evernote account.

The rest of the time your mobile device becomes your universal brain extension. You can just take out your cameraphone and snap a picture of what you want to remember and it automatically goes to Evernote. There your pictures, audio, text, web clips – whether they're from a phone or a desktop – are all synchronized onto our servers, where we index them by time, date, location, and tag

PHIL LIBIN
CEO, Evernote

Transformation_ Read my mind

them. You can search and find what you need and we make all this information available to you in Evernote, which you can access through any computer or phone.

Capturing content is one part of what we do. But we also share with friends and family. Is there a social aspect to your service?

We do let you share notebooks with people, but that's a relatively minor feature of Evernote. The choice not to focus on sharing was intentional because we wanted to be unlike every other Web 2.0 app that launched two years ago; we wanted to not be social. We decided not to target the extroverted market of people that just care about what their friends are doing; we focused on the two-thirds of the population whose primary concern is work, school, hobbies and what's in their head. As a result, our users tend to be older professionals. The more information-centric, introverted market was, by definition, large and under-served. That's where we saw the opportunity and the money.

How many users do you currently have and how do you generate revenues?

We have a growth rate that's faster than social apps such as Twitter. We are set to hit 2 million users before our 18-month anniversary. Twitter and Skype, which unlike Evernote are social and viral, took much longer to get to 2 million users.

We have a really simple business model. Our business model is we're going to make a service that's going to be used forever by hundreds of millions of people. We let people use it for free, without putting any time limits or big restrictions on usage. That gives users enough time to realize that it's worth paying $5 a month for a premium subscription. We're a straight premium play; we make money based on people converting to the premium version. The premium subscription gives you a few more features, such as general file attachments and a bigger allotment of new notes per month, but our goal is to make the free version good enough for 99 percent of our users.

Our conversion rate to premium goes up the longer people use the service. In the first month it's only a half of one percent. But after a year it's 2 percent, so 2 percent of all the people who sign up this month will be paying us 12 months from now. We only have about a year and a half of data at this point, but I can say that conversion is more than 6 percent, which is startling.

Having all my memories also allows you to recommend content and even advertising based on what I captured and what I think is important. Do you have ambitions to mine this data?

We don't want to show you ads and recommendations because we think it would just detract from our core mission. We also don't do data mining because it would require us to set up very comprehensive permissions and privacy policies.

However, I do see the great potential for using people's memories in Evernote as a platform upon which to build additional services. In fact, since we launched our API about a year ago, we have over 600 third-party developers currently creating Evernote apps. Some of these are about contextual recommendations and I know of one company that's writing a plug in that allows users to identify the wine a user is drinking and make suggestions of other wines based on that. Of course, the user has to give permission to the company first before it can deliver these recommendations.

What is the competitive landscape?

Our goal isn't to be better than anyone else; our goal is to be this great electronic memory. Going back to the wine recommendation application, we are seeing a lot of small companies that do some very smart things on the Evernote platform. We promote them and we do revenue-sharing on premium customers they bring to us. We see that as more than a way to get more of our functionality to our users: it's an interesting way to turn potential competitors into partners.

What are the exciting trends in 2010 and beyond?

I can tell you the trends I didn't get right. When I started at Evernote just over two years ago we had three viable platforms for smartphones: Blackberry, Windows Mobile and Symbian S60. I figured it would go from three to two, but it's actually grown to ten due to the advance of platforms including iPhone, Android and Palm Pre. The multiplication of mobile platforms is probably the biggest expense for us at this point.

On the positive side, another trend I got wrong - but I'm happy I got it wrong— is the new role of mobile operator in all of this. The carrier used to be the major roadblock that you had to overcome. But developments like iPhone and Android have weakened the carriers' grip, removing that obstacle as we move into 2010. In response, the carriers have become much more eager to innovate and much easier to deal with for a small company.

VIEWPOINTS

REGULATIONS
LEGAL
MARKET
GROWTH
DEVELOPMENT
INNOVATIONS

THE GLOBAL REGULATORY CHALLENGE

Setting the scene

The mobile industry is currently worth some $32 billion dollars globally. The consumer appetite for mobile content is fuelled by increasingly high quality products being offered in more innovative and user friendly ways.

Make no mistake; this is an exciting time to be involved in the mobile media industry. The ease and accessibility of mobile applications are further increasing this demand for mobile content. The 3rd MEF Business Confidence Index (BCI) Results published in November 2009 showed that:

- An average revenue growth of 33% has been predicted for the coming year, which is an increase of 6% on that being predicted at the beginning of 2009
- Respondents predicting that 63% of their revenue over the next quarter will come from both subscription and one off purchases. Games, video, music, social networking and infotainment continue to lead the way
- 14% of all revenue is now projected to come from applications

The problem of convergence

Surfing the internet, video and TV, music, radio, advertising, different payment mechanisms and more are all happening on one device. Convergence is real and it's finally happening. Whilst from a business development point of view this is very exciting, from a regulatory point of view it's an absolute nightmare.

Regulations and regulators are not equipped to deal with the challenges of regulating a converged market. Traditionally, each country will have specific regulators and/or regulations that deal with verticals. Rules on how to regulate advertising in print, TV or on the internet, the appropriateness of the content, different payment mechanisms (often for the same content) are treated differently depending on the regulator with jurisdiction. This creates regulatory overlap and event conflict which leads to significant confusion for the industry where it is not clear which regulations to comply with. This can make it very difficult for a company to globalise its offering or even determine which rules it needs to comply with in any given country.

SUHAIL BHAT

Policy and Initiatives Director, Mobile Entertainment Forum

For example, the chart above shows the complexity facing mobile media companies in the UK:

There is no easy fix and MEF has been increasingly approached by members throughout 2009 to deal specifically with regulatory issues. These relate predominantly to the possible implementation of new rules or changes to existing rules which the industry feel are onerous and damaging to industry. To counter this, MEF has been working hard to tackle regulatory issues throughout EMEA, South East Asia and the Americas.

Education

MEF has been trying to determine how best the industry and regulators can be served. The first important aspect we identified was education – not just letting the industry know what the rules are but also educating the regulators as to the types of services available, how they are purchased, what risks to consumers exist and how they can be managed. An important piece in this jigsaw that is often overlooked is educating consumers and ensuring there is trust in mobile media services.

In the UK we're supporting the regulator's media literacy programme which helps to educate consumers, particularly children, on the types of services available, how they operate, how they are charged etc. PhonepayPlus, as the regulator of premium rate (or VAS) services exists to ensure that consumers are treated fairly when using premium rate services. They state correctly that, for the long term success of mobile services, consumers need to have confidence that there are regulatory procedures in place to protect them and that there are mechanisms in place to assist them should things go wrong. PhonepayPlus undertake consumer campaigns aimed at providing useful and objective information to consumers on how best to use mobile media services.

The aim of this work is to empower consumers. There needs, however, to be a concerted joint effort from industry and regulators alike in each country to ensure consumers are better informed and have absolute clarity of costs or terms and conditions before they engage with a mobile service. This is not easy and it certainly is not cheap but it's absolutely essential. There have been some very high profile cases over the last year resulting in hefty fines to companies and a dip in consumer confidence. There have been instances of regulators threatening to close down segments of the industry caused by frustration and high levels of consumer complaints. Many of these issues can be resolved in part by educating the consumers, regulators and the industry better about how services should be advertised, ensuring appropriateness of content, so that consumers have all relevant information BEFORE they engage with services.

Key regulatory developments around the world

There have been, in a number of countries and regions, some key developments that are driving our regulatory work at MEF. Many tend to occur in the European Union. For this article we zoom in on two important ones: the Unfair Commercial Practices Directive and Audiovisual Media Services (AVMS) Directive.

- Unfair Commercial Practices Directive

This legislation introduced blanket regulations to protect consumers from unfair, misleading and aggressive selling practices throughout Europe. There were, for the first time, specific references to mobile media services. The Directive replaces or consolidates existing sector-specific and other consumer protection laws and mainly affected business-to-consumer transactions. The regulations apply before, during and after transactions.

In addition to the very widely worded general prohibition on "unfair commercial practices" and the more specifically worded prohibitions on misleading and aggressive practices, the regulations contain a blacklist of 31 practices that are always deemed unfair.

Businesses are not allowed to describe a product as "free" if consumers have to pay anything other than unavoidable cost of responding, or the costs of collecting or paying for the delivery of the products. With this rule the Directive addresses a common complaint from consumers. But while the extensive list suggests that the Directive achieves its set goals on consumer protection, it lacks clarity on some points that aid the industry in taking the right steps. What a rule that forbids "advertisements [containing] any direct exhortation to children to buy products or persuade their parents or other adults to buy products for them" means in practice is still far from clear.

The industry is desperate for some clarification particularly since the implications are severe. The means of enforcement range from self-regulatory and other informal procedures to civil action enforcement orders and – in serious cases – criminal proceedings. These may even lead to unlimited fines and up to two years imprisonment of company officers. In addition to producing a plain speaking Guide with Denton Wilde Sapte to the Unfair Commercial Practices Directive, we strongly urge businesses that have not already done so to be quick to assess whether their current practices may be deemed unfair under the new regulations.

- Audiovisual Media Services (AVMS) Directive

At present there is relatively limited regulation that needs to be considered in making audio-visual content available to the public on mobile devices and new media platforms in comparison with regulation applying to traditional television broadcasting. The AVMS Directive, transposed into national law by the 19th December 2009, changes this position for a range of audiovisual content service providers. Companies operating in this area may, in developing their business, need to consider more carefully the broadcast and content regulations, and rules and guidelines for advertising and sponsorship.

On a more positive note, the AVMS Directive has the potential to create opportunities by harmonising certain conflicting rules which currently apply in different EU member states and by making clear how the "country of origin" principle will apply to the mobile media sector. These changes may allow mobile companies operating across Europe to more fully exploit opportunities across the single market.

The examples above of new regulations are by no means exhaustive. There are literally hundreds of regulations that govern all the different services that are available to consumers on the mobile device. In order to try and make it easier to comply, we have produced and are continuing to produce an online Regulatory Database for 34 countries worldwide. This assists our members and regulators navigate the numerous Codes of Practice and legislation that impact their business strategies and bottom line. This online archive draws together information on the regulations applicable at a local, regional and international level, including access to guidance documents MEF has produced on specific codes; links to third-party resources for further reading; relevant contact details, etc.

- Regulatory Committees

With the increasing regulatory burdens imposed on the mobile entertainment ecosystem, MEF has set up an EMEA Regulatory Committee to consider, discuss and respond to the Codes that are impacting business strategies and revenues. The committee meets regularly via conference call with the following objectives:

Provide a platform for education, for example through webinars on specific topics to help members navigate any new and/or existing rules and proposals
- Discussion of specific issues and consultation for topics in individual territories
- Produce consensus reports so MEF can respond to issues

A solution?

There is no magic or quick solution to harmonise all applicable regulation globally. There is however an opportunity for the industry and regulators to sit together, discuss and manage risks in a sensible way that provides protection to consumers but does not stifle innovation. This is entirely feasible and we have been very encouraged by the willingness of all involved to engage.

The next few years will see new regulations replacing old ones, new services emerge, more consumer take up of services driven by better quality of user experience. Regulations get old very quickly and so we require all rules to be more goal based and meet a set objective – not to be prescriptive in a multitude of Codes. This may mean that some regulators and their Codes need to merge. We need to look long term and have some serious discussions and MEF is facilitating this worldwide.

Further information about the EU Directives mentioned in this article:
http://ec.europa.eu/avpolicy/
http://ec.europa.eu/consumers/rights/

THE APPETITE FOR MOBILE INTERNET

Approximately 227 million people age 13 and over held a mobile phone subscription within the EU5 (U.K., France, Germany, Italy, Spain) in September 2009. 61 million of these subscribers were mobile media users (consumers who used the Mobile Internet through their browser, an applications or they downloaded content), representing a reach of 27 per cent.

The number of mobile media users has grown 17 percent amongst European mobile subscribers during the past year, adding a further 8.5 million subscriber since September 2008. We expect the number of mobile media users in EU5 to rise even further in the fourth quarter of 2010 due to the increase in device sales and usage around the holiday period.

Growth of Key Market Enablers

Just as increased broadband penetration and the mass availability of computers cheaply and accessibly has accelerated the growth of Internet usage over the past decade, so too advancements in mobile technology are now beginning to spark an influx in mobile media usage.

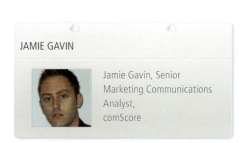

JAMIE GAVIN

Jamie Gavin, Senior Marketing Communications Analyst, comScore

ALISTAIR HILL

Analyst and Mobile Products, Europe, comScore

Two of these market enablers – smartphones and 3G devices – are now firmly entrenched in the market, as the popularity of the Apple iPhone, which already accounts for 8 percent of mobile media usage, demonstrates. The top 20 percent of mobile devices (277 different models) represent 79 percent of total mobile media usage in EU5, proving the 80/20 rule yet again.

However, the most important enabler, unlimited data plans, still has limited penetration across Europe, despite a growth rate of 55 percent on the previous year. The U.S. now has 20 percent penetration of unlimited data plans and 34 percent of the market using mobile media, in comparison to the EU5's level of 4 percent unlimited data plan penetration and 27 percent mobile media usage. To reiterate the importance of this enabler, 80

Viewpoints_ The Appetite for Mobile Internet

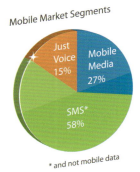

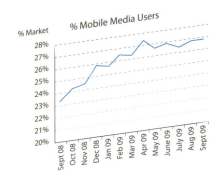

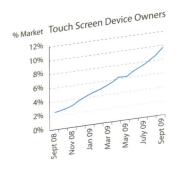

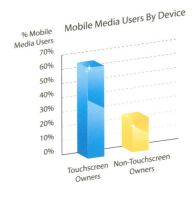

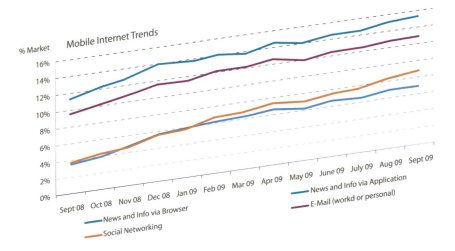

Source: comScore MobiLens, 3 month average ending September 2009.

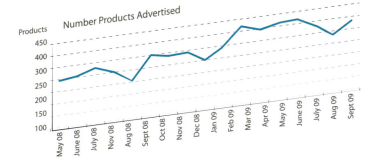

percent of unlimited data plan subscribers use mobile media, making them 199 percent more likely than the average mobile subscriber.

Touchscreen Devices

Since the European launch of the Apple iPhone in the summer of 2008, it has become the "must-have" gadget of the mobile world. Recognizing the popularity of this device, other manufactures have embraced touchscreens, meaning that over 10 percent of mobile owners now have one and 31 percent of new devices sold now have a touchscreen.

Not only do their owners love them (device satisfaction is 0.30 points higher than average on a 1-10 scale), but these users are over twice as likely to consume mobile media, and 13 percent less likely to want to switch mobile device.

Mobile Internet Services Continue to Boom

It is well over a year since the launch of the iPhone 3G and the initital boom in mobile servies, but the ability of the mobile device to attract new users shows no sign of waning. Social networking services and Apps are showing the highest gains with 130 percent and 95 percent growth in users on the previous year respectively, with email and news & information accessing also picking up.

Almost 12 percent of mobile owners now use information services on a daily basis, these being defined as news & info, email, IM, or social networking. Not only are the amount of Mobile Internet users growing but the amount of people who use information services on a daily basis has risen 43 percent during the past year, emphasizing how engrained the Mobile Internet is becoming in our day to day lives.

Steady Growth for Mobile Banner Advertising

Although there has not been the explosive growth in mobile advertising hoped for by many, there has been a constant and steady growth in the number of products being advertised on mobile devices during the past year in the UK. comScore Ad Metrix Mobile – a service dedicated to tracking Mobile Internet advertising campaigns – saw 383 separate products advertised using mobile banners in September 2009.

As smartphone, 3G and touchscreen devices begin to penetrate the market even further, and unlimited data plan availability grows, the Mobile Internet will become an even more attractive place for brands to advertise, which we predict will lend to further growth in Mobile Internet advertising.

Conclusion

In what has been a tough economic climate across the media and advertising world, consumer appetite for Mobile Internet services has shown steady growth during the past year. Device technology has evolved significantly — as the mass marketing of the Apple iPhone and other touch screen devices has indicated — providing a more appealing environment for increasingly compelling mobile-specific content, such as social networking services and apps.

There is still work to be done, particularly in the area of mass conversion to the unlimited data plans that will eventually result in the widespread uptake of Mobile Internet services, but the industry is now primed for marketers to utilize this emerging platform.

In correlation with this growth and in order to help facilitate it even further, Q1 of 2010 will see the introduction of the GSMA's Mobile Media Metrics service, provided by comScore in the UK. Through this unique and pioneering accountability service, advertisers will be able to plan and buy mobile advertising using robust Mobile Internet user data, which will in turn help to increase the size of the mobile advertising market.

THE CONQUEST OF MOBILE, THE CONQUEST OF SPACE

Our conquest of space has profoundly transformed the development of telecommunications and the dissemination of information. It initiated new areas of competition as well as cooperation in original ways. It is also a tremendous engine for innovation in many domains: electronics, information technology, energy, and mechanical engineering.

In many ways the developments in the mobile industry resemble the 50 year period that passed between the space flight of a monkey to the development of international space station ISS. In a time frame of just 7 years mobile gained an overall global penetration of 65 percent. This is the strongest and fastest adoption of the twentieth century, ahead of television (50 years for 92% penetration) and even the PC (25 years to reach 45% penetration).

In 1979 the first generation mobile telecommunications network was created in Japan. In late 2009 many operators opened 4th generation networks with the commercial launch of LTE, Long Term Evolution, the successor to UMTS. In 30 years we have moved from an era of voice calls and SMS messaging into the era of real-time information, TV, and video on our mobile screens.

We went from a heavy phone with a 2cm black and white screen in the 1980s to mobile phones as powerful as a PC with dozens of features that we only started to tame. And it doesn't stop there. In the coming years we'll see an unprecedented evolution of size, weight, autonomy and feature set.

The technological progress and growing breath of usages have been phenomenal and nothing short of a revolution, an explosion of services and application. In 2009 the rocket took off!

As the conquest of markets is taking shape, operators are under pressure to innovate their services to recruit but also retain their customer bases, while in parallel web giants are starting their programs. 2010 will provide a wealth of mobile services with plenty of application stores and web applications that will grow and further enhance the Mobile Internet use.

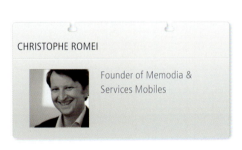

CHRISTOPHE ROMEI

Founder of Memodia & Services Mobiles

So what will application stores bring in the coming 12 months? A more fragmented offer, the emergence of several best applications, 3 to 4 winning application stores, a collapse of the offer, and the return of web applications in full force.

But if we put ourselves in the position of the consumers, it may be much simpler because their expectation is not the same as for the experts. A consumer buys his phone at the mobile network operator shop and gets a store preconfigured on his mobile. But constraining choice is not the answer. In the end the consumer wants to have a free access to any applications, pay using his mobile, regardless of who is behind the store front. As long as the application meets his needs and budget, the store is simple to use, applications can be downloaded with a single click, billing is clear, it's possible to back-up, and settings are easily retrieved when changing phones.

One of the key benefits of the conquest of space was the availability of household applications for anyone. The challenge for the mobile industry is to make available to the general public mobile services that are simple and useful, that facilitate the everyday life of billions of users. The tundra shepherd alerts his family of danger, fishermen sell their catch remotely in real time, a family sends money to one of her children thousands of miles away, doctors remotely monitor diabetes patients, firefighters send pictures of an accident for support in action, parents track their 10-year olds going to school, a blind person uses synthesized speech to read the daily newspaper, a businessman in an airport presents his mobile as flight ticket.

The mobile will also to be a simple means to connect people through social networks, with merchants and brands via mobile marketing and contactless technology, with their environment using augmented reality, and with life via mobile TV.

Most importantly, the mobile's voice and SMS messaging capabilities are the global language that allows one to get in touch with a person and to connect in real-time with family and community.

We'll see innovations that will not stop to surprise us because of man's infinite creative power. Perhaps already in a few years we'll experience a removal of Babylonian confusion of tongues, and voice recognition, automatic translation, speech synthesis and cloud computing work together to translate real-time conversion in thousands of languages.

The conquest of space has hardly begun, and so has the conquest of mobile. New players will emerge, new collaborations will form. On the horizon is a brave new world of mobile for the good of all "mobinauts!"

ABOUT NETSIZE

SOLUTIONS
EXPERIENCE
WORLDWIDE
PROMOTION
RETAIL
PAYMENT

SOLUTIONS THAT BOOST BUSINESS

Netsize offers a large portfolio of products that adapts to customer needs at different levels in the value chain. With this flexibility, Netsize has succeeded in launching mobile services for numerous market segments such as mobile device manufacturers, mobile service and content providers, marketing agencies, retail, public transportation, banking, and insurance.

The Netsize offer comprises connectivity products, applications, and professional & full services. These solutions are a combination of products throughout the value chain. Consequently, the product suite enables full flexibility to meet all customer needs.

NETSIZE ADDS VALUE AT MULTIPLE LEVELS

CONNECTIVITY PRODUCTS based on operator coverage
- Facilitates through a unique contract and technical platform access to 100+ operators for messaging, payment, and IP gateway
- Aggregates 800+ active customers, content and service providers to get the best traffic fee and pay-out

APPLICATIONS
- Ready to use solutions for executing standard services using Netsize connectivity
- Cross product use including statistical reporting through a unique portal

PROFESSIONAL AND FULL SERVICES
- Full service for hosting services, rolling-out marketing campaigns, and handling end user care (multi-lingual call center)
- Professional services for designing, validating, optimizing services, and obtaining authorization from operators and regulators

A BREADTH OF PRODUCTS
FOR MOBILIZING YOUR CUSTOMERS

CONNECTIVITY PRODUCTS based on the operators coverage

100+ MOBILE OPERATORS orange   T··Mobile

mMessaging
2-way SMS
- Worldwide
- Local enabling end-user initiated opt-in

Local MMS push

mProxy
Operator Billing
- SMS/MMS Premium
- WAP/WEB
- Direct (on IP, IMSI)

Credit card billing or e-Wallets

mPayment
- IP to Operator look-up
- Visitor authentication and browsing tracking
- Content download

APPLICATION

PROMOTE, ALERT, RETAIN ▶ **RETAIL** ▶ **CHARGE**

mPlug-in
Mobile extensions for corporate solutions (Messaging server, CRM, Emailer, BI, ERP)

mMarketing
CRM & Campaigns
Ready-to-use solution from a web browser

mStore
mCommerce solution for mobile storefront management

Smart Billing
Convergent solution for charging any end-user in application stores, or WAP/Web/SMS stores

PROFESSIONAL & FULL SERVICES

mServices

Roll-out Marketing Campaigns | Solution Management Audit for Regulator Compliancy | Yield Management | End-user Care

MANAGE ALL YOUR SERVICES THROUGH A SINGLE WEB PORTAL ...

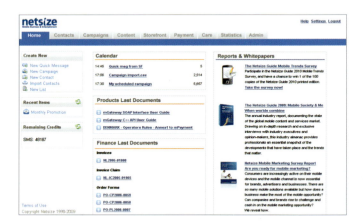

The Netsize portal is a web application that enables Netsize customers to manage all their mobile services from a single environment. The portal dashboard provides a unified view on product usage, traffic and transactions. Powerful tools are available for customised reporting and detailed analysis. Administrators can define user profiles and access rights on the portal's functionalities.

The Netsize portal also fully manages **the relationship between Netsize in its customers** including:
- Support case creation and tracking
- Legal and contractual document repository
- Developer resources and FAQs
- Account management and invoice area
- Newsletter and specific project follow-up

... AND A UNIFIED SERVICES DASHBOARD

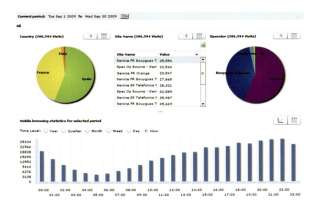

All Netsize products are designed on a common data warehouse, enabling unified statistics of all mobile service traffic. Detailed analysis may be performed on loyalty and conversion rates, including:
- SMS and browsing traffic analyzer by operator, service, and handset
- Real-time traffic statistics for instant analysis of marketing campaigns
- Conversion rate dashboard by service, content, operator, lead source, and handset
- Customizable reports including chart and table exporting
- End-user tracking enabling consumer care

Furthermore, Netsize mServices offers on-demand reports and dashboards creation that are sent periodically.

- Visitors browsing statistics report including full customization
- Lead sources tracking (campaign, operator portal, search engine)
- Payment & conversion report by service, by lead sources and by handset
- Real-time browsing and transactions statistics by operator and by handset

CONNECTIVITY EXTENSION: MORE COVERAGE & MORE CAPABILITIES

Netsize continuously extends the geographical reach for each connectivity product. In 2010, Netsize plans to invest in new local connections to mobile operator gateways. At least 10 additional countries are targeted for mobile service such as:
- Campaigning, alerting, and communication to mobile end-users
- SMS services supporting end-user opt-ins through local short codes
- Mobile Internet storefronts
- Mobile payment

CONNECTIVITY PRODUCTS	COVERAGE in number of countries 2009	2010	PRODUCTS CAPABILITIES
mMessaging	185	205	**Campaigning, alerting, and communicating** to end-users who opted in outside the SMS channel
mMessaging	24	35	Marketable services on local short code enabling **direct end-users opt-in by SMS**
mProxy	39	52	IP-to-Operator **look-up** **Content download** **End-user authentication** for tracking visitors
mPayment	29	41	**Premium SMS/MMS** billing **WAP** payment page **Direct** operator billing **Credit** card billing

mMARKETING: JUST A FEW CLICKS TO CAMPAIGN, ALERT, AND COMMUNICATE

With mMarketing sending mobile messaging campaigns from an Internet browser has never been easier. Campaigns may be just a simple message or they may be more advanced including interaction (managing end-user replies), multimedia (MMS), or links redirecting to promotional mobile micro-sites. Opt-in/out management as well as campaigning may be done in mMarketing or by external sources using the mMarketing web services. External sources are for example CRM systems, other web applications or even contactless (NFC) card readers. At each campaign completion, mMarketing automatically generates a detailed campaign status reports.

- Ready to use from your mobile browser
- SMS, MMS, push to mobile micro-sites
- Contact management included
- Detailed statistics on campaigns
- Opt-in management and leads generation

AS CUSTOMER RELATIONSHIPS TURN MULTICHANNEL ...

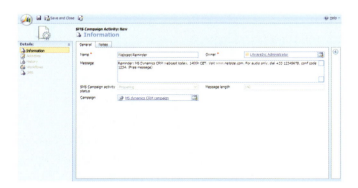

Neolane provides an enterprise marketing software platform encompassing all the essentials to manage campaigns, leads, dynamics content, marketing resources, customer data and analytics. This corporate solution enables companies to mix traditional communication channels with emerging technologies such as SMS and MMS to design and orchestrate cross-channel marketing campaigns. Netsize and Neolane have established a partnership enabling the delivery of SMS and MMS through the marketing software platform by the integration of Netsize's global messaging infrastructure.

Microsoft Dynamics

Netsize SMS Plug-in for Microsoft Dynamics CRM provides users with a simple and innovative way to interact with customers, partners and colleagues enabling a true multichannel solution in Microsoft Dynamics CRM. The mobile channel promotes a true two-way and real-time event-driven relationship with customers. Thanks to an easy integration with Microsoft Dynamics CRM environment, sending and receiving SMS has never been so easy. The plug-in will benefit all enterprises from all sectors with its multiple added-value features ranging from SMS campaign scheduling, to triggered SMS alerts based on user-defined events such as calendar updates, accounts creations and updates.

... NOW IS THE TIME TO PLUG-IN THE MOBILE CHANNEL INTO YOUR CRM & BUSINESS APPLICATIONS

Salesforce.com is the enterprise cloud computing company that provides CRM applications for sales and customer service. Netsize SMS Plug-in for Salesforce.com easily enables the mobile channel as a complete communication tool for supporting all sales phases:
- Campaigning: Operations targeting preselected Salesforce contacts
- Alerting: Reminder before a conference call
- Confirm: Order acknowledgement or for a delivery date confirmation
- Deliver: Reference code (number or bar code) for material pick-up

The plug-in adds the following features to Salesforce.com:
- Quick messaging from contacts
- SMS reminders to Sales or Contacts
- Setting campaigns from contacts selected according to settable criteria
- MMS/SMS digital content delivery

 Email server / SMTP

Netsize Mail-to-SMS is the quick and easy solution to send email from:
- E-mailer solutions
- Business intelligence solutions
- Information management systems

In many enterprises the integration of the mobile channel with existing information systems and business intelligence solutions usually is a complex and time-consuming project. Netsize Mail-to-SMS speeds the time to market by adapting SMS to the channel that is supported by all systems: email. Using the SMTP interface of Netsize Mail-to-SMS any information system can now send SMS messages as easily as sending email.

SMART BILLING ALWAYS FINDS THE BEST BILLING METHOD…

Netsize *Smart*Billing is a convergent Payment Service Provider that dynamically processes the best billing methods according to the following context of the transaction:
- The end-user device: mobile handset, smart phone, personal computer
- The network operator capability to authenticate end-users: ISP or mobile networks (land line, SMS, 3G, 4G, or other wireless networks)
- The storefront media: SMS service, WAP or Mobile Internet storefront, web storefront, on-device application, or application store
- The transaction details: the price and the business model (pay-per-use or subscription) supported by the payment operators

With *Smart*Billing, you choose the level of customization. This may be from no customization where the payment provider and billing method are automatically selected by *Smart*Billing or full customization where you choose which payment provider and billing method to be used.

3 Levels of selection

1. Full Automatic Selection

OR

2. Payment Provider Selection
   - Mobile Operator
   - Credit Card
   - eWallet

OR

3. Billing Method Selection
   - P-SMS
   - WAP billing
   - IP billing
   - …

> With SmartBilling, charging end-users becomes easy!

Netsize, the global mobile commerce enabler

... FOR CHARGING MOBILE USERS GLOBALLY FROM ANY STOREFRONT

OPERATOR PAYMENT PROVIDER
- Premium SMS
- WAP / Web billing
- Direct Billing

ALTERNATIVE PAYMENT PROVIDER
- Credit Card
- eWallets

Connect any Payment provider, and any billing method

Smart Billing
A unique payment service platform

Adapt to any storefront

| SMS Service | Mobile Internet WAP storefront | On-device application Application store | Web storefront |

SmartBilling provides an easy to use billing application platform for charging end-users from any type of media storefront such as SMS, website, Mobile Internet Storefront, and on-device application store. SmartBilling not only allows a seamless integration but also hides the complexity of payment providers.

SmartBilling is a unique and convergent payment provider

- Enable monetization of mobile or Web services
- Support any storefront, any network, any end-user device
- Reports and detailed statistics on transactions

MOBILE TRENDS SURVEY REPORT 2010

The Mobile Trends Survey 2010 was conducted by Netsize to determine the main trends and drivers behind the adoption of mobile technology among consumers and businesses globally. The survey addressed five trends for 2010: Activation, Interaction, Conversation, Transaction, and Transformation.

Key Findings

Activation – Mobile as a platform for applications;
- 87 percent of respondents believe Apple App Store will be the most successful. Google Android Market is runner-up with 60 percent, and Nokia Ovi Store is third with 30 percent, and mobile operator stores follow with 15 percent.
- The four C's - Convenience, Compatibility, Choice, and Charging are the top enablers of application store success (65 percent to 50 percent of respondents). Device or user "coolness" is not a factor (26 percent).

Interaction – Mobile to access content and communicate with our friends, peers and wider social networks
- Distribution channels are shifting. The importance of distribution through on-device portals and through handset vendors increases significantly over the period 2010 to 2012. 80 percent of respondents ranking these as top choice for 2012. Other channels will grow only slightly. Off-deck distribution is ranked first in 2012 by 76 percent, whereas the vote on application stores and on-deck operator portals remains stable with some 70 percent. Side-loading or content forwarding remains the most important distribution channel for mobile entertainment content, ranked first by 84 percent of respondents.
- The diversity of business models will increase. 93 percent of respondents estimate that the pay per MB (streaming) business model will be the most successful in the period 2010 to 2011. In-application billing and package deals receive 75 percent of votes, whereas subscription and ad-funded models are picked by 66 percent of the survey respondents.
- Asia Pacific and Europe are regarded as the main drivers for global mobile entertainment market growth, with respectively 65 percent and 50 percent of respondents indicating either region. North America is a clear third, getting 38 percent of the votes.

Conversation – Mobile to connect with brands, and direct, anytime, anywhere, two-way exchanges between people and the companies that serve them
- Industry, utility, healthcare and public sectors lead in the adoption of mobile for brand conversation, ranked first by 91 to 82 percent of respondents, followed by consumer products (brands, retail, financial services), marketing services and IT & telecommunications, that received some 76 to 70 percent of the votes.
- The most important combination of the mobile channel is noticeably with online media (web, email and social media). 92 percent of respondents consider it important, very important or critical in 2010. Strong growth is also observed in the combination of mobile with direct mail.

Transaction – Mobile for commerce and convenience, for browsing, shopping, buying, and customer service
- A good shopping experience on mobile starts with search, discovery, navigation of content and offers. 73 percent of respondents rate it as very important or critical. Choice of payment methods (cards or operator billing) was mentioned by 60 percent of respondents.
- The majority of survey respondents (68 percent) believed that it will take at least 2 years before contactless payments would take off in Europe in North America.

Transformation – Mobile as the remote control of our lives and an extension of our "selves"
- 2010 will see the take-off of permission-based commerce. 71 percent of respondents values receiving location-aware messages and marketing, whereas 57 percent estimates receiving offers and benefits via coupons and campaigns, both numbers up significantly from 2009.
- The modern mobile empowers us to have an impact on whom and what surrounds us in society. In 2010, over two-thirds of respondents regard mobile as a means to create content or engage in citizen journalism.

Activation

Mobile in 2010 is ACTIVATION: The mobile becomes a platform for applications, user engagement, a launch pad for Long Tail services and a marketplace for a plethora of application stores and developer ecosystems. What makes application stores winners?

Application stores are taking the mobile world by storm. When asked, which application stores will be most successful, respondents overwhelmingly (87 percent) pointed out Apple App Store. The top position doesn't come as a surprise, as it represents an attractive proposition for consumers and developers alike. **See Figure 1**.

Of the contenders, only Google Android Market comes close, being marked second successful store (60 percent). Nokia and Research in Motion both received less than 1/3 of the votes, and Microsoft 15 percent. In the eyes of the survey respondents, handset and operating system vendors clearly have work to do.

Respondents also found that application stores operated by mobile operators would not be among the winners, and votes varied between 2 percent (the recently announced Telefónica mstore) to 11 percent (Vodafone 360). A case of "unknown, unloved" perhaps?

But what is it about application stores that make them a leading destination for software applications? Here respondents were clear: it is the four C's - Convenience, Compatibility, Choice, and Charging. **See Figure 2**.

Convenience, everything you need for your mobile life conveniently in one place received 65 percent of votes. Some 50 percent of respondents mentioned compatibility (software applications specific to the device), choice (a large breadth of applications to choose from) and ease of payment (operator billing and credit card payment).

The application store brand was considered less important (mentioned by 37 percent only). Perhaps this is not a surprise as the well-known application stores are from trusted brands already **See Figure 2**. Also coolness was not seen as an important factor: it's not the application or the device that creates the application store success.

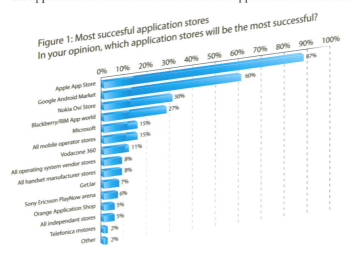

Figure 1: Most succesful application stores
In your opinion, which application stores will be the most successful?

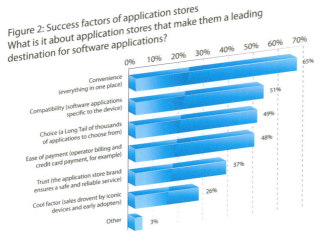

Figure 2: Success factors of application stores
What is it about application stores that make them a leading destination for software applications?

Interaction

Mobile in 2010 is INTERACTION: Mobile continues to gain traction as the way we access content and communicate with our friends, peers and wider social networks. What are the key drivers and what direction will this market take?

Side-loading or content forwarding remains the most important distribution channel for mobile entertainment content: for 84 percent of respondents this was their top choice. **See Figure 3**.

For 75 percent of respondents, the top performing distribution channels in 2010 and 2011 will be on-device portals, handset manufacturers, websites and off-deck portals. Application stores get 69 percent of votes. Looking ahead at 2012, respondents expect the importance of distribution through on-device portals and handset vendors to increase significantly (80 percent), more than websites and off-deck portals. The vote on application stores and on-deck operator portals remains stable (some 70 percent).

It appears to be congruent with the opinions that respondents expressed above on who will win the war of the application stores: the physically closer the brand to the consumer, the higher its chances as a successful distribution channel. **See Figure 3**

Respondents were more mixed about winning business models for the period 2010-2011.

The much-acclaimed but also much-criticized subscription model, depending on one's point of view, was mentioned by two-thirds as first choice and by one-third as second choice. With this somewhat undecided choice respondents seem to indicate that the market is in need for a new business model to replace the subscription model. Also the ad-funded model is not regarded as a winner, receiving similar scores.

In-application billing, package deals, flat rate and pay-per-use all received three quarters of the vote, with preference given to in-application billing. Once again we see that application stores are the disruptive factor, driving innovation in the way mobile entertainment content is distributed, and billed. **See Figure 4**

Asia Pacific and Europe are regarded as the main drivers for global mobile entertainment market growth, with respectively 65 percent and 50 percent of respondents

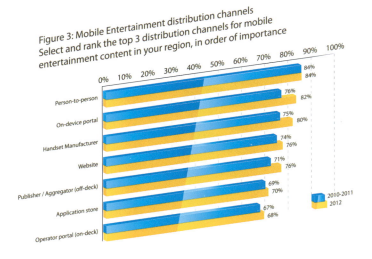

Figure 3: Mobile Entertainment distribution channels
Select and rank the top 3 distribution channels for mobile entertainment content in your region, in order of importance

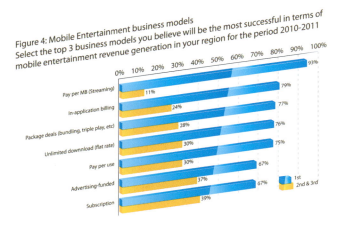

Figure 4: Mobile Entertainment business models
Select the top 3 business models you believe will be the most successful in terms of mobile entertainment revenue generation in your region for the period 2010-2011

indicating either region. North America is a clear third, getting 38 percent of the votes. **See Figure 5**

Conversation

Mobile in 2010 is CONVERSATION: consumers connect with brands they appreciate and brands talk back. The result is direct, anytime, anywhere, two-way exchanges between people and the companies that serve them. Are we ready for it? And where is the value?

We asked survey participants to select and rank the top three sectors that they expect will lead in developing and implementing effective strategies for mobile conversation. 91 to 82 percent of respondents ranked industry, utility, healthcare and public sectors as leading, followed by consumer products (brands, retail, financial services), marketing services and IT & telecommunications, that received some 76 to 70 percent of the votes. **See Figure 6.**

The latter sectors were also frequently ranked second or third, showing that opinions

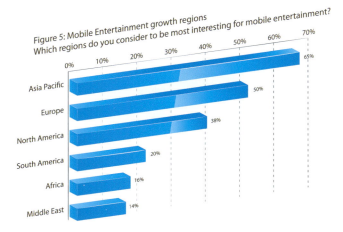

Figure 5: Mobile Entertainment growth regions
Which regions do you consider to be most interesting for mobile entertainment?

were mixed. This could be explained by the fact that especially these sectors have been among the early adopters of mobile in their marketing mix, and respondents expect new impetus to come from the sectors that have been lagging adoption of mobile so far. **See Figure 6**.

In September 2009 Netsize conducted an international survey on the adoption of mobile marketing and to identify its chief drivers and obstacles. The survey report "Mobile Marketing Survey 2009" Can companies and brands rise to challenge and cash in on the mobile marketing opportunity?," available from www.netsize.com. concludes that mobile marketing is set for strong growth in cross-media campaigns.

Mobile Trends Survey respondents confirmed this finding, and indicated a rising importance of mobile in combination with all other channels. The most important combination is noticeably with online media (web, email and social media). 87 percent of respondents currently consider it important, very important or critical, growing to 92 percent in 2010. Strong growth is also observed in the combination of mobile with direct mail, and importance leaps from 42 percent to 49 percent of respondents. **See Figure 7**.

Transaction

Mobile in 2010 is TRANSACTION: browsing, shopping, buying, customer service. It is all about commerce and convenience. What are the enablers?

A good shopping experience on mobile starts with search, discovery, navigation of content and offers. 73 percent of respondents rate it as very important or critical. See Figure 8. Choice of payment methods (cards or operator billing) was mentioned by 60 percent of respondents. It's an indication that the consumer applies the same criteria to a mobile shopping experience as to retail shopping in real life.

What makes mobile different is that it can link the real world with the digital world. Between 41 percent and 45 percent of respondents found the role of mobile to be very important for creating that integrated retail experience, providing location awareness and interaction in marketing campaigns that drive store traffic. **See Figure 8**

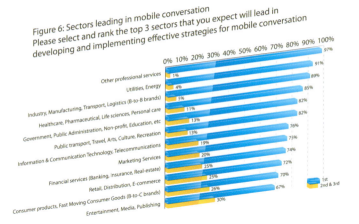

Figure 6: Sectors leading in mobile conversation
Please select and rank the top 3 sectors that you expect will lead in developing and implementing effective strategies for mobile conversation

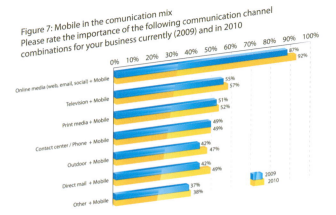

Figure 7: Mobile in the comunication mix
Please rate the importance of the following communication channel combinations for your business currently (2009) and in 2010

From the larger perspective of shopping and transaction, making a payment is one of the many functions of mobile, be it an important one. Contactless payments have made inroads in several Eastern Asian countries, enabled by a ubiquitous contactless payment infrastructure and societies that have been early adopters of mobile.

The majority of survey respondents (68 percent) believed that it will take at least 2 years before contactless payments would take off in Europe in North America. Just 6 percent thought that the use of contactless was too culturally linked to make it a success outside of Asia. **See Figure 9**

Transformation

Mobile in 2010 is TRANSFORMATION: the barriers between the physical and virtual worlds blurs – and both become actionable. The mobile phone becomes the remote control of our lives and an extension of our "selves." How quickly will we adopt?

By and large the mobile is a means to communicate using voice and text – the mobile has gradually become one of the bare necessities of modern life. Increasingly it is also affecting the way we live our lives: how we consume content like news and entertainment, capture what is happening, even how we socialize. For some 90 percent of respondents

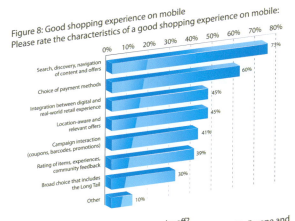

Figure 8: Good shopping experience on mobile
Please rate the characteristics of a good shopping experience on mobile:

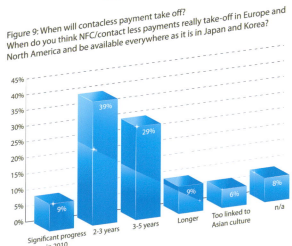

Figure 9: When will contactless payment take off?
When do you think NFC/contact less payments really take-off in Europe and North America and be available everywhere as it is in Japan and Korea?

this is being mobile, the 2010 way, up from some 80 percent in 2009. **See Figure 10**

We start to see the commercial benefits of being mobile, and trust others enough to provide them with the sensitive data on our location and needs, to receive location-aware messages and marketing (71 percent in 2010, up from 50 percent in 2009), and receive offers and benefits via coupons and campaigns (57 percent, up from 38 percent). That the motive is not always commercial is demonstrated by the fact that increasingly we regard mobile as suitable for improving education and healthcare (49 percent).

We are also learning that the modern mobile empowers us to have an impact on whom and what surrounds us in society. In 2010, over two-thirds of respondents regard mobile as a means to create content or engage in citizen journalism. For many too the days are coming closer that mobile stitches a seamless integration of digital and physical worlds and its different screens. With just half of respondents stating that this was the case in 2009, it is clear that we are fully embracing this ever cleverer device. **See Figure 10**

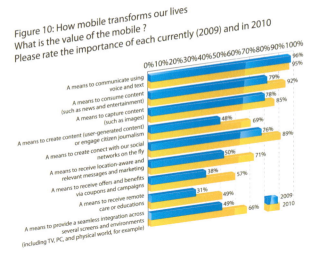

Figure 10: How mobile transforms our lives
What is the value of the mobile?
Please rate the importance of each currently (2009) and in 2010

Conclusion

Application stores are a disruptive force in the mobile industry and are impacting all elements and players in the content value chain. From the way an application is marketed to how it is billed for, how users search and discover, and enhance their mobile device.

Short term, the application store is a sure winner. Longer term, a fragmented offering due to a plethora of different mobile devices might swing the pendulum back to the mobile web.

The survey finds that handset vendors are well positioned and mobile network operators still have got work to do, where it comes to application store popularity. The vote is out on what will be the winning business model.

Mobile has become a mature instrument in the marketing mix, yet some media combinations are more of interest than others. The survey shows that web, email, and social media are the natural partner to mobile, while the combination with direct mail and outdoor is expected to grow strongly.

Mobile commerce is maturing. Contactless payments are around the corner, even if widespread adoption is expected still to be some two to three years away. In the mean time good search and navigation of content and offers, choice of mobile payment and promotions that are well-targeted will provide a teasing mobile shopping experience.

As consumers start to see the commercial benefits of "being mobile", they will trust brands with their sensitive data such as location and needs in exchange for benefits and offers.

For many the mobile still remains first and foremost a communications device. But as its capabilities develop and we discover new usages, we gradually realize that mobile is more than connecting with friends, social communities, or society. Increasingly mobile empowers us to interact with a world that surrounds us.

Methodology

The analysis includes answers from 1,003 respondents who completed the survey in the period from begin November to early December 2009. Respondents came from 67 countries globally, with 68.7 percent of respondents based in Europe, 9.9 percent in North America, 5.1 percent in South America, 11.5 percent in Asia Pacific, Australia and New Zealand, and 4.8 percent in Middle East and Africa.

Figure 11 shows the distribution of respondents by industry sector. The largest sector, at 42.1 percent of respondents, ICT & Telecommunications, comprises companies like network operators, telecom equipment vendors and technical service providers. Entertainment, media and publishing form the second largest sector in this survey, with 20.9 percent of respondents, followed by marketing services, at 12.2 percent of respondents. A quarter of respondents are from a mix of industry, services and public sectors.

In terms of area of responsibility, 45.4 percent of respondents fulfill a senior management role (CxO, VP, Director), 36.2 percent have a commercial function (business development, sales, marketing, product management), and 18.4 percent in technical, financial or other roles.

The survey results reflect the opinions and attitudes of the respondents.

The Netsize Mobile Trends Survey 2010 was conducted online and participation was anonymous.

To collect opinions we used multiple choice questions with single or multiple answer options, and to obtain ratings and rankings we used ordered response options (for instance, Unimportant – Slightly important – Important – Very important – Critical, plus an option Don't know / Not applicable). In addition we asked respondents to provide feedback in free format text.

Percentages are based on the proportion of respondents who answered the question.
See Figure 11

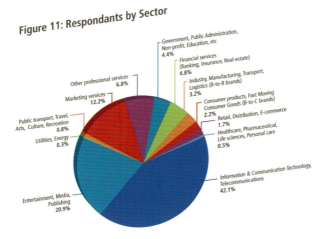

Figure 11: Respondents by Sector

COUNTRY DATA

166	AUSTRALIA	226	THE NETHERLANDS
170	AUSTRIA	229	NEW ZEALAND
173	BELGIUM	232	NORWAY
176	BRAZIL	235	POLAND
179	CANADA	238	PORTUGAL
181	CHINA	240	ROMANIA
183	CZECH REPUBLIC	241	RUSSIA
186	DENMARK	245	SINGAPORE
189	FINLAND	248	SLOVAKIA
192	FRANCE	250	SLOVENIA
196	GERMANY	252	SOUTH AFRICA
200	GREECE	255	SOUTH KOREA
203	HUNGARY	257	SPAIN
206	INDIA	260	SWEDEN
209	IRELAND	263	SWITZERLAND
212	ITALY	266	THAILAND
215	JAPAN	268	TURKEY
217	LUXEMBOURG	271	UNITED KINGDOM
219	MALAYSIA	275	UKRAINE
221	MEXICO	278	UNITED STATES OF AMERICA
223	MOROCCO		

THE MOBILE CONTENT MARKET IN 2010

Among the many things likely to happen next year in the mobile content and applications space, there are few worth highlighting: consolidation of the app-store market; greater operator focus on launching enhanced-address books and content services geared at all mobile users, not just their own subscribers; a re-emphasis on cellular-based mobile TV services, at least in Europe, and the rebirth of cellular broadcasting standard MBMS in its new IMB guise; increased emphasis by operators on DRM-free music; and emerging markets will continue to drive adoption of mobile-money services, as well as in verticals like mobile health and government.

App stores

The app-store bandwagon will slow down as many iPhone-copycat stores flounder and operators see more returns from enabling billing on third-party stores than from selling apps on their own stores. Application stores will inevitably continue to dominate the agenda over the next year, although we are likely to see enthusiasm wane in some industry quarters as many of the iPhone-copycat stores fail to get anywhere near as much market traction as the Apple App Store.

Operators will be the ones to most struggle to make a success of their application stores, unable in most cases to compete with Apple and other vendors in global reach, brand coolness and agility. Their biggest chance of retaining a significant role in the mobile applications value chain will be as billing enablers, since most handset/OS vendors realize they need carrier billing to get downloads going on their app stores.

Beyond Apple, Google will be the vendor to make the greatest headway with its Android Market, possibly matching or even exceeding the App Store's success. Symbian and Microsoft will have work to do to woo enough developer talent towards their respective stores.

MARK NEWMAN

Chief Research Officer, Informa Telecoms & Media

Enhanced address books

Over the next two years other mobile operators and handset vendors will follow Vodafone, T-Mobile and Motorola in enabling enhanced-address-book services for mobile subscribers. These will be made available by the mobile operators as an application that is pre-loaded onto the device or downloaded over-the-air, and also by the handset vendors as a native feature, possibly as part of the Rich Communications Suite (RCS) project but more likely to be independent of it, at least in the near-term.

Mobile operators will launch enhanced address books as a focal point around which to aggregate a range of community, messaging and content services and seize back the initiative from online brands that are increasingly capturing ground from cellcos on the mobile services front. But for enhanced-address-book services to succeed operators and device manufacturers need to make the application available on a critical mass of devices, accompanied by an appropriate, or worry-free, data plan. Enhanced-address-book providers also need to ensure that the application is as open as possible, to enable mobile subscribers to access all of the communities and social networks that they use on-line. That is in addition, of course, to making the user experience compelling, contemporary and reliable.

Early iterations of enhanced-address-book services that have been developed and launched by mobile operators appear to be limited in scope and therefore not fully delivering on their promise, leaving the way clear for the third party software developers and hosting providers that are already offering more comprehensive offerings either under a software-as-a-service (Saas) model, or direct-to-consumer. These companies are better able than mobile operators and handset vendors to deal with challenges such as application development and porting, and ensuring quality of service. Mobile operators and handset manufacturers may be better off, at least in the short-term, partnering with these companies in order to take advantage of the shared-risk business model.

Cellco cross-network apps

An increasingly number of operators will develop cross-network applications to break out beyond their physical footprints. They will launch applications accessible to other operators' subscribers in an attempt to compete with the global reach offered by online players and handset vendors.

We are likely to see more attempts by operators to break out beyond their footprints and offer content services to all mobile users, not just those subscribed to their networks. In April, Vodafone launched an iPhone app in the UK linking iPhone users to the carrier's new widget-driven My Web portal, at a time when O2 was still the UK's exclusive iPhone distributor. In other words, Vodafone was pitching the service to O2 subscribers. And its Vodafone 360 service is also designed to be downloaded by subscribers to any network with the right device.

Orange, meanwhile, is rolling out a widget service called Djinngo that will allow users on any mobile network around the world to download widgets from Orange, as long as they have the right kind of device.

One of the biggest drawbacks that operators have in competing in the mobile Web services arena is that their reach tends to be network and territory specific. More and more operators are likely to get around that with apps that can be accessed globally. But, will users be interested in such offerings? And how will operators monetize them?

Mobile TV and broadcasting

Cellular-based broadcast standard MBMS looks set to make a comeback in its new IMB guise, allowing operators to use a thus-far unused part of the 3G spectrum – TDD – to broadcast TV and other services to phones.

The new revamped standard, which has received the all-important endorsement of operator association the GSMA, has emerged just as interest in broadcast mobile TV standard DVB-H seems to be waning. DVB-H has seen deployment plans derailed in Germany and France, for example, and lacklustre results in Finland and Switzerland.

Orange France is one operator that intends to deploy IMB, after getting "sidetracked" by DVB-H over the past few years, and several other operators are also interested. There are 152 operators around the world that own TDD spectrum.

DVB-H has stalled in Europe because of numerous factors: lack of spectrum, lack of handsets, lack of a proven business case and the lack of an agreement between broadcasters and operators. DVB-H equipment tenders are in decline and there's renewed interest in cellular alternatives for delivering TV services to phones.

DRM-free music

More and more operators are likely to launch DRM-free music services to make their full-track offerings more appealing to users. Record labels will acquiesce as they look to operators to rival Apple as the main channel for consumers to pay for music.

The emergence of online digital music stores selling DRM-free tracks that can be easily sideloaded to mobile handsets threatens operators with being edged out of the mobile-music market. Many operators will therefore break from record labels' preferred mode of protecting against piracy – selling tracks with DRM software – to take the DRM-free route.

Emerging markets

The coming year will see further cementing of the mobile phone as the key communications and computing device in emerging markets – typically due to low penetration of fixed-line communications infrastructure and the non-universal availability of basic services such as electricity, banking and health.

Mobile networks and devices are increasingly being used in emerging markets not only for person-to-person communication but also by the corporate and government sector and non-government organizations to deliver a range of information and essential services via mainly SMS and voice that could not otherwise be accessed.

These services include information about healthcare, education and primary industries, as well as mobile phone top-up, banking and money transfer, among many other examples. While the still relatively low penetration of the mobile phone coupled with low GDP will likely continue to restrain messaging traffic and revenues in these markets in 2010/2011, the availability of such services will help stimulate local economies, and hopefully help contribute in some way to a cycle of wealth generation that will likely then result in further improvements in mobile communications infrastructure and services.

Informa Telecoms & Media also expect a number of mobile operators in emerging markets, especially in Africa, to roll out mobile e-mail services in 2010, whether these are services that are native to the device or SMS-based services. The demand for mobile e-mail will be led by both consumers and enterprises.

App-store billing

It looks like Apple's business model of leaving out carrier billing from payments on its App Store is not going to be emulated by most of the handset/OS vendors that are rolling out copycat application stores. Vendors such as Nokia and Microsoft realize that they need carrier billing to get sales going on their stores. But the large revenue share demanded by carriers is unlikely to please developers.

Most handset makers that are launching application stores are eager to connect to mobile operators to enable users to pay for downloads through their phone bills. And the biggest of them all, Nokia, has been willing to part with a substantial share of the revenue generated from application downloads to enable carrier billing on the Ovi Store. A source at Nokia told Informa Telecoms & Media that the same applies to other handset vendors offering mobile payments on their stores. Another vendor that is publicly seeking carrier billing for its app store is Microsoft, which launched the Windows Mobile Marketplace for Mobile only two weeks ago.

Handset/OS vendors would no doubt love to "own the customer" by establishing a direct billing relationship with app-store users, and they are all – including Nokia and Microsoft – offering users the option to pay them directly via credit or debit card. But they are painfully aware that most users are likely to be put off by having to register their card details before they can make their first purchase.

Apple is an exception. It has gotten away with billing all App Store transactions through online digital-content platform iTunes because people were accustomed to the idea of registering their card details with Apple to download digital content to the iPod well before the iPhone was launched. The iPhone just piggybacked on that.

Another case for carrier billing is that the vast majority of mobile users around the world don't own a credit or debit card – either because they are too young or because they live in the greater part of the world where bank accounts and plastic forms of payment are rare. So carrier billing is the only means they have to pay remotely for digital goods.

By the same token, it's in operators' interests to offer billing to third-party app stores, since although these stores compete with operators' own mobile content offerings, billing can secure operators a long-term place in the mobile content value chain – from which they are otherwise pretty much fated to be disintermediated.

But they have to be careful not to spoil this opportunity by being too greedy. The commission charged by operators for payments processed through their networks is far too high.

Operators should take a much smaller cut than they are used to, to secure a long-term role for mobile billing in app stores and other third-party services. But from the evidence so far, it seems that they might be able to get away with taking relatively moderate shares, rather than be forced to go down to the single-digit percentages typical of credit-card and online payment providers – in the short term at least. Certainly in the case of Nokia, it seems that operators have not had to make too much of a sacrifice.

Rich Communications Suite

Mobile operators' deployments of services based on the GSM Association's Rich Communications Suite are being deferred, because of a combination of delays by handset manufacturers in providing native RCS capabilities in their devices, the difficulties involved with enabling interoperability between mobile operator networks, and operators' concerns about business models.

The GSMA's Rich Communications Suite (RCS) initiative risks becoming irrelevant to the needs of the mobile industry, with the development and finalization of the RCS specifications lagging behind the rollout of RCS-like services by a significant margin. Those mobile operators that have deployed RCS-like services have seemingly cherry-picked features that are included in the RCS specifications (both finalized and in development) that they consider to be a priority and have rolled out proprietary services that include these capabilities. Specifically, Optimus, Vodafone, T-Mobile, SK Telecom, LG Telecom and KT Freetel have included in their various services their own proprietary implementations of one or more RCS features, including enhanced address books (various features of which are included in RCS 1.0 and 2.0), the ability to access voice and messaging services via multiple devices, including the PC (specified in RCS 2.0), and the integration and aggregation of social networking. Social networking is possibly included in RCS 3.0, but Informa Telecoms & Media believes it is more likely to be part of the RCS 4.0 set of specifications. Neither RCS 3.0 nor RCS 4.0 has been finalized. None of the services that are offered by the above operators are RCS-compliant, though most of the mobile operators involved would argue that their services are in the spirit of the RCS initiative, and the South Korean mobile operators say they will seek to make their services compliant with the RCS specifications.

It has been almost two years since a consortium of mobile operators and vendors announced the RCS initiative just before the Mobile World Congress in February 2008, and the industry is still unsure when the first RCS-compliant service will go live, even though there have been multiple rounds of interoperability testing involving mobile operators, infrastructure vendors, handset manufacturers and software developers. A long-awaited consumer market trial by French operators SFR, Orange and Bouygues Telecom has been delayed until Q1 2010 – it was expected to take place this past summer. The technical trials that have been under way in France are regarded as providing a template for the development of cross-network RCS services in other countries. In addition, Telecom Italia has been conducting its own internal trials of RCS 1.0 services.

It also appears that handset vendors are dragging their feet. It was revealed during the recent Rich Communications event in Paris, organized by Informa Telecoms & Media, that the world's largest handset vendor, Nokia, will not make a native RCS capability commercially available on any of its devices until end-2010. However, Nokia does plan to make a downloadable RCS 2.0 client for the N97 Mini available by the middle of 2010, according to Teppo Hyvonen, the vendor's director of new applications and technologies.

ABOUT THE COUNTRY DATA

Glossary
n/d: Technology not deployed.
n/a: Data not available.
Penetration rate 3Q09: Percentage of number of active SIM cards and/or connected lines versus total population, in the third quarter of 2009 (ends September).
Total subscriptions: Number of active SIM cards and/or connected lines carrying traffic.
3G WCDMA subscriptions: Number of SIM cards connected to a 3G WCDMA device. WCDMA is the 3G technology mainly adopted by GSM operators.
3G EV-DO subscriptions: Number of CDMA SIM cards or active lines connected to a CDMA2000 1xEV-DO device. EV-DO is the 3G technology adopted by CDMA networks. From 2007 onwards, many CDMA players (i.e. in Australia and Korea) decided to migrate from CDMA to WCDMA.
Total revenues: Total telecommunications revenues, including services and hardware sales.
Service revenues: Revenues generated by the use of the network by its customers for data and voice.
Data revenues: Data service revenues.
SMS revenues: Revenues generated by person-to-person text messages and person-to-application premium rate messages (such as SMS voting, and news/information requests) but not including content downloads.
Messaging revenues, Messaging ARPU: Total revenues of the whole messaging segment, including SMS, MMS, IM and Email (person-to-person, application-to-person and person-to-application).
Mobile content revenues, Content ARPU: Non-messaging data services, including value-added services that provide entertainment, information or a combination of the two. Mobile content can be delivered in a number of genres such as news, sports, games, video or picture messaging, and can be repackaged formats of existing media such as television, radio or Internet.
Mobile Music: Ringtones, ringback tones, full-track downloads, and streaming music content. Mode of delivery or access is via the voice network (Voice), download over-the-air (OTA), streaming over-the-air (OTA Streaming) or SMS.
Mobile Games: Game downloads and real-time game content.

Mobile Images: Image downloads.
Mobile TV: Mobile TV includes content delivered over cellular networks as well as over broadcast infrastructure. TV content is considered to be scheduled content. Any content that is requested on demand is considered to be video content.
Mobile Video: Unlike mobile TV, video content is content that is delivered to the user when requested, i.e. on-demand. Video content can either be downloaded and stored on the handset or streamed.
Mobile Internet: The Mobile Internet is defined as access to remotely-hosted server-based content via the medium of a mobile browser, widget, client-side application or web application. This content can reside on-deck or off-deck and is delivered using the cellular air interface of a wireless carrier's network.
Net additions 3Q09: Net increase in number of subscribers in third quarter of 2009.
ARPU 3Q09: Monthly Average Revenue per User in third quarter 2009 in euro. Prepaid and postpaid ARPU refer to the ARPU for prepaid and postpaid subscribers, respectively. Blended ARPU is defined as the weighted average of prepaid and postpaid ARPU.
Growth rate (%): Year-to-year growth of the number of subscribers.
Mobile Virtual Network Operators (MVNOs): Subscriptions numbers and financials of MVNOs are included in their host Mobile Network Operators.

All market and operator metrics in this report are based on September 2009 data. Financial data stated for a quarter refer to that quarter only. Messaging revenues and Mobile content revenues are annualized and are 2010 forecasts. Amounts denominated in US dollars have been converted into euros using an exchange rate of 1 euro = 1.4292 US$. Mobile content prices are in local currency, unless stated otherwise. Operator mobile content prices in US$ are based on second semester 2009 data.

informa
telecoms & media

Country information, Mobile telecommunications market (in €), Mobile operators data, Mobile content services (Mobile content revenues), Mobile content prices are based on Informa Telecoms & Media research.

netsize
Mobile Business & Entertainment

Mobile Operators added value services, Netsize Offer, Mobile content prices, Industry Associations, Regulators & Codes of practice are based on Netsize mServices research.

	COUNTRY	SUBSCRIPTION GROWTH RATE	PENETRATION 2009		COUNTRY	PENETRATION 2009	SUBSCRIPTION GROWTH RATE
1	India	45.3%	37.45%	1	Greece	170.03%	9.9%
2	Morocco	30.6%	78.13%	2	Singapore	150.19%	10.0%
3	Malaysia	17.9%	107.41%	3	Luxembourg	147.54%	5.7%
4	Brazil	17.1%	85.46%	4	Russia	145.72%	13.5%
5	China	14.0%	51.91%	5	Finland	142.86%	11.8%
6	Russia	13.5%	145.72%	6	Portugal	142.54%	4.7%
7	Finland	11.8%	142.86%	7	Romania	139.12%	11.6%
8	New Zealand	11.7%	111.92%	8	Italy	138.63%	-7.0%
9	Romania	11.6%	139.12%	9	Czech Republic	134.52%	1.2%
10	South Africa	10.5%	101.02%	10	Sweden	130.79%	5.1%
11	Singapore	10.0%	150.19%	11	Austria	130.24%	3.9%
12	Greece	9.9%	170.03%	12	Denmark	124.86%	3.9%
13	Mexico	8.2%	74.26%	13	UK	124.75%	2.3%
14	Australia	8.0%	118.72%	14	Germany	124.60%	2.0%
15	Canada	7.8%	66.98%	15	Norway	120.86%	1.5%
16	Korea	7.1%	98.92%	16	Spain	119.97%	-3.9%
17	Thailand	7.0%	99.41%	17	Switzerland	118.74%	5.6%
18	Netherlands	6.3%	116.90%	18	Australia	118.72%	8.0%
19	Luxembourg	5.7%	147.54%	19	Ireland	118.35%	-5.0%
20	Switzerland	5.6%	118.74%	20	Netherlands	116.90%	6.3%
21	Slovenia	5.1%	103.65%	21	Poland	116.51%	4.6%
22	Sweden	5.1%	130.79%	22	New Zealand	111.92%	11.7%
23	Portugal	4.7%	142.54%	23	Ukraine	111.79%	-8.8%
24	Poland	4.6%	116.51%	24	Belgium	109.97%	3.1%
25	Japan	4.3%	85.80%	25	Malaysia	107.41%	17.9%
26	France	4.1%	94.41%	26	Hungary	106.90%	0.9%
27	Denmark	3.9%	124.86%	27	Slovak Republic	104.42%	-2.5%
28	Austria	3.9%	130.24%	28	Slovenia	103.65%	5.1%
29	Belgium	3.1%	109.97%	29	South Africa	101.02%	10.5%
30	Turkey	2.7%	87.62%	30	Thailand	99.41%	7.0%
31	USA	2.7%	89.28%	31	Korea	98.92%	7.1%
32	UK	2.3%	124.75%	32	France	94.41%	4.1%
33	Germany	2.0%	124.60%	33	USA	89.28%	2.7%
34	Norway	1.5%	120.86%	34	Turkey	87.62%	2.7%
35	Czech Republic	1.2%	134.52%	35	Japan	85.80%	4.3%
36	Hungary	0.9%	106.90%	36	Brazil	85.46%	17.1%
37	Slovak Republic	-2.5%	104.42%	37	Morocco	78.13%	30.6%
38	Spain	-3.9%	119.97%	38	Mexico	74.26%	8.2%
39	Ireland	-5.0%	118.35%	39	Canada	66.98%	7.8%
40	Italy	-7.0%	138.63%	40	China	51.91%	14.0%
41	Ukraine	-8.8%	111.79%	41	India	37.45%	45.3%

Penetration rate of mobile subscribers in 2009

- > 130%
- < 130%
- < 120%
- < 110%
- < 100%
- < 50%

AUSTRALIA

COUNTRY INFORMATION

Population in 2009	21,204,500
Gross domestic product 2009 per capita, current prices	24,471
Penetration rate (%) 3Q09	118.72%
Language (s)	English
Currency	Australian Dollar (AUD)

MOBILE TELECOMMUNICATIONS MARKET

Total subscriptions 3Q09	25,173,700
3G WCDMA subscriptions 3Q09	13,677,800
3G EV-DO subscriptions 3Q09	n/d
Total revenues 3Q09 (EUR million)	2,468.40
Service revenues 3Q09 (EUR million)	2,051.94
Blended montly ARPU 3Q09 (EUR)	27.38
Data revenues 3Q09 (EUR million)	808.47
SMS revenues 3Q09 (EUR million)	n/a
Messaging revenues 2010 (EUR million)	n/a
Messaging ARPU 2010 (EUR)	n/a
Content ARPU 2010 (EUR)	n/a

MOBILE OPERATORS DATA

	TELSTRA	OPTUS	VODAFONE AUSTRALIA	3 AUSTRALIA
Total subscriptions 3Q09	10,400,700	8,225,000	4,191,000	2,357,000
Market share 3Q09	41.32%	32.67%	16.65%	9.36%
Prepaid subs 3Q09 (%)	34.50%	52.84%	65.30%	10.01%
Postpaid subs 3Q09 (%)	65.50%	47.16%	34.70%	89.99%
Growth rate (%) 3Q08 to 3Q09	8.47%	10.85%	11.05%	23.60%
Total net additions in 3Q09	209,700	223,000	31,000	87,000
WCDMA net additions in 3Q09	482,800	320,000	99,000	87,000
3G EV-DO net additions in 3Q09	n/d	n/d	n/d	n/d
Blended ARPU 3Q09	30.29	27.38	36.11	36.11
Prepaid ARPU 3Q09	9.03	16.31	0.00	0.00
Postpaid ARPU 3Q09	36.69	40.19	0.00	0.00

MOBILE OPERATORS VALUE ADDED SERVICES

	TELSTRA	OPTUS	VODAFONE AUSTRALIA	3 AUSTRALIA	VIRGIN MOBILE
SMS	Yes	Yes	Yes	Yes	Yes
Push SMS	Yes	Yes	Yes	Yes	Yes
Toll free SMS MO	Yes	No	Yes	Yes	Yes
Premium SMS MO	Yes - Up to AU$6.60	Yes - Up to AU$6.60	Yes - Up to AU$6.60	Yes - Up to AU$6.60	Yes - Up to AU$6.60
Premium SMS MT (subscription)	Yes - Up to AU$10.00	Yes - Up to AU$15.00	Yes - Up to AU$10.00	Yes - Up to AU$6.60	Yes - Up to AU$15.00
MMS	Yes	Yes	Yes	Yes	No
Push MMS	Yes	No – not a commercially available offering	Yes - Push Alerts (MMS) offered via Vodafone live!	Yes	
Toll free MMS MO	Yes	No	Yes - live! Push Alerts (MMS) service are 0 rated	No	No
Premium MMS MO	yes	No	No	No	No
Premium MMS MT (subscription)	Yes	No – not a commercially available offering	No	No	No
Maximum MMS weight	300kb	Current file size limitation of 300kb	Person2Machine = No size limit - Person 2 Person = 30KB for audio (60sec)/unlimited for picture and video. - Animated GIF = 100KB - Person to email - up to 8mb (WAP gateway limit; however, most handsets peak @ 300kb)	n/a	n/a
WAP	Yes	Yes	Yes	Yes	Yes
Operator portal	Bigpond Mobile	Optus Zoo	Vodafone live!	Planet 3	The Vibe
Billing type	PSMS only	WAP - Direct Billing	WAP Online for Vodafone live!; PSMS for off deck	WAP - Direct Billing	PSMS only
Pay per Use	n/a	Yes - Up to AU$15	Yes - Up to AU$6.60	Yes - Up to AU$15	n/a
Subscription	n/a	Yes - Up to AU$15	Yes - Up to AU$15	Yes - Up to AU$15	n/a
O-rate URL / Wholesale datacharge	Yes	Yes *	0 rate URL possible - Wholesale data only available via Wholesale business area for MVNO customers	Yes	No
Maximum WAP Gateway download	No	Unlimited **	WAP Gateway limit 8 gb but as per above, (most handsets have an imposed limit of 300 kb)	No	No

* Technically possible but this is strictly subject to a detailed understanding of the service / initiative and a mutual benefit of this to both Optus and the content partner. This will involve Optus commercial scrutiny of the initiative prior to any agreement of 0 rating a CP URL

**It is however strongly recommended that customers are well informed as to download file sizes wherever possible such that informed decisions can be made prior to the purchase / download. Customer should be well informed as to potential costs, and file sizes so they can ascertain if their phone has enough memory etc to download any file content.

NETSIZE OFFER

	TELSTRA	OPTUS	VODAFONE AUSTRALIA	3 AUSTRALIA	VIRGIN MOBILE
SMS					
Push SMS	Yes	Yes	Yes	Yes	Yes
Toll free SMS MO	Yes	Yes	Yes	Yes	Yes
Premium SMS MO	Yes - Up to AU$6.60	Yes - Up to AU$6.60	Yes - Up to AU$6.60	Yes - Up to AU$6.60	Yes - Up to AU$6.60
Premium SMS MT (subscription)	Yes - Up to AU$16.00 (project specific)	Yes - Up to AU$20.00 (project specific)	Yes - Up to AU$10.00	Yes - Up to AU$6.60	Yes - Up to AU$6.60
MMS					
Push MMS	Upon request	No	Upon request	Upon request	No
Toll free MMS MO	Upon request	No	Upon request	No	No
Premium MMS MO	Upon request	No	No	No	No
Premium MMS MT (subscription)	Upon request	No	No	No	No
Maximum MMS weight	n/a	n/a	n/a	n/a	n/a
WAP	Upon request	Yes	Upon request	Yes	Upon request
Operator portal	BigPond Mobile	Optus Zoo	Vodafone live!	Planet 3	The Vibe
Billing type	n/a	WAP - Direct Billing	WAP - Direct Billing (2Q10)	WAP - Direct Billing	n/a
Pay per Use	n/a	Yes - Up to AU$20.00 (project specific)	n/a	Yes - Up to AU$20.00 (project specific)	n/a
Subscription	n/a	Yes - Up to AU$20.00 (project specific)	n/a	Yes - Up to AU$20.00 (project specific)	n/a
0-rate URL / Wholesale datacharge	Yes	Yes	0 rate URL possible / Wholesale data only available via Wholesale business area for MVNO customers	Yes	Yes
Maximum WAP Gateway download	No limit	No limit	WAP Gateway limit 8 gb but as per above, (most handsets have an imposed limit of 300 kb)	No limit	No limit

AUSTRALIA

MOBILE CONTENT PRICES (Prices in EUR)

	PAY PER USE	SUBSCRIPTION
Sound	3.00 - 5.00	5.00 - 20.00 /wk depending on package
Polyphonics	3.00 - 5.00	5.00 - 20.00 /wk depending on package
True Tones	3.00 - 6.00	5.00 - 20.00 /wk depending on package
MP3	3.00 - 6.00	5.00 - 20.00 /wk depending on package
Images	1.00 - 5.00	5.00 - 20.00 /wk depending on package
Wallpapers	3.00 - 5.00	5.00 - 20.00 /wk depending on package
Videos	3.00 - 10.00	5.00 - 20.00 /wk depending on package
Games & Lottery	variable	n/a
Voting, Participation TV	0.55	n/a
Instant Win, quiz	2.00-2.50 each way	5.00 - 20.00 /wk depending on package
Java games	4.00 - 10.00	5.00 - 20.00 /wk depending on package
Community		5.00 - 20.00 /wk depending on package
Chat	2.00 - 4.00	n/a

INDUSTRY ASSOCIATIONS, REGULATORS & CODES OF PRACTICE

	NAME	WEBSITE
Telecom regulator	Australian Communications and Media Authority (ACMA)	www.acma.gov.au
Communications alliance	Australian Communications Industry Forum	www.commsalliance.com.au
Content classification	Classification Operation Branch of the Attorney General's department (previously OFLC)	www.classification.gov.au
Industry Association	Australian Direct Marketing Association (ADMA)	www.adma.com.au
Industry Association	Australian Interactive Media Industry Association (AIMIA)	www.aimia.com.au
Industry Association	Telecommunications Industry Ombudsman (TIO)	www.tio.com.au
Industry Association	Australian Mobile Telecommunications Association (AMTA)	www.amta.org.au

AUSTRIA

COUNTRY INFORMATION

Population in 2009	8,419,500
Gross domestic product 2009 per capita, current prices	30,486
Penetration rate (%) 3Q09	130.24%
Language (s)	German
Currency	Euro (EUR)

MOBILE TELECOMMUNICATIONS MARKET

Total subscriptions 3Q09	10,965,300
3G WCDMA subscriptions 3Q09	4,339,560
3G EV-DO subscriptions 3Q09	n/d
Total revenues 3Q09 (EUR million)	880.60
Service revenues 3Q09 (EUR million)	767.21
Blended montly ARPU 3Q09 (EUR)	26.18
Data revenues 3Q09 (EUR million)	253.05
SMS revenues 3Q09 (EUR million)	88.56
Messaging revenues 2010 (EUR million)	n/a
Messaging ARPU 2010 (EUR)	n/a
Content ARPU 2010 (EUR)	n/a

MOBILE OPERATORS DATA

	A1 MOBILKOM	T-MOBILE AUSTRIA	ORANGE AUSTRIA	HUTCHISON 3G (DREI)
Total subscriptions 3Q09	4,719,400	3,387,000	2,100,000	758,900
Market share 3Q09	43.04%	30.89%	19.15%	6.92%
Prepaid subs 3Q09 (%)	28.06%	32.89%	35.72%	14.50%
Postpaid subs 3Q09 (%)	71.94%	67.11%	64.28%	85.50%
Growth rate (%) 3Q08 to 3Q09	8.35%	1.62%	2.69%	68.19%
Total net additions in 3Q09	91,000	-15,000	15,100	81,300
WCDMA net additions in 3Q09	165,000	75,060	69,000	81,300
3G EV-DO net additions in 3Q09	n/d	n/d	n/d	n/d
Blended ARPU 3Q09	27.80	24.00	27.99	26.00
Prepaid ARPU 3Q09	7.70	7.00	0.00	11.89
Postpaid ARPU 3Q09	33.24	32.00	0.00	26.94

AUSTRIA

MOBILE OPERATORS VALUE ADDED SERVICES

	A1 MOBILKOM	T-MOBILE AUSTRIA	ORANGE AUSTRIA	HUTCHISON 3G (DREI)
SMS				
Push SMS	Yes	Yes	Yes	Yes
Toll free SMS MO / Non-premium SMS MO	Yes / Yes	Yes / Yes	Yes / Yes	Yes / Yes
Premium SMS MO	Yes - Up to €10.00	Yes - Up to €10.00	Yes - Up to €10.00	Yes - Up to €10.00
Premium SMS MT (subscription)	No	Yes - Up to €10.00	Yes - Up to €10.00	Yes - Up to €10.00
MMS				
Push MMS	Yes	Yes	Yes	Yes
Toll free MMS MO	Yes - as 0-priced MO-P	Yes	No	Yes
Premium MMS MO	Yes - Up to €10.00	No	Yes - Up to €10.00	Yes - Up to €10.00
Premium MMS MT (subscription)	No	Yes	Yes - Up to €10.00	Yes - Up to €10.00
Maximum MMS weight	300 kB	300 kb	300 kb	300 kb
WAP				
Operator portal	Vodafone live!	T-Zones	ChannelOne	Planet 3
Billing type	WAP billing	WAP billing from mid 2010	MIA Payment platform - WAP billing from 2010 H2	WAP billing from mid 2010
Pay per Use	Yes - Up to €10.00	Yes	Yes - Up to €25.00	n/a
Subscription	Yes - Up to €10.00	No	No	n/a
0-rate URL / Wholesale datacharge	No	No	No	n/a
Maximum WAP Gateway download	No	10 GB	No limit	n/a

NETSIZE OFFER

	A1 MOBILKOM	T-MOBILE AUSTRIA	ORANGE AUSTRIA	HUTCHISON 3G (DREI)
SMS				
Push SMS	Yes	Yes	Yes	Yes
Non-premium SMS MO	Yes	Yes	Yes	Yes
Premium SMS MO	Yes	Yes	Yes	Yes
Premium SMS MT (subscription)	No	Yes	Yes	Yes
MMS				
Push MMS	Upon request	Upon request	Upon request	Upon request
Toll free MMS MO	No	No	No	No
Premium MMS MO	No	No	No	No
Premium MMS MT (subscription)	No	No	No	No
Maximum MMS weight	300 kB	300 kB	300 kB	300 kB
WAP				
Operator portal	n/a	n/a	n/a	n/a
Billing type	WAP-billing	From 2010	From 2010	From 2010
Pay per Use	Yes	From 2010	From 2010	From 2010
Subscription	Yes	tbc	tbc	tbc
O-rate URL / Wholesale datacharge	No	Upon request	No	No
Maximum WAP Gateway download	No limit	No limit	No limit	No limit

MOBILE CONTENT PRICES (Prices in EUR)

	PAY PER USE	SUBSCRIPTION
Sound		
Polyphonics	1.50 - 2.00	0.40 - 0.60
True Tones	1.50 - 2.00	0.40 - 0.60
MP3	0,99 - 1,99	0.40 - 0.60
Images		
Wallpapers	1.50 - 2.00	0.40 - 0.60
Videos	2.00 - 3.00	0.40 - 0.60
Games & Lottery		
Voting, Participation TV	up to 0.50	n/a
Instant Win, quiz	up to 2.00	up to 2.00
Java games	2.00 - 5.00	0.40 - 0.60
Community		
Chat	0.40	n/a

OPERATOR MOBILE CONTENT PRICES (Prices in EUR)

	A1 MOBILKOM	T-MOBILE AUSTRIA	ORANGE AUSTRIA	HUTCHISON 3G (DREI)
Community	N/A	n/a	n/a	n/a
Music	1.5 €- 2.5 €	0,99 - 1,99 (T-Mobile Music)	2.0 €	1.29 € - 1.99 €
\Video	N/A	n/a	3.00 €	1.99 €; Mobile TV basic: 4€/month, 0.29 €/day; Mobile TV Premium: 6€/month, 0.49 €/day
Games	5.0 €	n/a	5.00 €	3.99 €
Images	1.5 €	n/a	2.00 €	n/a
Other	2.0 €	n/a	3.0 € (Ringtones, SMS tones)	1.99 € (True Tones)
MMS	n/a	n/a	2.0 € (Erotic MMS)	n/a

INDUSTRY ASSOCIATIONS, REGULATORS & CODES OF PRACTICE

TYPE	NAME	WEBSITE
Regulatory Authority for Broadcasting and Telecommunications	Rundfunk und Telekom Regulierungs-GmbH (RTR-GmbH)	www.rtr.at

BELGIUM

COUNTRY INFORMATION

Population in 2009	10,503,250
Gross domestic product 2009 per capita, current prices	28,001
Penetration rate (%) 3Q09	109.97%
Language (s)	Dutch, French
Currency	Euro (EUR)

MOBILE TELECOMMUNICATIONS MARKET

Total subscriptions 3Q09	11,550,530
3G WCDMA subscriptions 3Q09	830,000
3G EV-DO subscriptions 3Q09	n/d
Total revenues 3Q09 (EUR million)	1,070.49
Service revenues 3Q09 (EUR million)	940.69
Blended montly ARPU 3Q09 (EUR)	29.70
Data revenues 3Q09 (EUR million)	244.26
SMS revenues 3Q09 (EUR million)	159.93
Messaging revenues 2010 (EUR million)	n/a
Messaging ARPU 2010 (EUR)	n/a
Content ARPU 2010 (EUR)	n/a

MOBILE OPERATORS DATA

	BELGACOM MOBILE	MOBISTAR	KPN GROUP BELGIUM
Total subscriptions 3Q09	5,040,000	3,733,730	2,776,800
Market share 3Q09	43.63%	32.33%	24.04%
Prepaid subs 3Q09 (%)	46.01%	40.40%	76.74%
Postpaid subs 3Q09 (%)	53.99%	59.60%	23.26%
Growth rate (%) 3Q08 to 3Q09	4.54%	1.60%	5.77%
Total net additions in 3Q09	41,000	-53,850	56,940
WCDMA net additions in 3Q09	40,000	30,000	n/d
3G EV-DO net additions in 3Q09	n/d	n/d	n/d
Blended ARPU 3Q09	35.99	31.31	16.00
Prepaid ARPU 3Q09	23.60	17.85	8.00
Postpaid ARPU 3Q09	47.19	39.48	50.00

MOBILE OPERATORS VALUE ADDED SERVICES

	BELGACOM MOBILE	MOBISTAR	KPN GROUP BELGIUM
SMS			
Push SMS	Yes	Yes	Yes
Toll free SMS MO	Yes	Yes	Yes
Premium SMS MO	Yes - Up to €4.00	Yes - Up to €3.00	Yes - Up to €4.00
Premium SMS MT (subscription in the 9xxx range)	Yes - Up to €4.00	Yes - Up to €4.00	Yes - Up to €4.00
MMS			
Push MMS	Yes	Yes	No
Toll free MMS MO	Yes	No	No
Premium MMS MO	Yes - Up to €4.00	Yes - Up to €4.00	No
Premium MMS MT (subscription)	Yes - Up to €4.00	Yes - Up to €4.00	No
Maximum MMS weight	300kb	300kb	n/a
WAP			
Operator portal	Vodafone live!	Orange World	i-mode
Billing type	WAP or MSISDN Forwarding + PSMS MT	n/a	PSMS MT
Pay per Use	Yes - Up to €10.00	Yes - Up to €10.00	Yes - Up to €10.00
Subscription	Yes - Up to €10.00	Yes - Up to €10.00	Yes - Up to €10.00
O-rate URL / Wholesale datacharge	no	Special request	No
Maximum WAP Gateway download	depends on contract	No limit, end-user pays data charges	No limit, end-user pays data charges

NETSIZE OFFER

	BELGACOM MOBILE	MOBISTAR	KPN GROUP BELGIUM
SMS	Yes	Yes	Yes
Push SMS	Yes	Yes	Yes
Toll free SMS MO	Yes	Yes	Yes
Premium SMS MO	Yes - Up to €4.00	Yes - Up to €4.00	Yes - Up to €4.00
Premium SMS MT (subscription)	Yes - Up to €4.00	Yes - Up to €4.00	Yes - Up to €4.00
MMS	Yes	Yes	No
Push MMS	Yes	Yes	No
Toll free MMS MO	No	No	No
Premium MMS MO	No	No	No
Premium MMS MT (subscription)	Yes - Up to €4.00	Yes - Up to €4.00	No
Maximum MMS weight	300kb	300kb	300kb
WAP			
Operator portal	Vodafone live!/ PLAZZZA	Orange World/ PLAZZZA	i-mode/PLAZZA (Q1 2010)
Billing type	WAP-billing (on portal, off portal on PLAZZZA)	WAP-billing (on portal,"off portal" on PLAZZZA)	WAP-billing (on portal,"off portal" on PLAZZZA)
Pay per Use	Yes - Up to €10.00	Yes - Up to €10.00	Yes - Up to €10.00
Subscription	Yes - Up to €10.00	Yes - Up to €10.00	Yes - Up to €10.00
O-rate URL / Wholesale datacharge	No	No	No
Maximum WAP Gateway download	No limit	No limit	No limit

MOBILE CONTENT PRICES (Prices in EUR)

	PAY PER USE	SUBSCRIPTION
Sound		
Polyphonics	max 2 euro (MO+MT)	max 2 euro (MO max 0,15) (MO+MT)
True Tones	max 2 euro (MO+MT)	max 2 euro (MO max 0,15) (MO+MT)
MP3	max 2 euro (MO+MT)	max 2 euro (MO max 0,15) (MO+MT)
Images		
Wallpapers	max 2 euro (MO+MT)	max 2 euro (MO max 0,15) (MO+MT)
Videos	max 2 euro (MO+MT)	max 2 euro (MO max 0,15) (MO+MT)
Games & Lottery		
Voting, Participation TV	max 2 euro (MO+MT) only in 61xx range	n/a
Instant Win, quiz	max 2 euro (MO+MT)	max 2 euro (MO max 0,15) (MO+MT)
Java games	max 2 euro (MO+MT)	max 2 euro (MO max 0,15) (MO+MT)
Community		
Chat	max 2 euro (MO+MT)	n/a

INDUSTRY ASSOCIATIONS, REGULATORS & CODES OF PRACTICE

	NAME	WEBSITE
Telecom regulator	Institut Belge des services Postaux et de Télécommunications (BIPT)	www.bipt.be
Industry Association	WASP Forum	www.wasp-forum.be

BRAZIL

COUNTRY INFORMATION

Population in 2009	197,158,750
Gross domestic product 2009 per capita, current prices	4,566
Penetration rate (%) 3Q09	85.46%
Language (s)	Portuguese
Currency	Brazilian Real (BRL)

MOBILE TELECOMMUNICATIONS MARKET

Total subscriptions 3Q09	168,485,320
3G WCDMA subscriptions 3Q09	6,155,920
3G EV-DO subscriptions 3Q09	204,800
Total revenues 3Q09 (EUR million)	5,785.10
Service revenues 3Q09 (EUR million)	5,222.97
Blended montly ARPU 3Q09 (EUR)	9.77
Data revenues 3Q09 (EUR million)	655.27
SMS revenues 3Q09 (EUR million)	159.92
Messaging revenues 2010 (EUR million)	991.87
Messaging ARPU 2010 (EUR)	0.60
Content ARPU 2010 (EUR)	0.77

MOBILE OPERATORS DATA

	VIVO	CLARO	TIM BRASIL	TELEMAR PCS (OI)	BRASIL TELECOM GSM	NEXTEL TELECOMU-NICACOES	CTBC TELECOM	SERCOMTEL CELULAR	UNICEL DO BRASIL TELECOMU-NICACOES
Total subscriptions 3Q09	48,847,030	42,278,200	39,627,380	27,978,130	6,839,870	2,290,900	511,930	91,920	19,960
Market share 3Q09	28.99%	25.09%	23.52%	16.61%	4.06%	1.36%	0.30%	0.05%	0.01%
Prepaid subs 3Q09 (%)	81.48%	79.85%	84.46%	83.00%	91.74%	-	76.77%	88.61%	100.00%
Postpaid subs 3Q09 (%)	18.52%	20.15%	15.54%	17.00%	8.26%	100.00%	23.23%	11.39%	-
Growth rate (%) 3Q08 to 3Q09	15.56%	18.53%	12.50%	27.96%	30.39%	36.77%	18.22%	27.26%	446.85%
Total net additions in 3Q09	1,994,840	1,715,530	1,788,520	806,840	852,750	184,900	33,160	2,370	540
WCDMA net additions in 3Q09	491,620	364,400	80,880	61,890	16,110	n/d	8,100	450	r/d
3G EV-DO net additions in 3Q09	-23,360	n/d	n/d	n/d	n/d	n/d	n/d	n/d	r/d
Blended ARPU 3Q09	9.92	8.64	9.96	8.34	n/a	40.58	15.97	n/a	n/a
Prepaid ARPU 3Q09	0.00	0.00	0.00	0.00	n/a	0.00	0.00	n/a	n/a
Postpaid ARPU 3Q09	0.00	0.00	0.00	0.00	n/a	40.58	0.00	n/a	n/a

MOBILE CONTENT SERVICES

	TOTAL REVENUES 2010 (EUR MILLION)	CONTRIBUTION AS % OF TOTAL REVENUES
Mobile music market	204.15	9.63%
Mobile games market	68.28	3.22%
Mobile images market	29.22	1.38%
Mobile TV market	11.59	0.55%
Mobile video market	24.14	1.14%
Mobile internet market	790.47	37.29%
Mobile messaging market	991.87	46.79%

OPERATOR MOBILE CONTENT PRICES (Prices in US$)

	VIVO	TIM BRASIL
Community	Handset client (downloadable): 0.00 / Month - 0.00 / wk - Handset client (pre-inst.)/ SMS: 9.80 / month - 0.08 / message - GPRS/WAP/SMS: 0.11 / message - 0.03 / KB. Other data-pricing options available. No content charge.	GPRS/WAP: 9.07 / MB. Other data-pricing options available. No content charge. - 9.07 / MB. Other data-pricing options available. No content charge. - Handset client (downloadable): 9.07 / MB. Other data-pricing options available. No content charge.
Music	Ring tones: 1.64 / download - 2.14 / download - 2.14 / download - 3.22 / download (OTA) - Full-tracks: 2.43 / download. No addit. download/streaming traffic charges. (OTA/Streaming)	Full-tracks: 2.25 / download (OTA) - Ring tones: 3.38 / download - 2.25 / download (OTA) - Ring-back tones: 2.25 / tone for 60 days, + R$0.99 monthly subscr. fee. (OTA)
TV & Video	Mobile TV: 1.41 / 24 hrs - 2.88 / 30 days - 5.81 / 24 hrs - 8.75 / 30 days - 5.81 / 24 hrs - 11.69 / 30 days - 5.81 / 24 hrs - 11.69 / 30 days (Streamed) - Video-on-demand: 0.88 / download - 2.06 / download - 2.53 / download - 3.82 / download (Downloaded/streamed)	Mobile TV: 2.34 / 30 min - 3.52 / 120 min - 5.87 / 24 hrs (Streamed) - Video-on-demand: 1.76 / download, + data-traffic charges. Promotional price. - 1.23 / megabyte, + WAP portal browsing charges. (Download)
Location Based Services	Navigation: 2.82 / 3 days - 10.55 / month (GPS)	Navigation: 11.26 / month (GPS)

CANADA

COUNTRY INFORMATION

Population in 2009	33,529,250
Gross domestic product 2009 per capita, current prices	25,601
Penetration rate (%) 3Q09	66.98%
Language (s)	English, French
Currency	Canadian Dollar (CAD)

MOBILE TELECOMMUNICATIONS MARKET

Total subscriptions 3Q09	22,457,180
3G WCDMA subscriptions 3Q09	1,695,000
3G EV-DO subscriptions 3Q09	2,840,500
Total revenues 3Q09 (EUR million)	2,749.09
Service revenues 3Q09 (EUR million)	2,548.42
Blended montly ARPU 3Q09 (EUR)	38.11
Data revenues 3Q09 (EUR million)	517.20
SMS revenues 3Q09 (EUR million)	219.96
Messaging revenues 2010 (EUR million)	752.99
Messaging ARPU 2010 (EUR)	3.17
Content ARPU 2010 (EUR)	5.25

MOBILE OPERATORS DATA

	ROGERS WIRELESS COMMUNICATIONS	BELL WIRELESS AFFILIATES	TELUS MOBILITY	SASKTEL MOBILITY	MTS MOBILITY
Total subscriptions 4Q08	8,365,000	6,707,000	6,413,000	520,260	451,920
Market share	37.25%	29.87%	28.56%	2.32%	2.01%
Prepaid subs 3Q08 (%)	17.88%	25.96%	19.04%	2.00%	2.00%
Postpaid subs 3Q08 (%)	82.12%	74.04%	80.96%	98.00%	98.00%
Growth rate (%) 4Q07 to 4Q08	8.02%	4.00%	7.22%	5.33%	7.44%
Total net additions in 3Q08	209,000	135,000	125,000	7,680	5,630
WCDMA net additions in 4Q08	135,000	n/d	n/d	n/d	n/d
EV-DO net additions in 4Q08	n/d	100,000	28,000	4,000	5,500
Blended ARPU 3Q08	42.33	33.20	37.87	n/a	36.33
Prepaid ARPU 3Q08	11.97	11.69	0.00	n/a	0.00
Postpaid ARPU 3Q08	48.91	40.82	0.00	n/a	0.00

MOBILE CONTENT SERVICES

	TOTAL REVENUES 2010 (EUR MILLION)	CONTRIBUTION AS % OF TOTAL REVENUES
Mobile music market	82.46	4.40%
Mobile games market	56.35	3.01%
Mobile images market	16.44	0.88%
Mobile TV market	21.34	1.14%
Mobile video market	10.58	0.56%
Mobile internet market	933.28	49.82%
Mobile messaging market	752.99	40.19%

OPERATOR MOBILE CONTENT PRICES (Prices in US$)

	ROGERS WIRELESS COMMUNICATIONS	TELUS MOBILITY
Community	Handset client (pre-inst.): 0.95 / day of data use. Other data-pricing options available. No content charge. - 0.14 / SMS sent to Facebook	GPRS/WAP: 0.09 / web page. Other data-pricing options available. No content charge. - SMS: 0.14 / SMS sent and received - 0.14 / SMS sent and received - Handset client (downloadable): Variable Depending on app.
Music	Full-tracks: 1.37 / download, incl C$0.25 traffic fee - 18.32 / month. First month after signing up free. (OTA) - Ring-back tones: 1.83 / tone, + C$1 monthly subscr. fee. First tone free after signing up to service. - 2.74 / month for two tones (Voice) - Ring tones: 3.89 / download, incl C$0.25 traffic fee - 1.83 / download (OTA) - Mobile Radio: 13.74 / month. 33% discount when bought with a mobile browsing plan. (OTA Streaming)	Full-tracks: 0.63 / download (lowest price), + C$0.50 traffic charge. - 1.18 / download (highest price), + C$0.50 traffic charge. - 9.15 / download - 18.32 / month (OTA) - Ring tones: 1.83 / download, + C$0.50 traffic charge. (OTA) - Full-tracks: 7.32 / month - 13.74 / month - 2.74 / day (OTA Streaming)
Video	Video on demand: 4.71 / month (Streamed) - Mobile TV//Video on demand: 14.15 / month. 33% off when user buys C$10.00 unl. data package. - 1.17 / clip / 24hrs. 33% off when user buys C$10.00 unl. data package. - 23.59 / month. 33% off when user buys C$10.00 unl. data package. (Streamed) - Video on demand: 1.65 / download (Download)	Video on demand: 0.23 / download - 14.15 / month for unl. videos, incl data traffic. - 0.47 / YouTube stream (Streamed) - Mobile TV: 14.15 / month (Streamed)
Location Based Services	Navigation/ Local search: 9.25 / month (GPS) - Fitness tracker: 2.77 / month. Data charges may apply outside Canada (GPS)	Navigation/ Local search: 2.77 / day - 9.25 / month (GPS) - Family locator: 4.62 / month (GPS)

CHINA

COUNTRY INFORMATION

Population in 2009	1,345,732,500
Gross domestic product 2009 per capita, current prices	2,534
Penetration rate (%) 3Q09	51.91%
Language (s)	Chinese
Currency	Chinese Yuan Renminbi (CNY)

MOBILE TELECOMMUNICATIONS MARKET

Total subscriptions 3Q09	698,566,000
3G WCDMA subscriptions 3Q09	530,000
3G EV-DO subscriptions 3Q09	n/d
Total revenues 3Q09 (EUR million)	0.00
Service revenues 3Q09 (EUR million)	14,414.51
Blended montly ARPU 3Q09 (EUR)	6.90
Data revenues 3Q09 (EUR million)	4,472.15
SMS revenues 3Q09 (EUR million)	n/a
Messaging revenues 2010 (EUR million)	11,445.06
Messaging ARPU 2010 (EUR)	1.46
Content ARPU 2010 (EUR)	0.94

MOBILE OPERATORS DATA

	CHINA MOBILE	CHINA UNICOM	CHINA TELECOM
Total subscriptions 3Q09	508,457,000	143,329,000	46,780,000
Market share 3Q09	72.79%	20.52%	6.70%
Prepaid subs 3Q09 (%)	79.43%	48.43%	9.27%
Postpaid subs 3Q09 (%)	20.57%	51.57%	90.73%
Growth rate (%) 3Q08 to 3Q09	16.59%	-16.89%	11309.76%
Total net additions in 3Q09	15,333,000	2,861,500	7,089,000
WCDMA net additions in 3Q09	n/d	440,000	n/d
3G EV-DO net additions in 3Q09	n/d	n/d	n/d
Blended ARPU 3Q09	7.69	4.25	6.36
Prepaid ARPU 3Q09	0.00	0.00	0.00
Postpaid ARPU 3Q09	0.00	0.00	0.00

MOBILE OPERATORS VALUE ADDED SERVICES MOBILE CONTENT SERVICES

	TOTAL REVENUES 2010 (EUR MILLION)	CONTRIBUTION AS % OF TOTAL REVENUES
Mobile music market	2,177.03	11.82%
Mobile games market	204.23	1.11%
Mobile images market	392.05	2.13%
Mobile TV market	34.38	0.19%
Mobile video market	127.27	0.69%
Mobile internet market	4,045.70	21.96%
Mobile messaging market	11,445.06	62.11%

INDUSTRY ASSOCIATIONS, REGULATORS & CODES OF PRACTICE

	NAME	WEBSITE
Telecom regulator	Ministry of Information Industry	http://www.miit.gov.cn/

CZECH REPUBLIC

COUNTRY INFORMATION

Population in 2009	10,177,250
Gross domestic product 2009 per capita, current prices	11,673
Penetration rate (%) 3Q09	134.52%
Language (s)	Czech
Currency	Czech krona (CZK)

MOBILE TELECOMMUNICATIONS MARKET

Total subscriptions 3Q09	13,690,500
3G WCDMA subscriptions 3Q09	383,700
3G EV-DO subscriptions 3Q09	147,000
Total revenues 3Q09 (EUR million)	800.19
Service revenues 3Q09 (EUR million)	784.32
Blended montly ARPU 3Q09 (EUR)	19.30
Data revenues 3Q09 (EUR million)	191.13
SMS revenues 3Q09 (EUR million)	105.34
Messaging revenues 2010 (EUR million)	n/a
Messaging ARPU 2010 (EUR)	n/a
Content ARPU 2010 (EUR)	n/a

MOBILE OPERATORS DATA

	T-MOBILE CZECH REPUBLIC	TELEFONICA O2 CZECH REPUBLIC	VODAFONE CZECH REPUBLIC	MOBILKOM
Total subscriptions 3Q09	5,458,000	5,099,700	2,984,000	148,800
Market share 3Q09	39.87%	37.25%	21.80%	1.09%
Prepaid subs 3Q09 (%)	51.81%	42.68%	48.40%	
Postpaid subs 3Q09 (%)	48.19%	57.32%	51.60%	100.00%
Growth rate (%) 3Q08 to 3Q09	1.22%	5.33%	5.52%	105.81%
Total net additions in 3Q09	25,000	128,200	49,000	15,200
WCDMA net additions in 3Q09	n/d	22,900	6,000	n/d
3G EV-DO net additions in 3Q09	n/d	10,600	n/d	n/d
Blended ARPU 3Q09	18.00	20.02	20.45	n/a
Prepaid ARPU 3Q09	7.00	8.68	10.97	n/a
Postpaid ARPU 3Q09	30.00	29.17	31.34	n/a

MOBILE OPERATORS VALUE ADDED SERVICES

	T-MOBILE CZECH REPUBLIC	TELEFONICA O2 CZECH REPUBLIC	VODAFONE CZECH REPUBLIC
SMS			
Push SMS	Yes	Yes	Yes
Toll free SMS MO	No	No	No
Premium SMS MO	Yes - Up to CZK99.00	Yes - Up to CZK99.00	Yes - Up to CZK99.00
Premium SMS MT (subscription)	Yes - Up to CZK99.00	Yes - Up to CZK99.00	Yes - Up to CZK99.00
MMS			
Push MMS	Yes	Yes	Yes
Toll free MMS MO	No	No	No
Premium MMS MO	No	No	No
Premium MMS MT (subscription)	No	No	No
Maximum MMS weight	300 kB	300 kB	300 kB
WAP			
Operator portal	Yes - T-Zones	Yes - O2 Active	Yes - Vodafone Live!
Billing type	WAP-billing	WAP-billing	WAP-billing
Pay per Use	Yes	Yes	Yes
Subscription	No	No	No
O-rate URL / Wholesale datacharge	Yes	Yes	Yes
Maximum WAP download size (kB)	No limit	No limit	No limit

NETSIZE OFFER

	T-MOBILE CZECH REPUBLIC	TELEFONICA O2 CZECH REPUBLIC	VODAFONE CZECH REPUBLIC
SMS			
Push SMS	Yes	Yes	Yes
Toll free SMS MO	No	No	No
Premium SMS MO	Yes	Yes	Yes
Premium SMS MT (subscription)	No	No	No
MMS			
Push MMS	Upon request	Upon request	Upon request
Toll free MMS MO	No	No	No
Premium MMS MO	No	No	No
Premium MMS MT (subscription)	No	No	No
Maximum MMS weight	No limit	No limit	No limit
WAP			
Operator portal	Upon request	Upon request	Upon request
Billing type	Upon request	Upon request	Upon request
Pay per Use	No	No	No
Subscription	No	No	No
O-rate URL / Wholesale datacharge	No	No	No
Maximum WAP Gateway download	No limit	No limit	No limit

CZECH REPUBLIC

MOBILE CONTENT PRICES (Prices in CZK)

	PAY PER USE	SUBSCRIPTION
Sound		
Polyphonics	25.00 - 79.00	16.33 - 26.00
True Tones	30.00 - 79.00	16.33 - 26.00
MP3	59.00 - 79.00	26.00 - 27.50
Images		
Wallpapers	19.00 - 79.00	19.00
Videos	25.00 - 99.00	15.00 - 48.00
Games & Lottery		
Voting, Participation TV	1.00 - 9.00	n/a
Instant Win, quiz	1.00 - 50.00	n/a
Java games	49.00 - 89.00	39.00
Community	30.00 - 99.00	n/a
Chat	1.00 - 15.00	n/a

	T-MOBILE CZECH REPUBLIC	TELEFONICA O2 CZECH REPUBLIC
Community	n/a	Handset client (downloadable): 0.06 / message - 2.25 / wk (prepaid only) - 9.02 / month (postpaid only)
Music	Full-tracks: 13.16 / month - 5.76 / month (OTA) - Ring tones: 2.27 / download - 1.68 / download (OTA)	Ring-back tones: 1.46 / tone (Voice) - Ring tones: 2.32 / download - 1.15 / download - 1.15 / download (OTA)
TV & Video	Video-on-demand: 0.86 / download (lowest price). - 2.89 / download (highest price). - 0.86 / download - 1.43 / download (Download)	Video-on-demand: 2.87 / download - 0.23 / month, + traffic-download fees. - 0.57 / month, + traffic-download fees. (Download) - Traffic-camera streaming: 0.05 / streamed min (Streamed) - Traffic-camera streaming: 0.57 / 30 mins (Streamed) - Mobile TV: 1.15 / day for unl. viewing. - 4.31 / wk for unl. viewing. - 8.63 / month for unl. viewing. (Streamed) - Video-on-demand: 0.00 / download (lowest price). - 5.69 / download (highest price). (Streamed/downloaded)
Location Based Services	Local search: 0.16 / location request. Price shown for receiving SMS answer. Standard SMS charges apply when sending request. - 0.83 / location request. Same as above but price specifically to get answer for "find nearest night club." (Cell-ID)	Navigation: n/a (Information not available)

INDUSTRY ASSOCIATIONS, REGULATORS & CODES OF PRACTICE

	NAME	WEBSITE
Telecom regulator	Český telekomunikační úřad (ČTÚ)	www.ctu.cz
Premium Rate Services work group	Asociace Provozovatel Mobilních Sítí (APMS)	www.apms.cz

DENMARK

COUNTRY INFORMATION

Population in 2009	5,464,750
Gross domestic product 2009 per capita, current prices	36,954
Penetration rate (%) 3Q09	124.86%
Language (s)	Danish
Currency	Danish Krone (DKK)

MOBILE TELECOMMUNICATIONS MARKET

Total subscriptions 3Q09	6,823,300
3G WCDMA subscriptions 3Q09	1,630,000
3G EV-DO subscriptions 3Q09	n/d
Total revenues 3Q09 (EUR million)	683.02
Service revenues 3Q09 (EUR million)	567.94
Blended montly ARPU 3Q09 (EUR)	27.65
Data revenues 3Q09 (EUR million)	104.98
SMS revenues 3Q09 (EUR million)	n/a
Messaging revenues 2010 (EUR million)	n/a
Messaging ARPU 2010 (EUR)	n/a
Content ARPU 2010 (EUR)	n/a

MOBILE OPERATORS DATA

	TDC MOBIL	TELENOR DENMARK	TELIA DENMARK	HI3G DENMARK
Total subscriptions 3Q09	2,901,000	2,018,000	1,418,000	485,000
Market share 3Q09	42.52%	29.58%	20.78%	7.11%
Prepaid subs 3Q09 (%)	11.03%	41.18%	18.48%	0.31%
Postpaid subs 3Q09 (%)	88.97%	58.82%	81.52%	99.69%
Growth rate (%) 3Q08 to 3Q09	3.50%	13.18%	-3.80%	32.88%
Total net additions in 3Q09	-122,000	53,000	-31,000	37,000
WCDMA net additions in 3Q09	60,000	40,000	5,000	37,000
3G EV-DO net additions in 3Q09	n/d	n/d	n/d	n/d
Blended ARPU 3Q09	24.86	25.75	34.13	33.65
Prepaid ARPU 3Q09	0.00	13.96	11.69	10.50
Postpaid ARPU 3Q09	0.00	33.99	39.37	33.24

DENMARK

MOBILE OPERATORS VALUE ADDED SERVICES

	TDC MOBIL	TELENOR DENMARK	TELIA DENMARK	HI3G DENMARK
SMS				
Push SMS	Yes	Yes	Yes	Yes
Toll free SMS MO	No	No	No	No
Premium SMS MO	No	No	No	No
Premium SMS MT (subscription)	Yes - Up to DKK200	Yes - Up to DKK200	Yes - Up to DKK 200	Yes - Up to DKK 200
MMS				
Push MMS	Yes	Yes	Yes	Yes
Toll free MMS MO	No	No	No	No
Premium MMS MO	No	No	No	No
Premium MMS MT (subscription)	No	Yes - Max transaction price DKK200	Yes - Max transaction price DKK200	Yes - Max transaction price DKK200
Maximum MMS weight	300 kb	100 kb	500 kb	n/a
WAP				
Operator portal	Fly	e-go	Telia SurfPort	Planet 3
Billing type	MSISDN Forwarding + PSMS MT	WAP	WAP	WAP
Pay per Use	No	Yes - Max transaction price DKK150	Yes - Max transaction price DKK150	Yes - Max transaction price DKK150
Subscription	No	Yes - Max transaction price DKK200	Yes - Max transaction price DKK200	Yes - Max transaction price DKK200
O-rate URL / Wholesale datacharge	Yes	Yes	Yes	Yes
Maximum WAP Gateway download	no limit	no limit	no limit	no limit

NETSIZE OFFER

	TDC MOBIL	TELENOR DENMARK	TELIA DENMARK	HI3G DENMARK
SMS				
Push SMS	Yes	Yes	Yes	Yes
Toll free SMS MO	No	No	No	No
Premium SMS MO	No	No	No	No
Premium SMS MT (subscription)	Yes	Yes	Yes	Yes
MMS				
Push MMS	Upon request	Upon request	Upon request	Upon request
Toll free MMS MO	No	No	No	No
Premium MMS MO	No	No	No	No
Premium MMS MT (subscription)	No	Upon request	Upon request	Upon request
Maximum MMS weight	300 kb	100 kb	500 kb	n/a
WAP				
Operator portal	Fly	e-go	Telia SurfPort	Planet 3
Billing type	MSISDN Forwarding + PSMS MT	WAP	WAP	WAP
Pay per Use	Upon request	Upon request	Upon request	Upon request
Subscription	Upon request	Upon request	Upon request	Upon request
O-rate URL / Wholesale datacharge	No	No	No	No
Maximum WAP Gateway download	No limit	No limit	No limit	No limit

MOBILE CONTENT PRICES (Prices in DKK)

	PAY PER USE	SUBSCRIPTION
Sound	25- 45	45/week
Polyphonics	25-45	45/week
True Tones	25-45	45/week
MP3	25-45	45/week
Images	Dec-45	45/week
Wallpapers	Dec-45	45/week
Videos	25-45	n/a
Games & Lottery	45	45/week
Voting, Participation TV	n/a	n/a
Instant Win, quiz	n/a	n/a
Java games	30.00 - 50.00	
Community		
Chat	n/a	n/a

INDUSTRY ASSOCIATIONS, REGULATORS & CODES OF PRACTICE

	NAME	WEBSITE
Telecom regulator	Telestyrelsen - National Telecom Agency (NTA)	www.itst.dk
Operators Forum	Telecommunication Industries Association in Denmark	www.teleindustrien.dk
Codes of practices	Danish Consumer Ombudsman	www.forbrug.dk

FINLAND

COUNTRY INFORMATION

Population in 2009	5,311,000
Gross domestic product 2009 per capita, current prices	30,938
Penetration rate (%) 3Q09	142.86%
Language (s)	Finnish
Currency	Euro (EUR)

MOBILE TELECOMMUNICATIONS MARKET

Total subscriptions 3Q09	7,587,400
3G WCDMA subscriptions 3Q09	2,625,000
3G EV-DO subscriptions 3Q09	n/d
Total revenues 3Q09 (EUR million)	581.40
Service revenues 3Q09 (EUR million)	516.71
Blended montly ARPU 3Q09 (EUR)	22.90
Data revenues 3Q09 (EUR million)	98.16
SMS revenues 3Q09 (EUR million)	n/a
Messaging revenues 2010 (EUR million)	n/a
Messaging ARPU 2010 (EUR)	n/a
Content ARPU 2010 (EUR)	n/a

MOBILE OPERATORS DATA

	TELIASONERA	ELISA	DNA FINLAND	SAUNALAHTI	ÅLANDS MOBILTELEFON
Total subscriptions 3Q09	2,833,000	2,863,400	1,891,000	See Elisa	23,000
Market share 3Q09	37.34%	37.74%	24.92%		n/a
Prepaid subs 3Q09 (%)	10.31%	8.64%	16.70%		n/a
Postpaid subs 3Q09 (%)	89.69%	91.36%	83.30%		n/a
Growth rate (%) 3Q08 to 3Q09	7.11%	15.13%	19.31%		n/a
Total net additions in 3Q09	92,000	57,400	74,000		n/a
WCDMA net additions in 3Q09	40,000	50,000	65,000		n/d
3G EV-DO net additions in 3Q09	n/d	n/d	n/d		n/d
Blended ARPU 3Q09	23.00	23.20	22.30		n/a
Prepaid ARPU 3Q09	5.00	0.00	0.00		n/a
Postpaid ARPU 3Q09	25.00	0.00	0.00		n/a

MOBILE OPERATORS VALUE ADDED SERVICES

	TELIASONERA	ELISA	DNA FINLAND	SAUNALAHTI	ÅLANDS MOBILTELEFON
SMS					
Push SMS	Yes	Yes	Yes	Yes	n/a
Toll free SMS MO	Yes	Yes	Yes	Yes	n/a
Premium SMS MO	Yes - Up to €20.00	Yes - Up to €20.00	Yes - Up to €20.00	Yes - Up to €20.00	n/a
Premium SMS MT (subscription)	Yes - Up to €20.00	Yes - Up to €20.00	Yes - Up to € 20.00	Yes - Up to €20.00	n/a
MMS					
Push MMS	Yes	Yes	Yes	Yes	n/a
Toll free MMS MO	Yes	Yes	Yes	Yes	n/a
Premium MMS MO	Yes - Up to €20.00	Yes - Up to €20.00	Yes - Up to €20.00	Yes - Up to €20.00	n/a
Premium MMS MT (subscription)	Yes - Up to €20.00	Yes - Up to €20.00	Yes - Up to €20.00	Yes - Up to €20.00	n/a
Maximum MMS weight	MT MMS size 300 KB. MO MMS no limit	No limit	500 kb	No Limit	n/a
WAP					
Operator portal	SurfPort	WAP.Elisa.net	Oma DNA	SaunaWAP	n/a
Billing type	WAP	WAP	WAP	WAP	n/a
Pay per Use	Yes - Up to €20.00	Yes - Up to €20.00	Yes - Up to €20.00	Yes - Up to €20.00	n/a
Subscription	No	Yes, but billing is done through sms - Up to €20.00	Yes, but billing is done through sms - Up to €20.00	Yes, but billing is done through sms - Up to €20.00	n/a
O-rate URL / Wholesale datacharge	No	Yes	No	No	n/a
Maximum WAP Gateway download	No limit	Size 15 MB	10 MB	No Limit	n/a

NETSIZE OFFER

	SONERA	ELISA	DNA FINLAND	SAUNALAHTI	ÅLANDS MOBILTELEFON
SMS					
Push SMS	Yes	Yes	Yes	Yes	Upon request
Toll free SMS MO	Yes - Up to €20.00	Yes - Up to €20.00	Yes - Up to €20.00	Yes - Up to €20.00	Upon request
Premium SMS MO	Yes - Up to €20.00	Upon request	Upon request	Upon request	Upon request
Premium SMS MT (subscription)	Yes	Yes	Yes	Yes	Upon request
MMS					
Push MMS	Upon request	Upon request	Upon request	Upon request	Upon request
Toll free MMS MO	Upon request	Upon request	Upon request	Upon request	Upon request
Premium MMS MO	Upon request	Upon request	Upon request	Upon request	Upon request
Premium MMS MT (subscription)	Upon request	Upon request	Upon request	No	Upon request
Maximum MMS weight	MT MMS size 300 KB. MO MMS no limit	No limit	500 kb	No Limit	
WAP					
Operator portal	SurfPort	WAP.Elisa.net	Oma DNA	SaunaWAP	Upon request
Billing type	WAP	WAP	WAP	WAP	Upon request
Pay per Use	Yes - Up to €20.00	Yes - Up to €20.00	Yes - Up to €20.00	Yes - Up to €20.00	Upon request
Subscription	No	Yes, but billing is done through sms - Up to €20.00	Yes, but billing is done through sms - Up to €20.00	Yes, but billing is done through sms - Up to €20.00	Upon request
O-rate URL / Wholesale datacharge	No	Yes	No	No	Upon request
Maximum WAP Gateway download	No limit	Size 15 MB	10 MB	No Limit	No limit

MOBILE CONTENT PRICES (Prices in EUR)

	PAY PER USE	SUBSCRIPTION
Sound	3.00 - 4.00	1.5
Polyphonics	3.00 - 4.00	1.5
True Tones	3.00 - 4.00	1.5
MP3	3.00 - 4.00	0.4
Images	3.00 - 4.00	1
Wallpapers	1.50 - 4.00	1
Videos	3.00 - 5.00	n/a
Games & Lottery	5	0.8-1.50
Voting, Participation TV	0.95	n/a
Instant Win, quiz	n/a	n/a
Java games	5	n/a
Community		
Chat	n/a	n/a

INDUSTRY ASSOCIATIONS, REGULATORS & CODES OF PRACTICE

	NAME	WEBSITE
Telecom Regulator	Viestintävirasto Kommunikationsverket (Finnish Communications Regulatory Authority)	www.ficora.fi
Telecom Regulator	Finnish self regulatory committee for Premium Rate Services	www.mapel.fi
Codes of practices	Consumer agency and consumer Ombudsman	www.kuluttajavirasto.fi

FRANCE

COUNTRY INFORMATION

Population in 2009	62,279,750
Gross domestic product 2009 per capita, current prices	27,933
Penetration rate (%) 3Q09	94.41%
Language (s)	French
Currency	Euro (EUR)

MOBILE TELECOMMUNICATIONS MARKET

Total subscriptions 3Q09	58,798,000
3G WCDMA subscriptions 3Q09	15,669,000
3G EV-DO subscriptions 3Q09	n/d
Total revenues 3Q09 (EUR million)	6,256.91
Service revenues 3Q09 (EUR million)	5,814.92
Blended montly ARPU 3Q09 (EUR)	34.92
Data revenues 3Q09 (EUR million)	1,418.71
SMS revenues 3Q09 (EUR million)	732.87
Messaging revenues 2010 (EUR million)	2,379.35
Messaging ARPU 2010 (EUR)	3.79
Content ARPU 2010 (EUR)	3.68

MOBILE OPERATORS DATA

	ORANGE FRANCE	SFR	BOUYGUES TELECOM
Total subscriptions 3Q09	27,468,000	21,264,000	10,066,000
Market share 3Q09	46.72%	36.16%	17.12%
Prepaid subs 3Q09 (%)	36.07%	32.18%	23.84%
Postpaid subs 3Q09 (%)	63.93%	67.82%	76.16%
Growth rate (%) 3Q08 to 3Q09	4.80%	4.86%	7.92%
Total net additions in 3Q09	200,000	70,000	172,000
WCDMA net additions in 3Q09	523,000	649,000	160,000
3G EV-DO net additions in 3Q09	n/d	n/d	n/d
Blended ARPU 3Q09	33.17	34.33	41.00
Prepaid ARPU 3Q09	13.58	14.17	15.00
Postpaid ARPU 3Q09	42.25	43.42	50.00

FRANCE

MOBILE OPERATORS VALUE ADDED SERVICES

	ORANGE FRANCE	SFR	BOUYGUES TELECOM
SMS			
Push SMS	Yes	Yes	Yes
Toll free SMS MO	No	No	No
Premium SMS MO	Yes - Up to €3.00 - (€4.5 for Java or Video)	Yes - Up to €3.00 - (€4.5 for Java or Video)	Yes - Up to €3.00 - (€4.5 for Java or Video)
Premium SMS MT (subscription)	Yes - Up to €3.00 (€12.00 cumulated in a month)	Yes - Up to €3.00 (€12.00 cumulated in a month)	Yes - Up to €3.00 (€12.00 cumulated in a month)
MMS			
Push MMS	Yes	Yes	Yes
Toll free MMS MO	No	No	No
Premium MMS MO	Yes - Up to €3.00	Yes - Up to €3.00	Yes - Up to €3.00
Premium MMS MT (subscription)	yes	No	Yes
Maximum MMS weight	300 Ko	300 Ko	300 Ko
WAP			
Operator portal	Orange World, Gallery	Vodafone live!, Gallery	i-mode, 6ème Sens, Gallery
Billing type	WAP	WAP	WAP
Pay per Use	yes - up to €8.00	yes - up to €10.00	yes - up to €8.00
Subscription	yes - up to €12.00	yes - up to €12.00	yes - up to €10.00
O-rate URL / Wholesale datacharge	No	No	No
Maximum WAP Gateway download	n/a	n/a	n/a

NETSIZE OFFER

	ORANGE FRANCE	SFR	BOUYGUES TELECOM
SMS			
Push SMS	Yes	Yes	Yes
Toll free SMS MO	No	No	No
Premium SMS MO	Yes - Up to €3.00 - (€4.5 for Java or Video)	Yes - Up to €3.00 - (€4.5 for Java or Video)	Yes - Up to €3.00 - (€4.5 for Java or Video)
Premium SMS MT (subscription)	Yes - Up to €3.00 (€12.00 cumulated in a month)	Yes - Up to €3.00 (€12.00 cumulated in a month)	Yes - Up to €3.00 (€12.00 cumulated in a month)
MMS			
Push MMS	Yes	Yes	Yes
Toll free MMS MO	No	No	No
Premium MMS MO	Yes - Up to €3.00	Yes - Up to €3.00	Yes - Up to €3.00
Premium MMS MT (subscription)	No	No	No
Maximum MMS weight	300 kb	300 kb	300 kb
WAP			
Operator portal	Orange World, Gallery	Vodafone live!, Gallery	i-mode, ème Sens, Gallery
Billing type	WAP - Online Billing	WAP - Online Billing	WAP - Online Billing
Pay per Use	yes - up to €8.00	yes - up to €10.00	yes - up to €8.00
Subscription	yes - up to €12.00	yes - up to €12.00	yes - up to €10.00
O-rate URL / Wholesale datacharge	No	No	No
Maximum WAP Gateway download	No limit	No limit	No limit

MOBILE CONTENT SERVICES

	TOTAL REVENUES 2010 (EUR MILLION)	CONTRIBUTION AS % OF TOTAL REVENUES
Mobile music market	264.08	6.13%
Mobile games market	176.49	4.10%
Mobile images market	86.31	2.00%
Mobile TV market	87.03	2.02%
Mobile video market	38.93	0.90%
Mobile internet market	1,273.46	29.58%
Mobile messaging market	2,379.35	55.26%

MOBILE CONTENT PRICES (Prices in EUR)

	PAY PER USE	SUBSCRIPTION
Sound		
Polyphonics	1.50 - 3.00	0.30 - 12 through SMS subs offer - or 4.00 as common End-user price on Gallery
True Tones	1.50 - 3.00	0.50 - 12 through SMS subs offer - or 4.00 as common End-user price on Gallery
MP3	2.00 - 3.00	0.50 - 12 through SMS subs offer - or 4.00 as common End-user price on Gallery
Images		
Wallpapers	1.50 - 3.00	0.50-12 through SMS subs offer - or 4.00 as common End-user price on Gallery
Videos	3.00 - 4.50 (through SMS)	12 through SMS subs offer - or 4.00 as common End-user price on Gallery
Games & Lottery		
Voting, Participation TV	0.5	n/a
Instant Win, quiz	0.5	n/a
Java games	3.00 - 4.50 through SMS - 5.00 as common end-user price - through Gallery	3.00 - 4.50 through SMS - 5.00 as common end-user price - through Gallery
Community		
Chat	0.35/SMS (0.50/SMS if the end-user chat with a professional)	n/a

OPERATOR MOBILE CONTENT PRICES (Prices in US$)

	ORANGE FRANCE	SFR
Community	n/a	Handset client (downloadable): 5.97 / month - 0.15-0.22 / message (depending on plan)
Music	n/a	Full-tracks: 1.45 / download - 14.67 / download - 4.40 / month for 5 tracks - 21.88 / month for 20 tracks (OTA) - Ring tones: 4.40 / download - 7.34 / month for 3 tones (OTA)
TV & Video	Video-on-demand: 4.40 / download, + WAP data charges. (Download) - Mobile TV/Video-on-demand: 0.73 / 20 mins - 8.81 / month (cheapest option) - 13.22 / month (dearest option) - 0.00 Service bundled free with price of mobile contract. (Streamed)	Mobile TV: 8.81 / month - 11.75 / month - 14.69 / month (Streamed)
Location Based Services	Navigation/ Local search: 10.33 / month (GPS)	Navigation/ Local search: 2.21 / day - 7.37 / month (GPS)

INDUSTRY ASSOCIATIONS, REGULATORS & CODES OF PRACTICE

	NAME	WEBSITE
Electronical communications regulator	Autorité de Régulation des Communications Electroniques et des Postes (ARCEP)	www.arcep.fr
Industry Association	Agence Française du Multimédia Mobile	www.afmm.fr
Industry Association	Association Française du Multimédia Mobile (AFMM)	www.afmm.fr
Industry Association	Groupement des Editeurs de Services en Ligne (GESTE)	www.geste.fr
Industry Association	Association pour le Commerce et les Services En Ligne (ACSEL)	www.acsel.asso.fr
Industry Association	Forum des Droit sur Internet (FDI)	www.foruminternet.org
Industry Association	Association Française du multimedia Mobile	www.smsplus.org
Advertising regulator	Le bureau de vérification de la publicité (BVP)	www.bvp.org
Codes of practices	Operators Rules	www.afmm.fr

GERMANY

COUNTRY INFORMATION

Population in 2009	82,409,615
Gross domestic product 2009 per capita, current prices	26,104
Penetration rate (%) 3Q09	124.60%
Language (s)	German
Currency	Euro (EUR)

MOBILE TELECOMMUNICATIONS MARKET

Total subscriptions 3Q09	102,678,690
3G WCDMA subscriptions 3Q09	22,259,500
3G EV-DO subscriptions 3Q09	n/d
Total revenues 3Q09 (EUR million)	5,627.82
Service revenues 3Q09 (EUR million)	4,966.89
Blended montly ARPU 3Q09 (EUR)	15.22
Data revenues 3Q09 (EUR million)	1,415.66
SMS revenues 3Q09 (EUR million)	630.64
Messaging revenues 2010 (EUR million)	3,212.74
Messaging ARPU 2010 (EUR)	3.71
Content ARPU 2010 (EUR)	3.79

MOBILE OPERATORS DATA

	T-MOBILE	VODAFONE D2	E-PLUS	O2
Total subscriptions 3Q09	38,780,000	31,470,470	17,027,920	15,400,300
Market share 3Q09	37.77%	30.65%	16.58%	15.00%
Prepaid subs 3Q09 (%)	57.22%	48.51%	60.07%	51.69%
Postpaid subs 3Q09 (%)	42.78%	51.49%	39.93%	48.31%
Growth rate (%) 3Q08 to 3Q09	1.20%	-3.81%	9.90%	10.17%
Total net additions in 3Q09	197,000	-97,210	616,420	467,600
WCDMA net additions in 3Q09	512,050	723,860	67,210	548,000
3G EV-DO net additions in 3Q09	n/d	n/d	n/d	n/d
Blended ARPU 3Q09	15.00	15.90	14.00	15.70
Prepaid ARPU 3Q09	4.00	4.60	6.00	5.90
Postpaid ARPU 3Q09	30.00	28.90	27.00	26.10

GERMANY

MOBILE OPERATORS VALUE ADDED SERVICES

	T-MOBILE	VODAFONE D2	E-PLUS	O2	MOBILCOM-DEBITEL
SMS					
Push SMS	Yes	yes	yes	yes	Yes
Toll free SMS MO	Upon request	Upon request	Upon request	Upon request	Upon request
Premium SMS MO	Factoring up to 1,99 incl. Transport Costs	Factoring up to 1,99 incl. Transport Costs	Factoring up to 1,99 incl. Transport Costs	Factoring up to 1,99 incl. Transport Costs	Factoring up to 1,99 incl. Transport Costs
Premium SMS MT (subscription)	Up to €10,00 incl. Transport Costs	Up to €10,00 incl. Transport Costs	Up to €10,00 incl. Transport Costs	Up to €10,00 incl. Transport Costs	Up to €10,00 incl. Transport Costs
MMS					
Push MMS	Yes	Yes	Yes	Yes	No
Toll free MMS MO	n/a	n/a	n/a	n/a	No
Premium MMS MO	n/a	n/a	n/a	n/a	No
Premium MMS MT (subscription)	n/a	n/a	n/a	n/a	No
Maximum MMS weight	300kb	300kb	300kb	300kb	No
WAP					
Operator portal	T-Zones	Vodafone Live	e-plus	o2	www.debitel.de
Billing type	Direct Billing	Direct Billing	Direct Billing	Direct Billing	Direct Billing
Pay per Use	Up to €10,00 incl. Transport Costs	Up to €10,00 incl. Transport Costs	Up to €10,00 incl. Transport Costs	Up to €10,00 incl. Transport Costs	Up to €10,00 incl. Transport Costs
Subscription	Up to €10,00 incl. Transport Costs	Up to €10,00 incl. Transport Costs	Up to €10,00 incl. Transport Costs	Up to €10,00 incl. Transport Costs	Up to €10,00 incl. Transport Costs No WAP for Mobilcom
O-rate URL / Wholesale datacharge	n/a	n/a	n/a	n/a	
Maximum WAP Gateway download	n/a	n/a	n/a	n/a	n/a

NETSIZE OFFER

	T-MOBILE	VODAFONE D2	E-PLUS	O2	MOBILCOM-DEBITEL
SMS					
Push SMS	Yes	Yes	Yes	Yes	Yes
Toll free SMS MO	No	No	No	No	No
Premium SMS MO	Yes - up to € 1,.99	Yes - up to € 1,.99	Yes - up to €1.99	Yes - up to €1.99	Yes - up to €1.99
Premium SMS MT (subscription)	Yes - up to €9.99	Yes - up to €9.99	Yes - up to €9.99	Yes - up to €9.99	Yes - up to €9.99
MMS					
Push MMS	No	No	No	No	No
Toll free MMS MO	No	No	No	No	No
Premium MMS MO	No	No	No	No	No
Premium MMS MT (subscription)	No	No	No	No	No
Maximum MMS weight	300 kb	300 kb	300 kb	300 kb	n/a
WAP					
Operator portal	T-Zones	Vodafone live! GoDirect (direct linked off-net Partner Directory)	E-Plus Unlimited	O2 Active	www.debitel.de
Billing type	XTC	Vodafone Mobiles Bezahlen	mBilling and SMS MT	Payment Schnittstelle o2/ mPay	XCBI
Pay per Use	Yes - up to €9.99	Yes - up to €9.99	Yes - up to €9.99	Yes - up to €9.99	Yes - up to €9.99
Subscription	Yes - up to €9.99	Yes - up to €9.99	Yes - up to €9.99	Yes - up to €9.99	Yes - up to €9.99
O-rate URL / Wholesale datacharge	No	No	No	No	No
Maximum WAP Gateway download	No limit	No limit	No limit	No limit	No limit

MOBILE CONTENT SERVICES

	TOTAL REVENUES 2010 (EUR MILLION)	CONTRIBUTION AS % OF TOTAL REVENUES
Mobile music market	285.62	4.95%
Mobile games market	185.58	3.22%
Mobile images market	61.83	1.07%
Mobile TV market	131.95	2.29%
Mobile video market	45.33	0.79%
Mobile internet market	1,846.26	32.00%
Mobile messaging market	3,212.74	55.69%

MOBILE CONTENT PRICES (Prices in EUR)

	PAY PER USE	SUBSCRIPTION
Sound		
Polyphonics	1.00 - 1.99	2,99 - 4,99
True Tones	1.00 - 2.99	3,99 - 6,99
MP3	1.29 - 3.99	3,95 - 5,99
Images		
Wallpapers	0.99 - 1.99	1,99- 4,99
Videos	1.00 - 2.99	1,99 - 4,99
Games & Lottery	Not allowed	not allowed
Voting, Participation TV	n/a	n/a
Instant Win, quiz	n/a	n/a
Java games	1.99 - 9.99	1,99 - 4,99
Community		
Chat	0.20 - 0.40	n/a

OPERATOR MOBILE CONTENT PRICES (Prices in US$)

	T-MOBILE	VODAFONE D2
Community	Handset client (pre-inst./downloadable): 0.13 / min of GPRS/WAP connection. Other data-pricing options available. No content charge. - Handset client (downloadable): 7.39 / month - 2.91 / day from abroad	Handset client (pre-inst./downloadable): 0.28 / 10KB. Other data-pricing options available. No content charge.
Music	Full-tracks: 2.18 / download (OTA) - Ring-back tones: 2.92 / tone, + monthly renewal fee of €0.99. (Voice) - Ring tones: 3.65 / download (OTA) - Full-tracks: 2.18 / download - 17.60 / download (OTA)	Full-tracks: 1.45 / download - 14.67 / download - 13.20 / month (OTA) - Ring tones: 3.65 / download - 7.32 / month - 14.67 / month (OTA) - Message tones: 2.92 / download (OTA) - Ring tones: 2.92 / download - 4.39 / month - 8.79 / month (OTA) - Ring-back tones: 2.92 / tone, + € 0.99 monthly subscr. charge. - 4.39 / month - 8.79 / month (Voice)
TV & Video	Video on demand: 2.92 / download (Download) - Mobile TV: 2.93 / day - 11.02 / month - 2.86 / day - 7.27 / month - 4.40 / day - 14.69 / month (Streamed)	Mobile TV: 7.33 / month - 2.19 / wk - 14.68 / month - 4.39 / wk (Streamed) - Video on demand: 0.27 / download (lowest price) - 2.19 / download (highest price) (Download)
Location Based Services	Navigation/ Local search: 1.46 / day - 7.30 / month - 4.41 / day anywhere in EU or Switzerland. (GPS) - Navigation/ Local search: n/a (GPS)	Navigation/ Local search: 7.37 / month - 14.68 / month for Western Europe (GPS) - Friend finder/ Local search: 0.29 / SMS - 0.29 / min (WAP) (GPS/Cell-ID)

INDUSTRY ASSOCIATIONS, REGULATORS & CODES OF PRACTICE

	NAME	WEBSITE
Telecom regulator	Bundesnetzagentur für Elektrizität, Gas, Telekommunikation, Post und Eisenbahnen (BNETZA)	www.bundesnetzagentur.de
AVS	Freiwillige Selbstkontrolle der Filmwirtschaft	http://fst-ev.org/
AVS	Kommission für Jugendmedienschutz	www.kjm-online.de
Code of Conduct	Verhaltenskodex Premium SMS/Mobile Dienste und web-basierte Dienste	n/a

GREECE

COUNTRY INFORMATION

Population in 2009	11,197,750
Gross domestic product 2009 per capita, current prices	20,321
Penetration rate (%) 3Q09	170.03%
Language (s)	Greek
Currency	Euro (EUR)

MOBILE TELECOMMUNICATIONS MARKET

Total subscriptions 3Q09	19,039,760
3G WCDMA subscriptions 3Q09	3,245,000
3G EV-DO subscriptions 3Q09	n/d
Total revenues 3Q09 (EUR million)	1,066.39
Service revenues 3Q09 (EUR million)	1,025.47
Blended montly ARPU 3Q09 (EUR)	17.74
Data revenues 3Q09 (EUR million)	126.89
SMS revenues 3Q09 (EUR million)	93.90
Messaging revenues 2010 (EUR million)	n/a
Messaging ARPU 2010 (EUR)	n/a
Content ARPU 2010 (EUR)	n/a

MOBILE OPERATORS DATA

	COSMOTE	PANAFON	WIND HELLAS
Total subscriptions 3Q09	9,063,760	5,009,000	4,967,000
Market share 3Q09	47.60%	26.31%	26.09%
Prepaid subs 3Q09 (%)	72.98%	66.00%	78.78%
Postpaid subs 3Q09 (%)	27.02%	34.00%	21.22%
Growth rate (%) 3Q08 to 3Q09	22.31%	11.29%	1.43%
Total net additions in 3Q09	270,910	159,000	-106,460
WCDMA net additions in 3Q09	14,700	63,400	12,000
3G EV-DO net additions in 3Q09	n/d	n/d	n/d
Blended ARPU 3Q09	19.30	17.30	15.40
Prepaid ARPU 3Q09	6.00	5.40	0.00
Postpaid ARPU 3Q09	0.00	48.50	0.00

GREECE

MOBILE OPERATORS VALUE ADDED SERVICES

	COSMOTE	PANAFON	WIND HELLAS
SMS			
Push SMS	Yes	Yes	Yes
Toll free SMS MO	No	No	No
Premium SMS MO	Yes - Up to €3.50	Yes - Up to €3.50	Yes - Up to €3.50
Premium SMS MT (subscription)	Yes - Up to €2.00/SMS	Yes - Up to €2.00/SMS	Yes - Up to €2.00/SMS
MMS			
Push MMS	No	no	no
Toll free MMS MO	No	No	No
Premium MMS MO	No	No	No
Premium MMS MT (subscription)	No	No	No
Maximum MMS weight	No	No	No
WAP			
Operator portal	WAP or MSISDN Forwarding + PSMS MT	WAP or MSISDN Forwarding + PSMS MT	WAP or MSISDN Forwarding + PSMS MT
Billing type	i-mode-cosmote myview	Vodafone live!	Wind Plus
Pay per Use	Same price point as premium SMS need to get a contract with the operator	Same price point as premium SMS need to get a contract with the operator	Same price point as premium SMS need to get a contract with the operator
Subscription	n/a	n/a	n/a
O-rate URL / Wholesale datacharge	n/a	n/a	n/a
Maximum WAP Gateway download	n/a	n/a	n/a

NETSIZE OFFER

	COSMOTE	PANAFON	WIND HELLAS
SMS			
Push SMS	Yes	Yes	Yes
Toll free SMS MO	No	No	No
Premium SMS MO	Yes - Up to €3.50	Yes - Up to €3.50	Yes - Up to €3.50
Premium SMS MT (subscription)	Yes - Up to €2.00/SMS	Yes - Up to €2.00/SMS	Yes - Up to €2.00/SMS
MMS			
Push MMS	No	No	No
Toll free MMS MO	No	No	No
Premium MMS MO	No	No	No
Premium MMS MT (subscription)	No	No	No
Maximum MMS weight	No	No	No
WAP			
Operator portal	Upon request	Upon request	Upon request
Billing type	Upon request	Upon request	Upon request
Pay per Use	Upon request	Upon request	Upon request
Subscription	Upon request	Upon request	Upon request
O-rate URL / Wholesale datacharge	n/a	n/a	n/a
Maximum WAP Gateway download	No limit	No limit	No limit

MOBILE CONTENT PRICES (Prices in EUR)

	PAY PER USE	SUBSCRIPTION
Music		
Polyphonics	3.57 - 4.76	6.00 - 8.00
True Tones	3.57 - 4.76	6.00 - 8.00
MP3	3.57 - 4.76	6.00 - 8.00
Images		
Wallpapers	3.57 - 4.76	6.00 - 8.00
Videos	3.57 - 4.76	6.00 - 8.00
Games & Lottery		
Voting, Participation TV	0.25 - 1.19	6.00 - 8.00
Instant Win, quiz	1.19	6.00 - 8.00
Java games	3.57 - 4.76	6.00 - 8.00
Community		
Chat	0.25 - 1.19	6.00 - 8.00

INDUSTRY ASSOCIATIONS, REGULATORS & CODES OF PRACTICE

	NAME	WEBSITE
Telecom regulator	National Telecommunications and Post Commission - (EETT)	www.eett.gr
Operator	Cosmote	www.cosmote.gr
Operator	Vodafone	www.vodafone.gr
Operator	Wind	www.wind.gr

HUNGARY

COUNTRY INFORMATION

Population in 2009	9,961,750
Gross domestic product 2009 per capita, current prices	8,768
Penetration rate (%) 3Q09	106.90%
Language (s)	Hungarian (Magyar)
Currency	Hungarian Forint (HUF)

MOBILE TELECOMMUNICATIONS MARKET

Total subscriptions 3Q09	10,649,020
3G WCDMA subscriptions 3Q09	532,000
3G EV-DO subscriptions 3Q09	n/d
Total revenues 3Q09 (EUR million)	530.31
Service revenues 3Q09 (EUR million)	496.92
Blended montly ARPU 3Q09 (EUR)	14.71
Data revenues 3Q09 (EUR million)	92.71
SMS revenues 3Q09 (EUR million)	n/a
Messaging revenues 2010 (EUR million)	n/a
Messaging ARPU 2010 (EUR)	n/a
Content ARPU 2010 (EUR)	n/a

MOBILE OPERATORS DATA

	T-MOBILE	PANNON	VODAFONE
Total subscriptions 3Q09	4,751,840	3,542,570	2,354,610
Market share 3Q09	44.62%	33.27%	22.11%
Prepaid subs 3Q09 (%)	63.22%	55.88%	58.45%
Postpaid subs 3Q09 (%)	36.78%	44.12%	41.55%
Growth rate (%) 3Q08 to 3Q09	1.78%	1.97%	0.35%
Total net additions in 3Q09	11,010	-33,550	25,180
WCDMA net additions in 3Q09	40,000	19,000	39,000
3G EV-DO net additions in 3Q09	n/d	n/d	n/d
Blended ARPU 3Q09	14.00	14.76	16.07
Prepaid ARPU 3Q09	7.00	7.55	0.00
Postpaid ARPU 3Q09	26.00	23.12	0.00

MOBILE OPERATORS VALUE ADDED SERVICES

	T-MOBILE	PANNON	VODAFONE
SMS			
Push SMS	Yes	Yes	Yes
Non-Premium SMS MO	Yes	Yes	Yes
Premium SMS MO	Yes - Up to HUF 1000 (Ordinary) and HUF 1875 (Adult)	Yes - Up to HUF 1000 (Ordinary) and HUF 1875 (Adult)	Yes - Up to HUF 1000 (Ordinary) and HUF 1875 (Adult)
Premium SMS MT (subscription)	Yes - Up to HUF 1000 (Ordinary) and HUF 1875 (Adult)	Yes - Up to HUF 1000 (Ordinary) and HUF 1875 (Adult)	Yes - Up to HUF 1000 (Ordinary) and HUF 1875 (Adult)
MMS			
Push MMS	Yes	Yes	No
Toll free MMS MO	No	No	No
Premium MMS MO	Yes - Up to HUF 1000 (Ordinary) and HUF 1875 (Adult)	Yes - Up to HUF 1000 (Ordinary) and HUF 1875 (Adult)	No
Premium MMS MT (subscription)	Yes - Up to HUF 1160 (Ordinary) and HUF 1875 (Adult)	No	No
Maximum MMS weight	300 kb	300 kb	300 kb
WAP			
Operator portal	T-Zones	Djuice	Vodafone live!
Billing type	WAP billing	WAP billing	Offline billing not allowed
Pay per Use	Yes	Yes	n/a
Subscription	No (planned for 2010)	No (planned for 2010)	n/a
O-rate URL / Wholesale datacharge	No	No	No
Maximum WAP Gateway download	No limit	2 MB (or more based on agreement)	No limit

NETSIZE OFFER

	T-MOBILE	PANNON	VODAFONE
SMS			
Push SMS	Yes	Yes	Yes
Non-Premium SMS MO	Yes	Yes	Yes
Premium SMS MO	Yes - Up to HUF 1000 (Ordinary) and HUF 1875 (Adult)	Yes - Up to HUF 1000 (Ordinary) and HUF 1875 (Adult)	Yes - Up to HUF 1000 (Ordinary) and HUF 1875 (Adult)
Premium SMS MT (subscription)	Yes - Up to HUF 1000 (Ordinary) and HUF 1875 (Adult)	Yes - Up to HUF 1000 (Ordinary) and HUF 1875 (Adult)	Yes - Up to HUF 1000 (Ordinary) and HUF 1875 (Adult)
MMS			
Push MMS	No	No	No
Toll free MMS MO	No	No	No
Premium MMS MO	No	No	No
Premium MMS MT (subscription)	No	No	No
Maximum MMS weight	n/a	n/a	n/a
WAP			
Operator portal	No	No	No
Billing type	No (planned for 2010)	No (planned for 2010)	No
Pay per Use	No (planned for 2010)	No (planned for 2010)	No
Subscription	No	No (planned for 2010)	No
O-rate URL / Wholesale datacharge	No	No	No
Maximum WAP Gateway download	No limit	2 MB	No limit

MOBILE CONTENT PRICES (Prices in HUF)

	PAY PER USE	SUBSCRIPTION
Sound		
Polyphonics	125-315	60 - 300
True Tones	500-1000	210-1000
MP3	500-1000	250-400
Images		
Wallpapers	200-500	125-400
Videos	250-500	200-500
Games & Lottery		
Voting, Participation TV	100-300	n/a
Instant Win, quiz	100-500	100-500
Java games	500-1875	330-500
Community		
Chat	16-50	n/a

INDUSTRY ASSOCIATIONS, REGULATORS & CODES OF PRACTICE

	NAME	WEBSITE
Telecom regulator	National Communications Authority of Hungary (NCAH)	www.nhh.hu
Industry association	Magyar Mobilmarketing és Tartalomipari Egyesület (MMTE) Hungarian Mobile Marketing and Content Industry Association	www.mmte.hu
Govermental body	Közlekedési, Hírközlési és Energiaügyi Minisztérium (KHEM) - Ministry of Transport, Telecommunication and Energy	www.khem.gov.hu/en

INDIA

COUNTRY INFORMATION

Population in 2009	1,207,315,000
Gross domestic product 2009 per capita, current prices	687
Penetration rate (%) 3Q09	37.45%
Language (s)	Hindi, English
Currency	Indian Rupee (INR)

MOBILE TELECOMMUNICATIONS MARKET

Total subscriptions 3Q09	452,195,300
3G WCDMA subscriptions 3Q09	64,900
3G EV-DO subscriptions 3Q09	n/d
Total revenues 3Q09 (EUR million)	4,411.71
Service revenues 3Q09 (EUR million)	4,374.86
Blended montly ARPU 3Q09 (EUR)	2.96
Data revenues 3Q09 (EUR million)	416.13
SMS revenues 3Q09 (EUR million)	n/a
Messaging revenues 2010 (EUR million)	1,628.96
Messaging ARPU 2010 (EUR)	0.34
Content ARPU 2010 (EUR)	0.38

INDIA

MOBILE OPERATORS DATA

	BHARTI AIRTEL	RELIANCE COMMUNICA-TIONS	VODAFONE ESSAR	BSNL	IDEA CELLULAR	TATA TELESERVICES	AIRCEL	MTNL	LOOP MOBILE	SHYAM	HFCL INFOTEL
Total subscriptions 3Q09	110,511,410	84,099,190	82,846,070	53,422,400	51,454,400	35,273,930	25,728,640	4,371,000	2,495,090	1,801,170	192,000
Market share 3Q09	24.44%	18.60%	18.32%	11.81%	11.38%	7.80%	5.69%	0.97%	0.55%	0.40%	0.04%
Prepaid subs 3Q09 (%)	95.17%	94.49%	93.40%	96.35%	90.42%	90.62%	92.38%	83.12%	91.08%	79.59%	68.33%
Postpaid subs 3Q09 (%)	4.83%	5.51%	6.60%	3.65%	9.58%	9.38%	7.62%	16.88%	8.92%	20.41%	31.67%
Growth rate (%) 3Q08 to 3Q09	42.65%	57.21%	51.66%	36.40%	51.43%	58.59%	85.39%	18.85%	49.95%	3575.86%	8.47%
Total net additions in 3Q09	8,143,520	6,654,940	6,396,470	4,444,800	4,365,500	6,406,930	3,929,880	73,180	189,450	752,350	0
WCDMA net additions in 3Q09	n/d	n/d	n/d	52,670	n/d	n/d	n/d	900	n/d	n/d	n/d
3G EV-DO net additions in 3Q09	n/d	n/d	n/d	n/d	n/d	n/d	n/d	n/d	n/d	n/d	n/d
Blended ARPU 3Q09	3.65	2.58	3.22	2.66	3.03	2.73	1.68	1.45	2.38	2.31	1.40
Prepaid ARPU 3Q09	0.00	0.00	2.62	0.00	0.00	0.00	0.00	1.16	0.00	0.00	0.00
Postpaid ARPU 3Q09	0.00	0.00	11.53	0.00	0.00	0.00	0.00	2.75	0.00	0.00	0.00

MOBILE CONTENT SERVICES

	TOTAL REVENUES 2010 (EUR MILLION)	CONTRIBUTION AS % OF TOTAL REVENUES
Mobile music market	765.15	23.08%
Mobile games market	62.73	1.89%
Mobile images market	38.51	1.16%
Mobile TV market	9.12	0.28%
Mobile video market	19.95	0.60%
Mobile internet market	790.08	23.84%
Mobile messaging market	1,628.96	49.15%

OPERATOR MOBILE CONTENT PRICES (Prices in US$)

	BHARTI AIRTEL	VODAFONE ESSAR
Community	WAP/SMS: 0.02 / SMS - Handset client (downloadable): 1.07 / month (incl unl. messaging) - Voice: 0.64 / month (call charges of INR2.00 / min apply)	GPRS/WAP: 0.00 / 10KB. Other data-pricing options available. No content charge.
Music	Ring-back tones: 0.30 / tone. + monthly subscr. fee of INR30.00, or 3-monthly for INR60.00, 6-monthly for INR120.00 or yearly for INR200.00. Service set-up costs: calls INR3.00 / min and SMS INR3.00 / message. - 0.61 / 4 tones. + monthly subscr. fee of INR30.00, or 3-monthly for INR60.00, 6-monthly for INR120.00 or yearly for INR200.00. Service set-up costs: calls INR3.00 / min and SMS INR3.00 / message. - 0.61 / 4 tones. + monthly subscr. fee of INR15.00, or 3-monthly for INR30.00, 6-monthly for INR60.00 or yearly for INR100.00. Service set-up costs: calls INR3.00 / min and SMS INR3.00 / message. (Voice) - Full-tracks: 0.61 / month for 30 mins airtime. Top-ups of INR 10 avaiable to add 10-mins airtime. - 0.20 / song - 0.20 / song - 0.20 / 10 days (Voice) - Ring tones: 0.10 / download. Cost of setting up service using IVR INR2.00/ min. - 0.20 / download. Cost of setting up service using IVR INR2.00/min. (OTA) - Full-tracks: 0.30 / download. Cost of setting up service using IVR INR2.00/min. (OTA)	Ring-back tones: 0.30 / tone, + 3-monthly renewal charge of INR 15 and monthly subscr. fee of INR 30. Setting up service costs INR 3 / SMS or INR 60 / voice min. - 0.20 / match / day. Set-up costs via SMS INR 3 / message. - 1.02 / entire cricket-match series. Set-up costs via SMS INR 3 / message. - 0.51 / 3 tones - 0.82 / 5 tones - 1.02 / 7 tones - 2.03 / 30 tones (Voice) - Full-tracks: 0.61 / month for 30 mins airtime. Top-ups of INR 10 avaiable to add 10-mins airtime. (Voice) - Radio: 1.02 / month - 0.01 / min, pay as you go (Voice) - Full-tracks: 0.61 / month (Voice) - Ring tones: 0.10 / download (lowest price), + IVR charge of INR 6/min whilst ordering - 0.41 / download (highest price), + IVR charge of INR 6/min whilst ordering - 0.20 / download (Via SMS) - Full-tracks: 2.03 / month - 0.51 / download (OTA)
TV & Video	Mobile TV: 0.41 / day - 2.06 / month (Streamed)	Video-on-demand: 0.41 / download - 0.06 / download (lowest price) - 0.20 / download (highest price) (Download)
Location Based Services	Navigation: 4.19 / month, + standard data charges. (GPS) - Navigation: n/a Standard data charges apply. (GPS)	Vehicle tracker: n/a (GPS)

INDUSTRY ASSOCIATIONS, REGULATORS & CODES OF PRACTICE

	NAME	WEBSITE
Telecom regulator	Telecom Regulatory Authority of India	www.trai.gov.in

IRELAND

COUNTRY INFORMATION

Population in 2009	4,469,000
Gross domestic product 2009 per capita, current prices	34,352
Penetration rate (%) 3Q09	118.35%
Language (s)	Irish (Gaelic), English
Currency	Euro (EUR)

MOBILE TELECOMMUNICATIONS MARKET

Total subscriptions 3Q09	5,289,100
3G WCDMA subscriptions 3Q09	1,498,500
3G EV-DO subscriptions 3Q09	n/d
Total revenues 3Q09 (EUR million)	659.79
Service revenues 3Q09 (EUR million)	623.46
Blended montly ARPU 3Q09 (EUR)	38.60
Data revenues 3Q09 (EUR million)	157.95
SMS revenues 3Q09 (EUR million)	89.15
Messaging revenues 2010 (EUR million)	n/a
Messaging ARPU 2010 (EUR)	n/a
Content ARPU 2010 (EUR)	n/a

MOBILE OPERATORS DATA

	VODAFONE IRELAND	O2	METEOR COMMUNICATIONS	HUTCHISON 3G
Total subscriptions 3Q09	2,119,000	1,717,500	1,046,000	406,600
Market share 3Q09	40.06%	32.47%	19.78%	7.69%
Prepaid subs 3Q09 (%)	68.70%	60.62%	86.04%	64.40%
Postpaid subs 3Q09 (%)	31.30%	39.38%	13.96%	35.60%
Growth rate (%) 3Q08 to 3Q09	-5.02%	0.26%	4.39%	49.49%
Total net additions in 3Q09	-10,000	800	20,000	36,980
WCDMA net additions in 3Q09	37,250	31,500	7,000	36,980
3G EV-DO net additions in 3Q09	n/d	n/d	n/d	n/d
Blended ARPU 3Q09	38.80	39.90	36.02	n/a
Prepaid ARPU 3Q09	0.00	25.80	0.00	n/a
Postpaid ARPU 3Q09	0.00	62.10	0.00	n/a

MOBILE OPERATORS VALUE ADDED SERVICES

	VODAFONE IRELAND	O2	METEOR COMMUNICATIONS	HUTCHISON 3G
SMS				
Push SMS	Yes	Yes	Yes	Yes
Toll free SMS MO	Yes	Yes	Yes	Yes
Premium SMS MO	Yes - Up to €10.00	Yes - Up to € 2.50	Yes - Up to €10.00	Yes - Up to €10.00
Premium SMS MT (subscription)	Yes - Up to €5.00 with special permission	Yes - Up to € 5.00	Yes - Up to €10.00	Yes - Up to €10.00
MMS				
Push MMS	No	Yes	No	Yes
Toll free MMS MO	No	No	No	Yes
Premium MMS MO	No	No	No	Yes
Premium MMS MT (subscription)	No	No	No	Yes
Maximum MMS weight	300 kb	300 kb	n/a	300kb
WAP				
Operator portal	Vodafone live!	O2 Active i-mode	Meteor Mobile	Planet 3
Billing type	MSISDN Forwarding + PSMS MT	n/a	n/a	MSISDN Forwarding + PSMS MT
Pay per Use	Yes	n/a	n/a	Yes
Subscription	Yes	n/a	n/a	Yes
O-rate URL / Wholesale datacharge	No	No	No	Yes
Maximum WAP Gateway download	300 kb	300 kb	300 kb	No WAP Gateway. xHTML and WAP to xHTML conversion

NETSIZE OFFER

	VODAFONE IRELAND	O2	METEOR COMMUNICATIONS	HUTCHISON 3G
SMS				
Push SMS	Yes	Yes	Yes	Yes
Toll free SMS MO	Available on request	Available on request	Available on request	Available on request
Premium SMS MO	Yes - Up to €10.00	Yes - Up to € 2.50	Yes - Up to €8.00	Yes - Up to €10.00
Premium SMS MT (subscription)	Yes - Up to €5.00 with operator approval	Yes - Up to € 5.00	Yes - Up to €8.00	Yes - Up to €10.00
MMS				
Push MMS	No	Upon request	No	Upon request
Toll free MMS MO	No	No	No	Upon request
Premium MMS MO	No	No	No	Upon request
Premium MMS MT (subscription)	No	No	No	Upon request
Maximum MMS weight	Operator max	Operator max	Operator max	Operator max
WAP				
Operator portal	Vodafone live!	O2 Active i-mode	Meteor Mobile	Planet 3
Billing type	Available on request	n/a	n/a	Available on request
Pay per Use	Yes	n/a	n/a	Yes
Subscription	Yes	n/a	n/a	Yes
O-rate URL / Wholesale datacharge	Upon request	Upon request	Upon request	Upon request
Maximum WAP Gateway download	No limit	No limit	No limit	No limit

IRELAND

MOBILE CONTENT PRICES (Prices in EUR)

	PAY PER USE
Sound	
Polyphonics	2.00 - 4.00
True Tones	4.00 - 5.00
MP3	4.00 - 5.00
Images	
Wallpapers	2.00 - 4.00
Videos	2.00 - 4.00
Games & Lottery	
Voting, Participation TV	0.20 - 1.00
Instant Win, quiz	1.00 - 1.50
Java games	3.00 - 5.00
Community	
Chat	0.35 - 1.50

INDUSTRY ASSOCIATIONS, REGULATORS & CODES OF PRACTICE

	NAME	WEBSITE
Independent Regulator of the content and promotion of Premium Rate Telecommunications Services	Regtel	www.regtel.ie
Telecom regulator	Commission for Communications Regulation (ComReg)	www.odtr.ie

ITALY

COUNTRY INFORMATION

Population in 2009	58,972,769
Gross domestic product 2009 per capita, current prices	23,267
Penetration rate (%) 3Q09	138.63%
Language (s)	Italian (italiano)
Currency	Euro (EUR)

MOBILE TELECOMMUNICATIONS MARKET

Total subscriptions 3Q09	81,754,980
3G WCDMA subscriptions 3Q09	27,817,480
3G EV-DO subscriptions 3Q09	n/d
Total revenues 3Q09 (EUR million)	5,148.25
Service revenues 3Q09 (EUR million)	4,868.07
Blended montly ARPU 3Q09 (EUR)	20.72
Data revenues 3Q09 (EUR million)	1,239.77
SMS revenues 3Q09 (EUR million)	671.66
Messaging revenues 2010 (EUR million)	3,025.56
Messaging ARPU 2010 (EUR)	4.95
Content ARPU 2010 (EUR)	4.87

MOBILE OPERATORS DATA

	TELECOM ITALIA	VODAFONE ITALIA	WIND	H3G
Total subscriptions 3Q09	31,921,000	25,941,500	17,901,000	5,991,480
Market share 3Q09	39.04%	31.73%	21.90%	7.33%
Prepaid subs 3Q09 (%)	80.00%	85.94%	94.09%	53.60%
Postpaid subs 3Q09 (%)	20.00%	14.06%	5.91%	46.40%
Growth rate (%) 3Q08 to 3Q09	-9.51%	-3.09%	8.91%	5.39%
Total net additions in 3Q09	-709,000	-213,790	401,000	117,480
WCDMA net additions in 3Q09	-123,000	851,420	198,500	117,480
3G EV-DO net additions in 3Q09	n/d	n/d	n/d	n/d
Blended ARPU 3Q09	20.70	22.20	17.50	24.00
Prepaid ARPU 3Q09	0.00	18.30	0.00	11.89
Postpaid ARPU 3Q09	0.00	48.70	0.00	37.43

ITALY

MOBILE OPERATORS VALUE ADDED SERVICES

	TELECOM ITALIA	VODAFONE ITALIA	WIND	H3G
SMS				
Push SMS	Yes	Yes	Yes	Yes
Toll free SMS MO	No	No	No	No
Premium SMS MO	No	No	No	No
Premium SMS MT (subscription)	Yes - Up to €24.00 (per month)	Yes - Up to €24.00 (per month)	Yes - Up to €24.00 (per month)	Yes - Up to €24.00 (per month)
MMS				
Push MMS	Yes	Yes	Yes	Yes
Toll free MMS MO	No	No	No	No
Premium MMS MO	No	No	No	No
Premium MMS MT (subscription)	Yes - Up to €24.00 (per month)	Yes - Up to €24.00 (per month)	Yes - Up to €24.00 (per month)	Yes - Up to €24.00 (per month)
Maximum MMS weight	30 KB	300 Kb	300 Kb	100kb
WAP				
Operator portal	WAP.i.tim.it (i-tim)	Vodafone live!	Mobile libero	mobile.3.it/hb (Pianeta3)
Billing type	WAP	WAP	WAP	WAP
Pay per Use	Yes - Up to €10.00	Yes - Up to €8.00	Yes - Up to €10.00	Yes - Up to €10.00
Subscription	Yes - no set thresholds	Yes - no set thresholds	No	Yes - no set thresholds
O-rate URL / Wholesale datacharge	No	No	No	No
Maximum WAP Gateway download	n/a	400 k if you connect from foreign country- 8Mb (general maximum size)	n/a	12 Mb

NETSIZE OFFER

	TIM	VODAFONE	WIND	H3G
SMS				
Push SMS	Yes	Yes	Yes	Yes
Toll free SMS MO	No	No	No	No
Premium SMS MO	No	No	No	No
Premium SMS MT (subscription)	Yes - Up to €24.00 (per month)	Yes - Up to €24.00 (per month)	Yes - Up to €24.00 (per month)	Yes - Up to €24.00 (per month)
MMS				
Push MMS	Yes	Yes	Yes	Yes
Toll free MMS MO	No	No	No	No
Premium MMS MO	No	No	No	No
Premium MMS MT (subscription)	No	Yes	No	No
Maximum MMS weight	30 KB	300 Kb	300 Kb	100kb
WAP				
Operator portal	i-TIM	Vodafone live!	Mobile libero	Pianeta3
Billing type	Direct billing	WAP online billing	MSISDN forwarding +PSMS MT	Upon request
Pay per Use	Yes - Up to €10.00	Yes - Up to €8.00	Yes - Up to €2.40	Yes - Up to €10.00
Subscription	Yes - no set thresholds	Yes - no set thresholds	Yes - Up to €24.00 (per month)	Yes - no set thresholds
O-rate URL / Wholesale datacharge	No	No	No	No
Maximum WAP Gateway download	No limit	No limit	No limit	No limit

MOBILE CONTENT SERVICES

	TOTAL REVENUES 2010 (EUR MILLION)	CONTRIBUTION AS % OF TOTAL REVENUES
Mobile music market	241.96	4.47%
Mobile games market	171.47	3.17%
Mobile images market	62.61	1.16%
Mobile TV market	161.65	2.99%
Mobile video market	51.96	0.96%
Mobile internet market	1,696.88	31.35%
Mobile messaging market	3,025.56	55.90%

MOBILE CONTENT PRICES (Prices in EUR)

	PAY PER USE	SUBSCRIPTION
Sound		
Polyphonics	1.90 - 3.00	1.00 - 5.00
True Tones	3.00 - 4.00	2.00 - 5.00
MP3	1.50 - 2.50	1.00 - 2.00
Images		
Wallpapers	1.50 - 3.00	1.00 - 2.00
Videos	3.00 - 4.00	2.50 - 3.00
Games & Lottery		
Voting, Participation TV	0.30 - 1.00	4
Instant Win, quiz	0.50 - 1.00	n/a
Java games	4.00 - 5.00	2.00 - 5.00
Community		
Chat	0.5	4

INDUSTRY ASSOCIATIONS, REGULATORS & CODES OF PRACTICE

	NAME	WEBSITE
Telecom regulator	Autorità per le Garanzie nelle Comunicazioni (Agcom)	www.agcom.it
Authority over competition	Autorità Garante della Concorrenza e del Mercato	www.agcm.it

JAPAN

COUNTRY INFORMATION

Population in 2009	127,779,000
Gross domestic product 2009 per capita, current prices	27,369
Penetration rate (%) 3Q09	85.80%
Language (s)	Japanese
Currency	Japanese Yen (JPY)

MOBILE TELECOMMUNICATIONS MARKET

Total subscriptions 3Q09	109,634,100
3G WCDMA subscriptions 3Q09	73,393,800
3G EV-DO subscriptions 3Q09	22,928,000
Total revenues 3Q09 (EUR million)	16,454.84
Service revenues 3Q09 (EUR million)	13,354.17
Blended montly ARPU 3Q09 (EUR)	39.02
Data revenues 3Q09 (EUR million)	5,771.76
SMS revenues 3Q09 (EUR million)	n/a
Messaging revenues 2010 (EUR million)	5,976.17
Messaging ARPU 2010 (EUR)	4.72
Content ARPU 2010 (EUR)	13.94

MOBILE OPERATORS DATA

	NTT DOCOMO	KDDI	SOFTBANK MOBILE	EACCESS
Total subscriptions 3Q09	55,186,500	31,233,000	21,316,900	1,897,700
Market share 3Q09	50.34%	28.49%	19.44%	1.73%
Prepaid subs 3Q09 (%)	0.07%	1.28%	4.54%	2.49%
Postpaid subs 3Q09 (%)	99.93%	98.72%	95.46%	97.51%
Growth rate (%) 3Q08 to 3Q09	2.32%	2.57%	8.58%	133.79%
Total net additions in 3Q09	322,500	236,900	360,700	225,400
WCDMA net additions in 3Q09	1,012,300	n/d	782,700	225,400
3G EV-DO net additions in 3Q09	n/d	660,000	n/d	n/d
Blended ARPU 3Q09	40.50	41.85	31.01	n/a
Prepaid ARPU 3Q09	0.00	0.00	0.00	n/a
Postpaid ARPU 3Q09	0.00	0.00	0.00	n/a

MOBILE CONTENT SERVICES

	TOTAL REVENUES 2010 (EUR MILLION)	CONTRIBUTION AS % OF TOTAL REVENUES
Mobile music market	617.22	3.10%
Mobile games market	660.55	3.32%
Mobile images market	131.62	0.66%
Mobile TV market	544.74	2.74%
Mobile video market	271.62	1.37%
Mobile internet market	11,685.49	58.76%
Mobile messaging market	5,976.17	30.05%

OPERATOR MOBILE CONTENT PRICES (Prices in US$)

	NTT DOCOMO	KDDI
Community	n/a	n/a
TV & Video	Ring-back tones: 2.33 / month (tax incld) - 1.16 / month (tax incld) (Voice) - Full-tracks: Varies Flat-rate tariffs for unl. music downloads depend on individual i-mode sites. - Varies Content-download charges depend on individual i-mode sites. (OTA) - Ring tones: Varies Content-download charges depend on individual i-mode sites. (OTA)	n/a
TV & Video	Video-on-demand: 3.52 / month, incl VAT. Flat-rate data subscr. required to cover traffic charges. - Varied Content charges depend on individual i-mode content providers. Flat-rate data subscr. required to cover traffic charges. - Varied Video content charges depend on individual i-mode content providers signed up to Vlive. For ¥180 (¥189 incl. tax) a month, Vlive users can subscribe to Yu Yu Call and designate in advance number common to all Vlive access numbers as one of their discounted numbers to receive a 30% discount on videophone charges when viewing all Vlive content. - Varied Content charges depend on individual i-mode content providers. Flat-rate data subscr. required to cover traffic charges. (Download) - Mobile TV: 0.00 Free-to-air service (ISDB-T broadcast)	n/a
Location Based Services	Family locator/ Distress alarm: 2.33 / month (incl. tax). + charge for each location request of JPY5.00. (GPS/Cell-ID) - Self locator: 3.49 / location request. (GPS) - Local search: 0.00 Free (GPS/Cell-ID) - Navigation: 0.00 Free (GPS)	Fitness tracker: 1.16 / month for "basic package." - 3.49 / month for "premium package." (GPS) - Navigation: 0.00 Free for checking some maps. - 1.05 / day for full service. - 3.49 / month for full service. (GPS)

INDUSTRY ASSOCIATIONS, REGULATORS & CODES OF PRACTICE

	NAME	WEBSITE
Telecom regulator	Ministry of Internal Affairs and Communications	http://www.soumu.go.jp/english/index.html

LUXEMBOURG

COUNTRY INFORMATION

Population in 2009	479,250
Gross domestic product 2009 per capita, current prices	66,063
Penetration rate (%) 3Q09	147.54%
Language (s)	German, French, Luxembourgish
Currency	Euro (EUR)

MOBILE TELECOMMUNICATIONS MARKET

Total subscriptions 3Q09	707,100
3G WCDMA subscriptions 3Q09	152,500
3G EV-DO subscriptions 3Q09	n/d
Total revenues 3Q09 (EUR million)	74.01
Service revenues 3Q09 (EUR million)	59.47
Blended montly ARPU 3Q09 (EUR)	26.86
Data revenues 3Q09 (EUR million)	n/a
SMS revenues 3Q09 (EUR million)	n/a
Messaging revenues 2010 (EUR million)	n/a
Messaging ARPU 2010 (EUR)	n/a
Content ARPU 2010 (EUR)	n/a

MOBILE OPERATORS DATA

	P&T LUXEMBOURG	TANGO	ORANGE LUXEMBOURG
Total subscriptions 3Q09	375,000	252,000	80,100
Market share 3Q09	53.03%	35.64%	11.33%
Prepaid subs 3Q09 (%)	44.75%	50.40%	36.20%
Postpaid subs 3Q09 (%)	55.25%	49.60%	63.80%
Growth rate (%) 3Q08 to 3Q09	1.35%	3.28%	3.34%
Total net additions in 3Q09	800	6,000	520
WCDMA net additions in 3Q09	4,300	10,000	1,500
3G EV-DO net additions in 3Q09	n/d	n/d	n/d
Blended ARPU 3Q09	n/a	24.20	35.16
Prepaid ARPU 3Q09	n/a	0.00	0.00
Postpaid ARPU 3Q09	n/a	0.00	0.00

MOBILE OPERATORS VALUE ADDED SERVICES

	P&T LUXEMBOURG	TANGO	ORANGE LUXEMBOURG
SMS			
Push SMS	Yes	Yes	Yes
Toll free SMS MO	No	No	No
Premium SMS MO	Yes - Up to €3.00	Yes - Up to €3.00	Yes - Up to €3.00
Premium SMS MT (subscription)	Yes - Up to €3.00	Yes - Up to €3.00	Yes - Up to €3.00
MMS			
Push MMS	Yes	Yes	Yes
Toll free MMS MO	No	No	No
Premium MMS MO	No	No	No
Premium MMS MT (subscription)	No	No	No
Maximum MMS weight	300kb	300kb	300kb
WAP			
Operator portal	Vodafone live!, Mobile Fun	TanGoLive!	WapVOX
Billing type	WAP or MSISDN Forwarding + PSMS MT	WAP or MSISDN Forwarding + PSMS MT	WAP or MSISDN Forwarding + PSMS MT
Pay per Use	as PSMS	as PSMS	as PSMS
Subscription	as PSMS	as PSMS	as PSMS
O-rate URL / Wholesale datacharge	No	No	No
Maximum WAP Gateway download	Unlimited, end-user pays	Unlimited, end-user pays	Unlimited, end-user pays

NETSIZE OFFER

	P&T LUXEMBOURG	TANGO	ORANGE LUXEMBOURG
SMS			
Push SMS	Yes	Yes	Yes
Toll free SMS MO	No	No	No
Premium SMS MO	Yes - Up to €3.00	Yes - Up to €3.00	Yes - Up to €3.00
Premium SMS MT (subscription)	Yes - Up to €3.00	Yes - Up to €3.00	Yes - Up to €3.00
MMS			
Push MMS	Yes	Yes	Yes
Toll free MMS MO	No	No	No
Premium MMS MO	No	No	No
Premium MMS MT (subscription)	No	No	No
Maximum MMS weight	n/a	n/a	n/a
WAP			
Operator portal	Vodafone live !	TanGoLive!	WapVOX
Billing type	PSMS	PSMS	PSMS
Pay per Use	Yes	Yes	Yes
Subscription	Yes	Yes	Yes
O-rate URL / Wholesale datacharge	No	No	No
Maximum WAP Gateway download	No limit	No limit	No limit

INDUSTRY ASSOCIATIONS, REGULATORS & CODES OF PRACTICE

	NAME	WEBSITE
Telecom regulator	Institut Luxembourgeois de Régulation (ILR)	www.ilr.etat.lu

MALAYSIA

COUNTRY INFORMATION

Population in 2009	27,579,500
Gross domestic product 2009 per capita, current prices	5,355
Penetration rate (%) 3Q09	107.41%
Language (s)	Malay
Currency	Malaysian Ringgit (MYR)

MOBILE TELECOMMUNICATIONS MARKET

Total subscriptions 3Q09	29,623,000
3G WCDMA subscriptions 3Q09	7,424,000
3G EV-DO subscriptions 3Q09	n/d
Total revenues 3Q09 (EUR million)	1,006.45
Service revenues 3Q09 (EUR million)	940.94
Blended montly ARPU 3Q09 (EUR)	10.75
Data revenues 3Q09 (EUR million)	n/a
SMS revenues 3Q09 (EUR million)	n/a
Messaging revenues 2010 (EUR million)	n/a
Messaging ARPU 2010 (EUR)	n/a
Content ARPU 2010 (EUR)	n/a

MOBILE OPERATORS DATA

	MAXIS COMMUNICATIONS	DIGI	CELCOM	U MOBILE
Total subscriptions 3Q09	11,735,000	7,393,000	10,142,000	353,000
Market share 3Q09	39.61%	24.96%	34.24%	1.19%
Prepaid subs 3Q09 (%)	75.29%	83.77%	77.53%	80.00%
Postpaid subs 3Q09 (%)	24.71%	16.23%	22.47%	20.00%
Growth rate (%) 3Q08 to 3Q09	6.29%	8.67%	22.87%	194.17%
Total net additions in 3Q09	312,000	163,000	444,000	159,000
WCDMA net additions in 3Q09	500,000	11,000	450,000	159,000
3G EV-DO net additions in 3Q09	n/d	n/d	n/d	n/d
Blended ARPU 3Q09	10.77	10.96	10.57	n/a
Prepaid ARPU 3Q09	8.17	9.77	8.37	n/a
Postpaid ARPU 3Q09	20.53	17.14	18.14	n/a

MOBILE OPERATORS VALUE ADDED SERVICES

	MAXIS COMMUNICATIONS	DIGI	CELCOM	U MOBILE
SMS				
Push SMS	Yes	Yes	Yes	n/a
Toll free SMS MO	Yes	No	No	n/a
Premium SMS MO	Yes - Up to MYR 10	Yes - Up to MYR 10	Yes - Up to MYR 10	n/a
Premium SMS MT (subscription)	Yes - Up to MYR 10	Yes - Up to MYR 10	Yes - Up to MYR 10	n/a
MMS				
Push MMS		Yes	Yes	
Toll free MMS MO		No	No	
Premium MMS MO		No	No	
Premium MMS MT (subscription)		Yes	Yes	
Maximum MMS weight		300kb		
WAP	Yes	Yes	Yes	
Operator portal	My Maxis	My DiGi	Channel X	n/a
Billing type	WAP - Direct Billing	WAP - Online Blling	WAP - Direct Billing	n/a
Pay per Use	Yes - Up to MYR 30	Yes - Up to MYR 10	Yes - Up to MYR 10	n/a
Subscription	Yes	Yes	Yes	n/a
O-rate URL / Wholesale datacharge	Yes - Specific agreement	n/a	n/a	n/a
Maximum WAP Gateway download	n/a	n/a	n/a	n/a

NETSIZE OFFER

	MAXIS COMMUNICATIONS	DIGI	CELCOM	U MOBILE
SMS				
Push SMS	Yes	Yes	Yes	Yes
Toll free SMS MO	No	No	No	No
Premium SMS MO	No	No	No	No
Premium SMS MT (subscription)	No	No	No	No
MMS				
Push MMS	No	No	No	No
Toll free MMS MO	No	No	No	No
Premium MMS MO	No	No	No	No
Premium MMS MT (subscription)	No	No	No	No
Maximum MMS weight	n/a	n/a	n/a	No
WAP	Yes	No	No	No
Operator portal	My Maxis	n/a	n/a	No
Billing type	WAP - Direct Billing	n/a	n/a	No
Pay per Use	Yes - Up to MYR 30	n/a	n/a	No
Subscription	Yes	n/a	n/a	No
O-rate URL / Wholesale datacharge	Yes	n/a	n/a	No
Maximum WAP Gateway download	No limit	n/a	n/a	n/a

INDUSTRY ASSOCIATIONS, REGULATORS & CODES OF PRACTICE

	NAME	WEBSITE
Telecom regulator	Malaysian Communications and Multimedia Commission	www.skmn.gov.my

MEXICO

COUNTRY INFORMATION

Population in 2009	109,388,500
Gross domestic product 2009 per capita, current prices	5,390
Penetration rate (%) 3Q09	74.26%
Language (s)	Spanish
Currency	Mexican Peso (MXN)

MOBILE TELECOMMUNICATIONS MARKET

Total subscriptions 3Q09	81,230,900
3G WCDMA subscriptions 3Q09	957,990
3G EV-DO subscriptions 3Q09	n/d
Total revenues 3Q09 (EUR million)	9,268.78
Service revenues 3Q09 (EUR million)	2,698.51
Blended montly ARPU 3Q09 (EUR)	9.49
Data revenues 3Q09 (EUR million)	558.20
SMS revenues 3Q09 (EUR million)	n/a
Messaging revenues 2010 (EUR million)	n/a
Messaging ARPU 2010 (EUR)	n/a
Content ARPU 2010 (EUR)	n/a

MOBILE OPERATORS DATA

	TELCEL (RADIOMÓVIL DIPSA)	TELEFÓNICA MÓVILES MEXICO	IUSACELL CELULAR	NEXTEL MEXICO
Total subscriptions 3Q09	3,442,800	2,909,700	58,360,000	16,518,400
Market share 3Q09	4.24%	3.58%	71.84%	20.34%
Prepaid subs 3Q09 (%)	68.42%		98.30%	94.18%
Postpaid subs 3Q09 (%)	31.58%	100.00%	1.70%	5.82%
Growth rate (%) 3Q08 to 3Q09	-15.43%	12.57%	7.32%	12.51%
Total net additions in 3Q09	-104,200	74,800	279,000	575,900
WCDMA net additions in 3Q09	n/d	n/d	276,400	42,590
3G EV-DO net additions in 3Q09	n/d	n/d	n/d	n/d
Blended ARPU 3Q09	13.99	32.89	9.09	6.80
Prepaid ARPU 3Q09	0.00	0.00	0.00	0.00
Postpaid ARPU 3Q09	0.00	32.89	0.00	0.00

OPERATOR MOBILE CONTENT PRICES (Prices in US$)

	TELCEL (RADIOMÓVIL DIPSA)
Community	SMS: 0.09 / SMS sent (VAT incld). - GPRS/WAP: 0.39 / day, unl. access via GPRS (VAT incld). - 1.97 / wk, unl. access via GPRS (VAT incld). - GPRS/WAP: 0.63 / day, unl. access via GPRS (VAT incld). incl cost of uploading photos or videos. It doesn't incl video downloading costs. - 3.16 / wk, unl. access via GPRS (VAT incld). incl cost of uploading photos or videos. It doesn't incl video downloading costs. - GPRS/WAP: 1.97 / wk, unl. access via GPRS. Sending MMS carries addit. charge of MXN 2 / message and sending SMS an addit. charge of MXN 0.85 / message (all prices incl VAT).
Music	Ring tones: 1.11 / download - 1.70 / download - 1.70 / download - 0.37 / download (OTA) - Message tones: 1.11 / download (OTA) - Ring-back tones: 1.11 / tone for 12-month rental, + MXN 5 monthly service charge and MXN 25 service set-up fee (prices incl VAT). (Voice) - Full-tracks: 1.27 / download (incl. VAT) (OTA)
TV & Video	Mobile TV: 2.30 / day - 6.12 / wk - 11.48 / month (Streamed) - Video-on-demand: 1.53 / download - 1.15 / download - 1.15 / download - 0.00 / KB (Download)
Location Based Services	Navigation / Local search: 28.83 / month. Handset subscr. package incl 500MB of data usage. Beyond that users charged MXN$0.04 / KB. - 34.16 / month. Handset subscr. package incl 3GB of data usage. Beyond that users charged MXN$0.04 / KB. (GPS)

MOROCCO

COUNTRY INFORMATION

Population in 2009	32,098,250
Gross domestic product 2009 per capita, current prices	1,858
Penetration rate (%) 3Q09	78.13%
Language (s)	Arabic, French
Currency	Moroccan Dirham (MAD)

MOBILE TELECOMMUNICATIONS MARKET

Total subscriptions 3Q09	25,077,000
3G WCDMA subscriptions 3Q09	n/a
3G EV-DO subscriptions 3Q09	301,200
Total revenues 3Q09 (EUR million)	575.90
Service revenues 3Q09 (EUR million)	0.00
Blended montly ARPU 3Q09 (EUR)	6.97
Data revenues 3Q09 (EUR million)	98.26
SMS revenues 3Q09 (EUR million)	93.08
Messaging revenues 2010 (EUR million)	n/a
Messaging ARPU 2010 (EUR)	n/a
Content ARPU 2010 (EUR)	n/a

MOBILE OPERATORS DATA

	ITTISSALAT AL-MAGHRIB	MÉDI TÉLÉCOM	WANA
Total subscriptions 3Q09	15,239,000	9,209,000	629,000
Market share 3Q09	60.77%	36.72%	2.51%
Prepaid subs 3Q09 (%)	95.61%	97.08%	86.00%
Postpaid subs 3Q09 (%)	4.39%	2.92%	14.00%
Growth rate (%) 3Q08 to 3Q09	4.17%	24.38%	144.75%
Total net additions in 3Q09	951,000	575,000	17,000
WCDMA net additions in 3Q09	31,020	29,260	n/d
3G EV-DO net additions in 3Q09	n/d	n/d	35,300
Blended ARPU 3Q09	8.65	4.20	n/a
Prepaid ARPU 3Q09	0.00	0.00	n/a
Postpaid ARPU 3Q09	0.00	0.00	n/a

MOBILE OPERATORS VALUE ADDED SERVICES

	ITTISSALAT AL-MAGHRIB	MÉDI TÉLÉCOM	WANA
SMS			
Push SMS	Yes	Yes	Yes
Toll free SMS MO	No	No	No
Premium SMS MO	Yes - Up to MAD20.00	Yes - Up to MAD20.00	Yes - Up to MAD20.00
Premium SMS MT (subscription)	No	No	No
MMS			
Push MMS	No	No	No
Toll free MMS MO	No	No	No
Premium MMS MO	No	No	No
Premium MMS MT (subscription)	No	No	No
Maximum MMS weight	n/a	n/a	n/a
WAP			
Operator portal	Menara	Imédia	CDMA
Billing type	n/a	n/a	n/a
Pay per Use	n/a	n/a	n/a
Subscription	n/a	n/a	n/a
O-rate URL / Wholesale datacharge	n/a	n/a	n/a
Maximum WAP Gateway download	n/a	n/a	n/a

NETSIZE OFFER

	ITTISSALAT AL-MAGHRIB	MÉDI TÉLÉCOM	WANA
SMS			
Push SMS	Yes	Yes	Yes
Toll free SMS MO	No	No	No
Premium SMS MO	Yes - Up to MAD20.00	Yes - Up to MAD20.00	Yes - Up to MAD20.00
Premium SMS MT (subscription)	No	no	n/a
MMS			
Push MMS	No	No	n/a
Toll free MMS MO	No	No	n/a
Premium MMS MO	No	No	n/a
Premium MMS MT (subscription)	No	No	n/a
Maximum MMS weight	n/a	n/a	n/a
WAP	No	No	n/a
Operator portal	No	No	n/a
Billing type	No	No	n/a
Pay per Use	No	No	n/a
Subscription	No	No	n/a
O-rate URL / Wholesale datacharge	No	No	n/a
Maximum WAP Gateway download	No limit	No limit	No limit

MOBILE CONTENT PRICES (Prices in MAD)

	PAY PER USE
Sound	
Polyphonics	6.00
True Tones	6.00
MP3	6.00
Images	
Wallpapers	6.00
Videos	6.00
Games & Lottery	
Voting, Participation TV	5.00
Instant Win, quiz	5.00
Java games	7.50
Community	
Chat	0.80

INDUSTRY ASSOCIATIONS, REGULATORS & CODES OF PRACTICE

	NAME	WEBSITE
Telecom regulator	Agence Nationale de Réglementation des Télécomunication (ANRT)	www.anrt.net.ma

THE NETHERLANDS

COUNTRY INFORMATION

Population in 2009	16,475,750
Gross domestic product 2009 per capita, current prices	30,968
Penetration rate (%) 3Q09	116.90%
Language (s)	Dutch
Currency	Euro (EUR)

MOBILE TELECOMMUNICATIONS MARKET

Total subscriptions 3Q09	19,259,370
3G WCDMA subscriptions 3Q09	4,612,000
3G EV-DO subscriptions 3Q09	n/d
Total revenues 3Q09 (EUR million)	1,719.11
Service revenues 3Q09 (EUR million)	1,602.71
Blended montly ARPU 3Q09 (EUR)	25.52
Data revenues 3Q09 (EUR million)	403.00
SMS revenues 3Q09 (EUR million)	n/a
Messaging revenues 2010 (EUR million)	n/a
Messaging ARPU 2010 (EUR)	n/a
Content ARPU 2010 (EUR)	n/a

MOBILE OPERATORS DATA

	KPN MOBILE	VODAFONE LIBERTEL	T-MOBILE NETHERLANDS	TELE2
Total subscriptions 3Q09	9,477,550	4,307,820	5,474,000	n/a
Market share 3Q09	49.21%	22.37%	28.42%	n/a
Prepaid subs 3Q09 (%)	48.60%	34.53%	56.45%	n/a
Postpaid subs 3Q09 (%)	51.40%	65.47%	43.55%	n/a
Growth rate (%) 3Q08 to 3Q09	8.53%	6.66%	2.76%	n/a
Total net additions in 3Q09	125,100	77,230	61,000	n/a
WCDMA net additions in 3Q09	167,500	234,520	77,400	n/a
3G EV-DO net additions in 3Q09	n/d	n/d	n/d	n/a
Blended ARPU 3Q09	23.00	34.30	23.00	n/a
Prepaid ARPU 3Q09	0.00	8.80	6.00	n/a
Postpaid ARPU 3Q09	0.00	51.40	45.00	n/a

* Telfort operator data are consolidated in KPN Mobile, and Orange Netherlands operator data are consolidated in T-Mobile Netherlands.

MOBILE OPERATORS VALUE ADDED SERVICES

	KPN MOBILE	TELFORT	VODAFONE LIBERTEL	T-MOBILE NETHERLANDS	TELE2
SMS					
Push SMS	Yes	Yes	Yes	Yes	Yes
Toll free SMS MO	no	no	No	No	No
Premium SMS MO	Yes - Up to €2.25	Yes - Up to €1.50	Yes - Up to €5.00	Yes - Up to €1.50	Yes - Up to €5.00
Premium SMS MT (subscription)	Yes - Up to €6.00	Yes - Up to €1.50	Yes - Up to €10.00	Yes - Up to €3.00	Yes - Up to €5.00
MMS					
Push MMS	Yes	Yes	Yes	Yes	Yes
Toll free MMS MO	No	No	No	No	No
Premium MMS MO	No	No	Yes - Up to €5.00	Yes - Up to €5.00	No
Premium MMS MT (subscription)	No	No	No	No	No
Maximum MMS weight	300kb	300kb	300kb	300kb	300kb
WAP					
Operator portal	i-mode/KPN portal	Spot	Vodafone live!	T-Zones	n/a
Billing type	WAP Billing	No	content billing	No (2010)	no (2010)
Pay per Use	Yes - max €10	Yes - Up to €1.50	Yes - Up to €10.00	Yes - max €3.00	Yes - Up to €5.00
Subscription	Yes - max €10	No	Yes - Up to €10.00	No	No
O-rate URL / Wholesale datacharge	Depends on end-user rateplan	Depends on end-user rateplan	Depends on end-user rateplan	Depends on end-user rateplan	na
Maximum WAP Gateway download	According to contract	According to contract	According to contract	According to contract	na

NETSIZE OFFER

	KPN MOBILE	TELFORT	VODAFONE LIBERTEL	T-MOBILE NETHERLANDS	TELE2
SMS					
Push SMS	Yes	Yes	Yes	Yes	Yes
Toll free SMS MO	yes	yes	No	No	No
Premium SMS MO	Yes	Yes	Yes	Yes	Yes
Premium SMS MT (subscription)	Yes	Yes	Yes	Yes	Yes
MMS					
Push MMS	Yes	Yes	Yes	No	No
Toll free MMS MO	No	No	No	No	No
Premium MMS MO	No	No	Yes - Up to €5.00	No	No
Premium MMS MT (subscription)	No	No	No	No	No
Maximum MMS weight	300kb	300kb	300kb	n/a	n/a
WAP					
Operator portal	i-mode/kpn portal	Spot	Vodafone live!	T-Zones	n/a
Billing type	WAP-billing	No	WAP-billing	WAP-billing (only on portal)	n/a
Pay per Use	Yes	n/a	Yes	Yes	n/a
Subscription	Yes	n/a	Yes	Yes	n/a
O-rate URL / Wholesale datacharge	Depends on end-user rateplan	n/a	Depends on end-user rateplan	Depends on end-user rateplan	n/a
Maximum WAP Gateway download	No limit	No limit	No limit	No limit	n/a

MOBILE CONTENT PRICES (Prices in EUR)

	PAY PER USE	SUBSCRIPTION
Sound		
Polyphonics	1.50 - 3.30	up to 9.00 weekly
True Tones	2.00 - 4.50	up to 9.00 weekly
MP3	1.10 - 3.30	up to 9.00 weekly
Images	1.10 - 1.50	no data
Wallpapers	1.00 - 3.30	up to 9.00 weekly
Videos	2.00 - 3.30	up to 9.00 weekly
Games & Lottery	Lotteries not allowed	lotteries not allowed
Voting, Participation TV	max 60ct per event	n/a
Instant Win, quiz	n/a	n/a
Java games	3.50 - 6.00	up to 12.00 weekly
Community	no data	no data
Chat	< 1.50	n/a

INDUSTRY ASSOCIATIONS, REGULATORS & CODES OF PRACTICE

	NAME	WEBSITE
Telecom regulator	OPTA	www.opta.nl
Consumer Law Supervisor	Consumentenautoriteit	www.consumentenautoriteit.nl
Industry Association	Stichting SMS-Gedragscode	www.smsgedragscode.nl
Industry Association	SMS dienstenfilter	www.smsdienstenfilter.nl
Industry Association	mijn mobiele betalingen	www.mijnmobielebetalingen.nl

NEW ZEALAND

COUNTRY INFORMATION

Population in 2009	4,256,500
Gross domestic product 2009 per capita, current prices	14,666
Penetration rate (%) 3Q09	111.92%
Language (s)	English
Currency	New Zealand Dollar (NZD)

MOBILE TELECOMMUNICATIONS MARKET

Total subscriptions 3Q09	4,764,000
3G WCDMA subscriptions 3Q09	935,000
3G EV-DO subscriptions 3Q09	n/d
Total revenues 3Q09 (EUR million)	217.07
Service revenues 3Q09 (EUR million)	189.94
Blended montly ARPU 3Q09 (EUR)	12.39
Data revenues 3Q09 (EUR million)	66.34
SMS revenues 3Q09 (EUR million)	n/a
Messaging revenues 2010 (EUR million)	n/a
Messaging ARPU 2010 (EUR)	n/a
Content ARPU 2010 (EUR)	n/a

MOBILE OPERATORS DATA

	TELECOM NEW ZEALAND	VODAFONE NEW ZEALAND	TWO DEGREES MOBILE
Total subscriptions 3Q09	2,250,000	2,484,000	30,000
Market share 3Q09	47.23%	52.14%	0.63%
Prepaid subs 3Q09 (%)	60.80%	70.80%	100.00%
Postpaid subs 3Q09 (%)	39.20%	29.20%	
Growth rate (%) 3Q08 to 3Q09	2.74%	2.35%	
Total net additions in 3Q09	64,000	-27,000	30,000
WCDMA net additions in 3Q09	82,000	82,000	n/d
3G EV-DO net additions in 3Q09	n/d	n/d	n/d
Blended ARPU 3Q09	12.39	17.91	n/a
Prepaid ARPU 3Q09	4.18	0.00	n/a
Postpaid ARPU 3Q09	25.54	0.00	n/a

MOBILE OPERATORS VALUE ADDED SERVICES

	TELECOM NEW ZEALAND	VODAFONE NEW ZEALAND	TWO DEGREES MOBILE
SMS			
Push SMS	Yes	Yes	Yes
Toll free SMS MO	Yes	Yes	Yes
Premium SMS MO	Yes	Yes - Up to NZ$8	Yes - Up to NZ$8
Premium SMS MT (subscription)	Yes	Yes - Up to NZ$8	Yes - Up to NZ$8
MMS			
Push MMS	n/a	Yes	No
Toll free MMS MO	n/a	No	No
Premium MMS MO	n/a	No	No
Premium MMS MT (subscription)	n/a	Yes	No
Maximum MMS weight	n/a	Person2Machine = No size limit Person 2 Person = 30KB for NZDio (60sec)/unlimited for picture and video. Animated GIF = 100KB	
WAP			
Operator portal	xTra	Vodafone live!	2degrees Mobile Portal
Billing type	PSMS for off deck	WAP Online for Vodafone live! PSMS for off deck	PSMS for off deck
Pay per Use	Yes	Yes	Yes
Subscription	Yes	Yes	Yes
0-rate URL / Wholesale datacharge	Yes	0 rate URL possible / Wholesale data only available, via Wholesale business area for MVNO customers	
Maximum WAP Gateway download	n/a	WAP Gateway limit 8 gb but as per above, most handsets have an imposed limit of 300 kb	

NETSIZE OFFER

	TELECOM NEW ZEALAND	VODAFONE NEW ZEALAND	TWO DEGREES MOBILE
SMS			
Push SMS	Available in 2010	Available in 1H10	Available in 1H10
Toll free SMS MO	Available in 2010	Available in 1H10	Available in 1H10
Premium SMS MO	Available in 2010	Available in 1H10	Available in 1H10
Premium SMS MT (subscription)	Available in 2010	Available in 1H10	Available in 1H10
MMS			
Push MMS	No	Yes	No
Toll free MMS MO	No	No	No
Premium MMS MO	No	No	No
Premium MMS MT (subscription)	No	No	No
Maximum MMS weight	n/a	Operator limit stated above	n/a
WAP			
Operator portal	Upon request	Upon request	Upon request
Billing type	No	No	No
Pay per Use	No	No	No
Subscription	No	No	No
0-rate URL / Wholesale datacharge	No	No	No
Maximum WAP Gateway download	No limit	No limit	No limit

MOBILE CONTENT PRICES (Prices in NZD)

	PAY PER USE
Sound	
Polyphonics	2.00 - 4.00
True Tones	2.00 - 4.00
MP3	2.00 - 6.00
Images	
Wallpapers	3.00 - 4.00
Videos	1.00 - 4.00
Games & Lottery	
Voting, Participation TV	n/a
Instant Win, quiz	n/a
Java games	4.00 - 8.00
Community	
Chat	n/a

INDUSTRY ASSOCIATIONS, REGULATORS & CODES OF PRACTICE

	NAME	WEBSITE
Operator Forum	Telecommunications Carriers Forum Inc	www.tcf.gov.nz
Advertising Association	Advertising Standards Authority Incorporated of New Zealand	www.asa.co.nz
Regulatory Body	Department of Internal Affairs	www.dia.govt.nz

NORWAY

COUNTRY INFORMATION

Population in 2009	4,763,250
Gross domestic product 2009 per capita, current prices	49,429
Penetration rate (%) 3Q09	120.86%
Language (s)	Norwegian
Currency	Norwegian Kroner (NOK)

MOBILE TELECOMMUNICATIONS MARKET

Total subscriptions 3Q09	5,757,000
3G WCDMA subscriptions 3Q09	1,800,000
3G EV-DO subscriptions 3Q09	n/d
Total revenues 3Q09 (EUR million)	647.91
Service revenues 3Q09 (EUR million)	545.68
Blended montly ARPU 3Q09 (EUR)	32.66
Data revenues 3Q09 (EUR million)	145.68
SMS revenues 3Q09 (EUR million)	n/a
Messaging revenues 2010 (EUR million)	n/a
Messaging ARPU 2010 (EUR)	n/a
Content ARPU 2010 (EUR)	n/a

MOBILE OPERATORS DATA

	TELENOR MOBIL	NETCOM	TELE2 - MOBILE NORWAY)	NETWORK NORWAY
Total subscriptions 3Q09	3,117,000	2,153,000	See NetCom	455,000
Market share 3Q09	54.14%	37.40%		7.90%
Prepaid subs 3Q09 (%)	25.09%	22.57%		19.23%
Postpaid subs 3Q09 (%)	74.91%	77.43%		80.77%
Growth rate (%) 3Q08 to 3Q09	-0.10%	4.46%		30.00%
Total net additions in 3Q09	49,000	36,000		25,000
WCDMA net additions in 3Q09	60,000	30,000		n/d
3G EV-DO net additions in 3Q09	n/d	n/d		n/d
Blended ARPU 3Q09	31.74	34.10		n/a
Prepaid ARPU 3Q09	13.05	13.05		n/a
Postpaid ARPU 3Q09	46.46	42.68		n/a

NORWAY

MOBILE OPERATORS VALUE ADDED SERVICES

	TELENOR MOBIL	NETCOM	TELE2 - MOBILE NORWAY)	NETWORK NORWAY
SMS				
Push SMS	Yes	Yes	Yes	Yes
Toll free SMS MO	No	No	No	No
Premium SMS MO	No	No	No	No
Premium SMS MT (subscription)	Yes - Up to NOK 200.00	Yes - Up to NOK 200	Yes - Up to NOK 200	Yes - Up to NOK 200
MMS				
Push MMS	Yes	Yes	Yes	Yes
Toll free MMS MO	No	No	No	No
Premium MMS MO	NO	No	No	No
Premium MMS MT (subscription)	Yes - Up to NOK200	Yes - Up to NOK200	Yes - Up to NOK 200	Yes - Up to NOK 200
Maximum MMS weight	300 kb	300 kb	300 kb	300 kb
WAP				
Operator portal	WAP.telenormobil.no	Netcom Surfport WAP.netcom.no	WAP.tele2.no	http://wap.networknorway.no
Billing type	WAP	WAP	WAP	WAP
Pay per Use	Yes - Max transaction price NOK200	Yes - Max NOK 200	Yes - Max NOK 200	Yes - Max NOK 200
Subscription	Yes, but billing through sms. Max transaction price NOK 200	Yes, but billing through sms. Max transaction price NOK 200	Yes - Max NOK 200	Yes, but billing through sms. Max transaction price NOK 200
O-rate URL / Wholesale datacharge	No	Yes	Yes	No
Maximum WAP Gateway download	No limit	1 MB	No limit	1 MB

NETSIZE OFFER

	TELENOR MOBIL	NETCOM	TELE2 - MOBILE NORWAY)	NETWORK NORWAY
SMS				
Push SMS	Yes	Yes	Yes	Yes (From 2010)
Toll free SMS MO	No	No	No	No
Premium SMS MO	No	No	No	No
Premium SMS MT (subscription)	Yes - Up to NOK 200	Yes - Up to NOK 200	Yes - Up to NOK 200	Yes (From 2010) - Up to NOK 200
MMS				
Push MMS	Yes	Yes	Yes	Yes (From 2010)
Toll free MMS MO	No	No	No	No
Premium MMS MO	No	No	No	No
Premium MMS MT (subscription)	Yes - Up to NOK 200	Yes - Up to NOK 200	Yes - Up to NOK 200	Yes (From 2010) - Up to NOK 200
Maximum MMS weight	300 kb	300 kb	300 kb	300 kb
WAP				
Operator portal	WAP.telenormobil.no	Netcom Surfport WAP.netcom.no	WAP.tele2.no	http://wap.networknorway.no
Billing type	WAP	WAP	WAP	WAP
Pay per Use	Yes - Max transaction price NOK 2100	Yes - Max NOK100	Yes - Max transaction price NOK100	Yes (From 2010) - Max NOK100
Subscription	Yes - Up to NOK 200	Yes - Up to NOK 200	Yes - Up to NOK 200	Yes (From 2010) - Up to NOK 200
O-rate URL / Wholesale datacharge	No	No	No	No
Maximum WAP Gateway download	No limit	1 MB	No limit	1 MB

MOBILE CONTENT PRICES (Prices in NOK)

	PAY PER USE	SUBSCRIPTION
Sound		
Polyphonics	29.00 - 50.00	10-50
True Tones	29.00 - 50.00	10-50
MP3	10.00 - 15.00	10-50
Images		
Wallpapers	25.00- 30.00	10-50
Videos	30	10-50
Games & Lottery		
Voting, Participation TV	n/a	10-50
Instant Win, quiz	n/a	10-50
Java games	30-70	10-50
Community		
Chat	n/a	n/a

INDUSTRY ASSOCIATIONS, REGULATORS & CODES OF PRACTICE

	NAME	WEBSITE
Telecom regulator	Post- og teletilsynet (PT)	www.npt.no
Authority for Lottery	Lotteri- og stiftelsestilsynet	www.lottstift.no
The ombudsman	Forbrukerombudet	www.forbrukerombudet.no/index.gan - id=490&subid=
CPA guidelines	Cpa riktlinjer	cpa.telenor.no/cpa/guidelines/2004-12-01%20CPA%20 Retningslinjer%20ver%201.1.pdf

POLAND

COUNTRY INFORMATION

Population in 2009	37,946,250
Gross domestic product 2009 per capita, current prices	7,405
Penetration rate (%) 3Q09	116.51%
Language (s)	Polish
Currency	Polish Zloty (PLN)

MOBILE TELECOMMUNICATIONS MARKET

Total subscriptions 3Q09	44,212,500
3G WCDMA subscriptions 3Q09	12,471,000
3G EV-DO subscriptions 3Q09	n/d
Total revenues 3Q09 (EUR million)	1,475.38
Service revenues 3Q09 (EUR million)	1,444.07
Blended montly ARPU 3Q09 (EUR)	10.82
Data revenues 3Q09 (EUR million)	359.88
SMS revenues 3Q09 (EUR million)	345.60
Messaging revenues 2010 (EUR million)	n/a
Messaging ARPU 2010 (EUR)	n/a
Content ARPU 2010 (EUR)	n/a

MOBILE OPERATORS DATA

	ORANGE POLAND (CENTERTEL)	POLKOMTEL (PLUS)	PTC (ERA)	P4 (PLAY)
Total subscriptions 3Q09	13,784,000	14,143,000	13,482,000	2,800,000
Market share 3Q09	31.18%	31.99%	30.49%	6.33%
Prepaid subs 3Q09 (%)	52.44%	52.10%	51.22%	66.67%
Postpaid subs 3Q09 (%)	47.56%	47.90%	48.78%	33.33%
Growth rate (%) 3Q08 to 3Q09	-2.07%	0.85%	3.60%	78.04%
Total net additions in 3Q09	-32,050	-321,940	73,000	175,000
WCDMA net additions in 3Q09	51,000	19,400	101,400	175,000
3G EV-DO net additions in 3Q09	n/d	n/d	n/d	n/d
Blended ARPU 3Q09	10.96	10.75	11.00	9.55
Prepaid ARPU 3Q09	5.07	0.00	4.00	0.00
Postpaid ARPU 3Q09	19.15	0.00	11.00	0.00

MOBILE OPERATORS VALUE ADDED SERVICES

	ORANGE POLAND (CENTERTEL)	POLKOMTEL (PLUS)	PTC (ERA)	P4 (PLAY)
SMS				
Push SMS	Yes	Yes	Yes	Yes
Non-premium SMS MO	Yes	Yes	Yes	Yes
Premium SMS MO	Yes - Up to PLN25.00 net	Yes - Up to PLN25.00 net	Yes - Up to PLN25.00 net	Yes - Up to PLN25.00 net
Premium SMS MT (subscription)	Operator managed renewal service	Under trial period	Operator managed renewal service	Operator managed renewal service
MMS	Yes	Yes	Yes	Yes
Push MMS	No	No	No	No
Toll free MMS MO	No	No	No	No
Premium MMS MO	Yes - Up to PLN25.00 net	Yes - Up to PLN20.00 net	Yes - Up to PLN9.00	Yes - Up to PLN19.00
Premium MMS MT (subscription)	No	No	No	No
Maximum MMS weight	100 kb	100 kb	100 kb	100 kb
WAP				
Operator portal	Orange World	Plus.pl	Era OMNIX	PlayNet
Billing type	WAP	WAP	WAP	n/a
Pay per Use	Yes	Yes	Yes	n/a
Subscription	No	No	No	n/a
O-rate URL / Wholesale datacharge	n/a	n/a	n/a	n/a
Maximum WAP Gateway download	100 kb	100 kb	100 kb	n/a

NETSIZE OFFER

	ORANGE POLAND (CENTERTEL)	POLKOMTEL (PLUS)	PTC (ERA)	P4 (PLAY)
SMS				
Push SMS	Yes	Yes	Yes	Yes
Non-premium SMS MO	Yes	Yes	Yes	Yes
Premium SMS MO	Yes - Up to PLN25.00 net	Yes - Up to PLN25.00 net	Yes - Up to PLN25.00 net	Yes - Up to PLN25.00 net
Premium SMS MT (subscription)	Upon request	No	Upon request	Upon request
MMS				
Push MMS	No	No	No	No
Toll free MMS MO	No	No	No	No
Premium MMS MO	No	No	No	No
Premium MMS MT (subscription)	No	No	No	No
Maximum MMS weight	n/a	n/a	n/a	n/a
WAP				
Operator portal	No	No	No	No
Billing type	WAP	WAP	WAP	No
Pay per Use	Upon request	Upon request	Upon request	n/a
Subscription	No	No	No	n/a
O-rate URL / Wholesale datacharge	n/a	n/a	n/a	n/a
Maximum WAP Gateway download	No limit	No limit	No limit	n/a

MOBILE CONTENT PRICES (Prices in PLN)

	PAY PER USE
Sound	
Polyphonics	2.44 - 7.32
True Tones	2.44 - 7.32
MP3	2.44 - 7.32
Images	
Wallpapers	1.22 - 7.32
Videos	2.44 - 10.98
Games & Lottery	
Voting, Participation TV	1.22 - 2.44
Instant Win, quiz	1.22 - 2.44
Java games	2.44 - 10.98
Community	
Chat	1.22 - 2.44

OPERATOR MOBILE CONTENT PRICES (Prices in US$)

	POLKOMTEL (PLUS)	PTC (ERA)
Community	n/a	n/a
Music	n/a	n/a
TV & Video	n/a	n/a
Location Based Services	Family locator: 0.42 / location request - 2.11 / 8-request bundle - 3.79 / 15-request bundle (Cell-ID)	Family locator: 0.42 / location request. Additionl registration fee of PLN1.22 / user. Users being registered must confirm at cost of PLN1.22 also. (Cell-ID)

INDUSTRY ASSOCIATIONS, REGULATORS & CODES OF PRACTICE

	NAME	WEBSITE
Telecom regulator	Urz d Komunikacji Elektronicznej (UKE)	www.uke.gov.pl

PORTUGAL

COUNTRY INFORMATION

POPULATION IN 2009	10,695,000
Gross domestic product 2009 per capita, current prices	13,731
Penetration rate (%) 3Q09	142.54%
Language (s)	Portuguese
Currency	Euro (EUR)

MOBILE TELECOMMUNICATIONS MARKET

Total subscriptions 3Q09	15244930
Total subscriptions 3Q09	15,244,930
3G WCDMA subscriptions 3Q09	5,171,390
3G EV-DO subscriptions 3Q09	n/d
Total revenues 3Q09 (EUR million)	850.23
Service revenues 3Q09 (EUR million)	768.36
Blended montly ARPU 3Q09 (EUR)	16.96
Data revenues 3Q09 (EUR million)	130.64
SMS revenues 3Q09 (EUR million)	43.07
Messaging revenues 2010 (EUR million)	n/a
Messaging ARPU 2010 (EUR)	n/a
Content ARPU 2010 (EUR)	n/a

MOBILE OPERATORS DATA

	TMN	VODAFONE PORTUGAL	SONAECOM SERVICOS COMUNICACOES
Total subscriptions 3Q09	7,084,000	5,349,700	2,811,230
Market share 3Q09	46.47%	35.09%	18.44%
Prepaid subs 3Q09 (%)	69.50%	77.94%	69.00%
Postpaid subs 3Q09 (%)	30.50%	22.06%	31.00%
Growth rate (%) 3Q08 to 3Q09	5.23%	6.49%	16.61%
Total net additions 3Q09	104,000	125,810	65,530
WCDMA net additions in 3Q09	104,120	41,510	52,370
3G EV-DO net additions in 3Q09	n/d	n/d	n/d
Blended ARPU 3Q09	16.80	18.10	15.20
Prepaid ARPU 3Q09	0.00	0.00	0.00
Postpaid ARPU 3Q09	0.00	0.00	0.00

PORTUGAL

MOBILE OPERATORS VALUE ADDED SERVICES

	TMN	VODAFONE PORTUGAL	SONAECOM SERVICOS COMUNICACOES
SMS			
Push SMS	Yes	Yes	Yes
Toll free SMS MO	Yes	Yes	Yes
Premium SMS MO	Yes - Up to €5.00	Yes - Up to €4.00	Yes - Up to €5.00
Premium SMS MT (subscription)	Yes - Up to €2.00	Yes - Up to €5.00	Yes - Up to €2.00
Premium MO-MTP Pay per use (new service)	Yes	Yes	Yes
MMS			
Push MMS	Yes	Yes	Yes
Toll free MMS MO	No	No	Yes
Premium MMS MO	Yes	Yes	Yes
Premium MMS MT (subscription)	No	Yes	No
Maximum MMS weight	99 kb	300 kb	300 k
WAP			
Operator portal	i9	Vodafone live!	Zone
Billing type	WAP or MSISDN Forwarding + PSMS MT	WAP or MSISDN Forwarding + PSMS MT	WAP or MSISDN Forwarding + PSMS MT
Pay per Use	Yes- Up to €10.00	Yes - Up to €7.5	Yes- Up to €5.00
Subscription	No	Planned	No
O-rate URL / Wholesale datacharge	No	No	Yes
Maximum WAP Gateway download	n/a	n/a	n/a

NETSIZE OFFER

	TMN	VODAFONE PORTUGAL	SONAECOM SERVICOS COMUNICACOES
SMS			
Push SMS	Yes	Yes	Yes
Toll free SMS MO	No	No	No
Premium SMS MO	Yes - Up to €4.00	Yes - Up to €4.00	Yes - Up to €4.00
Premium SMS MT (subscription)	Yes - Up to €2.00	Yes - Up to €5.00	Yes - Up to €2.00
Premium MO-MTP Pay per use (new service)	Yes	Yes	Yes
MMS			
Push MMS	Upon request	Upon request	Upon request
Toll free MMS MO	Upon request	Upon request	Upon request
Premium MMS MO	Upon request	Upon request	Upon request
Premium MMS MT (subscription)	Upon request	Upon request	Upon request
Maximum MMS weight	99 kb	300 kb	300 k
WAP			
Operator portal	i9	Vodafone live!	Zone
Billing type	WAP	WAP	WAP
Pay per Use	Yes - Up to €10.00	Yes - Up to €7.50	Yes - Up to €5.00
Subscription	No	No	No
O-rate URL / Wholesale datacharge	No	No	No
Maximum WAP Gateway download	n/a	n/a	n/a

INDUSTRY ASSOCIATIONS, REGULATORS & CODES OF PRACTICE

	NAME	WEBSITE
Telecom regulator	Autoridade Nacional de Comunicações (ANACOM)	www.anacom.pt
Industry Association	Associação Portuguesa de Informação, Tecnologia e Entretenimento Digital (APITED)	www.apited.com

ROMANIA

COUNTRY INFORMATION

Population in 2009	21,219,750
Gross domestic product 2009 per capita, current prices	5,439
Penetration rate (%) 3Q09	139.12%
Language (s)	Romanian
Currency	Romanian Lei (RON)

MOBILE TELECOMMUNICATIONS MARKET

Total subscriptions 3Q09	29,520,710
3G WCDMA subscriptions 3Q09	4,328,900
3G EV-DO subscriptions 3Q09	11,000
Total revenues 3Q09 (EUR million)	668.80
Service revenues 3Q09 (EUR million)	572.73
Blended montly ARPU 3Q09 (EUR)	7.54
Data revenues 3Q09 (EUR million)	n/a
SMS revenues 3Q09 (EUR million)	n/a
Messaging revenues 2010 (EUR million)	n/a
Messaging ARPU 2010 (EUR)	n/a
Content ARPU 2010 (EUR)	n/a

MOBILE OPERATORS DATA

	ORANGE ROMANIA	VODAFONE ROMANIA	COSMOTE ROMANIA	RCS&RDS	TELEMOBIL	ROM TELEKOM
Total subscriptions 3Q09	10,694,000	9,535,000	6,599,290	2,300,000	390,900	1,520
Market share 3Q09	36.23%	32.30%	22.35%	7.79%	1.32%	0.01%
Prepaid subs 3Q09 (%)	64.66%	61.60%	80.00%	100.00%	68.28%	
Postpaid subs 3Q09 (%)	35.34%	38.40%	20.00%		31.72%	100.00%
Growth rate (%) 3Q08 to 3Q09	4.76%	0.20%	25.79%	101.81%	13.11%	
Total net additions in 3Q09	340,000	2,000	268,970	150,000	15,900	170
WCDMA net additions in 3Q09	66,700	20,000	n/d	150,000	3,900	n/d
3G EV-DO net additions in 3Q09	n/d	n/d	n/d	n/d	-1,000	n/d
Blended ARPU 3Q09	8.33	8.10	5.00	n/a	14.50	n/a
Prepaid ARPU 3Q09	0.00	2.70	2.00	n/a	0.00	n/a
Postpaid ARPU 3Q09	0.00	16.00	14.00	n/a	0.00	n/a

RUSSIA

COUNTRY INFORMATION

Population in 2009	140,863,250
Gross domestic product 2009 per capita, current prices	5,758
Penetration rate (%) 3Q09	145.72%
Language (s)	Russian
Currency	Russian Rouble (RUB)

MOBILE TELECOMMUNICATIONS MARKET

Total subscriptions 3Q09	205,268,960
3G WCDMA subscriptions 3Q09	6,182,600
3G EV-DO subscriptions 3Q09	n/d
Total revenues 3Q09 (EUR million)	4,091.98
Service revenues 3Q09 (EUR million)	3,757.64
Blended montly ARPU 3Q09 (EUR)	6.59
Data revenues 3Q09 (EUR million)	690.55
SMS revenues 3Q09 (EUR million)	287.57
Messaging revenues 2010 (EUR million)	1,613.55
Messaging ARPU 2010 (EUR)	1.29
Content ARPU 2010 (EUR)	2.05

MOBILE OPERATORS DATA

	MOBILE TELE-SYSTEMS	VIMPELCOM (BEELINE)	MEGAFON	TELE2	URALSVYAZIN-FORM	SIBIRTELECOM	NIZHEGORODS-KAYA CELLULAR COMMUNICA-TIONS	SMARTS	NOVAYA TELEFONNAYA COMPANIYA	SKYLINK	OTHERS
Total subscriptions 3Q09	68,700,000	51,028,000	48,324,600	13,302,000	5,700,000	5,487,200	3,169,640	2,900,000	1,393,400	1,196,270	4,067,850
Market share 3Q09	33.47%	24.86%	23.54%	6.48%	2.78%	2.67%	1.54%	1.41%	0.68%	0.58%	1.98%
Prepaid subs 3Q09 (%)	87.69%	91.69%	88.71%	90.00%	78.66%	88.27%	91.47%	87.00%	83.00%		71.83%
Postpaid subs 3Q09 (%)	12.31%	8.31%	11.29%	10.00%	21.34%	11.73%	8.53%	13.00%	17.00%	100.00%	28.17%
Growth rate (%) 3Q08 to 3Q09	10.99%	11.87%	16.76%	33.90%	2.74%	15.53%	26.79%	2.83%	14.60%	40.25%	11.85%
Total net additions in 3Q09	1,280,000	648,800	2,963,810	996,800	0	231,900	189,110	52,940	41,400	96,270	110,970
WCDMA net additions in 3Q09	435,000	435,100	88,500	n/d	n/d	n/d	n/d	n/d	n/d	n/d	n/d
3G EV-DO net additions in 3Q09	n/d	n/d	n/d	n/d	n/d	n/d	n/d	n/d	n/d	n/d	n/d
Blended ARPU 3Q09	5.74	7.42	7.30	4.71	4.14	10.07	6.02	2.96	n/a	19.03	n/a
Prepaid ARPU 3Q09	3.50	0.00	0.00	0.00	0.00	0.00	0.00	0.00	n/a	0.00	n/a
Postpaid ARPU 3Q09	17.49	0.00	0.00	0.00	0.00	0.00	0.00	0.00	n/a	0.00	n/a

RUSSIA

MOBILE OPERATORS VALUE ADDED SERVICES

	MOBILE TELESYS-TEMS	VIMPELCOM (BEELINE)	MEGAFON	TELE2	URALSVYAZIN-FORM
SMS					
Push SMS	Yes*	Yes*	Yes*	Yes*	Yes*
Toll free SMS MO	Yes	Yes	Yes	Yes	Yes
Premium SMS MO	Yes - RUB 5.00 - 305.00	Yes - RUB 5.00 - 300.00	Yes - RUB 5.90 - 354.00	Yes - RUB 5.30 - 339.00	Yes - RUB 5.90 - 354.00
Premium SMS MT (subscription)	Yes (subscription platform - 1,27 - 160,89 RUB	Yes (subscription platform - 1,27 - 160,89 RUB	n/a	n/a	n/a
MMS	Yes	Yes	Yes	Yes	n/a
Push MMS					
Toll free MMS MO	Yes	n/a	Yes	n/a	n/a
Premium MMS MO	Yes - 1,27 - 258,30 RUB	n/a	Yes - 1,50 -177,00 RUB	n/a	n/a
Premium MMS MT (subscription)	n/a	n/a	n/a	n/a	n/a
Maximum MMS weight	300 Kb	500 Kb	300 Kb	n/a	n/a
WAP					
Operator portal	WAP.mts.ru	WAP.beeline.ru	WAP.megafon.ru	wap.tele2.ru	n/a
Billing type	MSISDN Forwarding + PSMS MT	IVR	WAP	n/a	n/a
Pay per Use	Yes	Yes	Yes	n/a	n/a
Subscription	n/a	n/a	n/a	n/a	n/a
O-rate URL / Wholesale datacharge	n/a	n/a	n/a	n/a	n/a
Maximum WAP Gateway download	2000 kb	2000 kb	2000 kb	n/a	n/a

NETSIZE OFFER

	MOBILE TELESYSTEMS	VIMPELCOM (BEELINE)	MEGAFON	TELE2	OTHERS
SMS					
Push SMS	Yes	Yes	Yes	Yes	Yes
Non-premium free SMS MO	Yes - (shared SC only)	Yes - (shared SC only)	Yes - (shared SC only)	Yes - (shared SC only)	Yes - (shared SC only)
Premium SMS MO	Yes - Up to RUB 304	Yes - Up to RUB 300	Yes - Up to RUB 354	Yes - Up to RUB 338	Yes - Up to RUB 354
Premium SMS MT (subscription)	Yes (subscription platform - 1,27 - 160,89 RUB	Yes (subscription platform - 1,27 - 160,89 RUB	No	No	No
MMS					
Push MMS	No	No	No	No	No
Toll free MMS MO	No	No	No	No	No
Premium MMS MO	Upon request	No	Upon request	No	No
Premium MMS MT (subscription)	No	No	No	No	No
Maximum MMS weight	no data	no data	no data	no data	no data
WAP					
Operator portal	No	No	No	No	No
Billing type	MSISDN Forwarding + PSMS MT	No	WAP	No	No
Pay per Use	Upon request	No	Upon request	No	No
Subscription	No	No	No	No	No
O-rate URL / Wholesale datacharge	No	No	No	No	No
Maximum WAP Gateway download	n/a	n/a	n/a	n/a	n/a

* Opt-in required.

MOBILE CONTENT SERVICES

	TOTAL REVENUES 2010 (EUR MILLION)	CONTRIBUTION AS % OF TOTAL REVENUES
Mobile music market	368.13	9.05%
Mobile games market	109.13	2.68%
Mobile images market	24.38	0.60%
Mobile TV market	7.05	0.17%
Mobile video market	7.52	0.18%
Mobile internet market	1,938.17	47.64%
Mobile messaging market	1,613.55	39.67%

MOBILE CONTENT PRICES (Prices in RUB)

	PAY PER USE
Sound	
Polyphonics	24-30
True Tones	55-65
MP3	60-80
Images	
Wallpapers	24-30
Videos	60-80
Games & Lottery	
Voting, Participation TV	8 – 60
Instant Win, quiz	8 – 60
Java games	80-150
Community	
Chat	24 – 150

OPERATOR MOBILE CONTENT PRICES (Prices in US$)

	MOBILE TELESYSTEMS	MEGAFON
Community	Handset client (downloadable): 0.05 / day - 0.02 / outgoing message (determined by half of user's standard SMS charge. RUB1.05 most common SMS charge. - GPRS/WAP: 0.28 / MB between 8.45am and 0.00am. Other data-pricing options available. No content charge. - 0.12 / MB between 0.00am and 8.45am. Other data-pricing options available. No content charge.	Handset client (downloadable): 0.17 / day - 0.00 / outgoing message
Music	Ring-back tones: 1.24 / tone (lowest price), + monthly subscr. of RUB 50.30 - 3.14 / tone (highest price), + monthly subscr. of RUB 50.30 (Voice) - Ring tones: 0.81 / download (OTA) - Full-track: 2.09 / download (OTA)	n/a
TV & Video	Video-on-demand: 2.01 / download (Download)	n/a
Location Based Services	Location-based dating: 1.08 / wk (Cell-ID) - Family locator: 1.71 / month. incl unl. searches of 3 numbers / month. - 0.17 / location request. For numbers other than selected 3. (Cell-ID)	n/a

INDUSTRY ASSOCIATIONS, REGULATORS & CODES OF PRACTICE

	NAME	WEBSITE
Providers association	Association of providers of mobile services and content	www.cspa.ru
Goverment (Ministry)	Russian Ministry of Telecommunications	english.minsvyaz.ru/enter.shtml
DM Association	Russian Direct Marketing Association	www.radm.ru/pages/79

SINGAPORE

COUNTRY INFORMATION

Population in 2009	4,552,250
Gross domestic product 2009 per capita, current prices	26,007
Penetration rate (%) 3Q09	150.19%
Language (s)	English
Currency	Singapore Dollar (SGD)

MOBILE TELECOMMUNICATIONS MARKET

Total subscriptions 3Q09	6,836,800
3G WCDMA subscriptions 3Q09	2,927,700
3G EV-DO subscriptions 3Q09	n/d
Total revenues 3Q09 (EUR million)	440.33
Service revenues 3Q09 (EUR million)	414.59
Blended montly ARPU 3Q09 (EUR)	22.23
Data revenues 3Q09 (EUR million)	118.74
SMS revenues 3Q09 (EUR million)	n/a
Messaging revenues 2010 (EUR million)	n/a
Messaging ARPU 2010 (EUR)	n/a
Content ARPU 2010 (EUR)	n/a

MOBILE OPERATORS DATA

	SINGTEL MOBILE	MOBILEONE	STARHUB	DNA COMMS
Total subscriptions 3Q09	3,100,000	1,718,000	1,884,000	134,800
Market share 3Q09	45.34%	25.13%	27.56%	1.97%
Prepaid subs 3Q09 (%)	49.71%	47.96%	51.01%	
Postpaid subs 3Q09 (%)	50.29%	52.04%	48.99%	100.00%
Growth rate (%) 3Q08 to 3Q09	7.86%	5.98%	8.09%	29.74%
Total net additions in 3Q09	109,000	49,000	35,000	7,400
WCDMA net additions in 3Q09	60,000	90,600	37,800	n/d
3G EV-DO net additions in 3Q09	n/d	n/d	n/d	n/d
Blended ARPU 3Q09	24.32	18.58	22.15	n/a
Prepaid ARPU 3Q09	6.81	7.15	11.19	n/a
Postpaid ARPU 3Q09	41.34	29.13	33.56	n/a

MOBILE OPERATORS VALUE ADDED SERVICES

	SINGTEL MOBILE	MOBILEONE	STARHUB	DNA COMMS
SMS				
Push SMS	Yes	Yes	Yes	n/a
Toll free SMS MO	Yes	Yes	Yes	n/a
Premium SMS MO	Yes - Up to SG$10	Yes - Up to SG$20	Yes - Up to SG$10	n/a
Premium SMS MT (subscription)	Yes - Up to SG$10	Yes - Up to SG$20	Yes - Up to SG$10	n/a
MMS				
Push MMS	Yes	Yes	Yes	n/a
Toll free MMS MO	n/a	Yes	n/a	n/a
Premium MMS MO	n/a	Yes - Up to SG$20	n/a	n/a
Premium MMS MT (subscription)	n/a	Yes - Up to SG$20	n/a	n/a
Maximum MMS weight	n/a	100-300kB	n/a	n/a
WAP				
Operator portal	IDEAS	Miworld	Starhub Gee!	n/a
Billing type	WAP -Direct Billing	WAP -Direct Billing	WAP -Direct Billing	n/a
Pay per Use	Yes - Up to SG$20	Yes - Up to SG$20	Yes - Up to SG$20	n/a
Subscription	Yes - Up to SG$20	Yes - Up to SG$20	Yes - Up to SG$20	n/a
O-rate URL / Wholesale datacharge	Yes	Yes	Yes	n/a
Maximum WAP Gateway download	No	No	No	n/a

NETSIZE OFFER

	SINGTEL MOBILE	MOBILEONE	STARHUB	DNA COMMS
SMS				
Push SMS	Yes	Yes	Yes	Yes
Toll free SMS MO	No	No	Yes	n/a
Premium SMS MO	No	No	Yes - Up to SG$10	n/a
Premium SMS MT (subscription)	No	No	Yes - Up to SG$10.00	n/a
MMS				
Push MMS	No	No	No	n/a
Toll free MMS MO	No	No	No	n/a
Premium MMS MO	No	No	No	n/a
Premium MMS MT (subscription)	No	No	No	n/a
Maximum MMS weight	n/a	n/a	n/a	n/a
WAP	Yes	Yes	No	
Operator portal	IDEAS	Miworld	Starhub Gee!	n/a
Billing type	WAP - Direct Billing	WAP - Direct Billing	n/a	n/a
Pay per Use	Yes - Up to SG$20	Yes - Up to SG$20	n/a	n/a
Subscription	Yes - Up to SG$20	Yes - Up to SG$20	n/a	n/a
O-rate URL / Wholesale datacharge	Yes	Yes	n/a	n/a
Maximum WAP Gateway download	No	No	n/a	n/a

SINGAPORE

MOBILE CONTENT PRICES

	PAY PER USE
Sound	
Polyphonics	1.50 - 3.00
True Tones	2.00 - 4.00
MP3	2.00 - 6.00
Images	
Wallpapers	1.50 - 3.00
Videos	1.50 - 4.00
Games & Lottery	
Voting, Participation TV	n/a
Instant Win, quiz	3.00 - 5.00
Java games	3.00 - 9.00
Community	
Chat	2.00 - 5.00

INDUSTRY ASSOCIATIONS, REGULATORS & CODES OF PRACTICE

	NAME	WEBSITE
Telecom regulator	Infocomm Development Authority of Singapore (IDA)	www.ida.gov.sg

SLOVAKIA

COUNTRY INFORMATION

Population in 2009	5,394,500
Gross domestic product 2009 per capita, current prices	11,364
Penetration rate (%) 3Q09	104.42%
Language (s)	Slovak
Currency	Euro (EUR)

MOBILE TELECOMMUNICATIONS MARKET

Total subscriptions 3Q09	5,633,000
3G WCDMA subscriptions 3Q09	1,292,600
3G EV-DO subscriptions 3Q09	n/d
Total revenues 3Q09 (EUR million)	372.10
Service revenues 3Q09 (EUR million)	346.91
Blended montly ARPU 3Q09 (EUR)	20.57
Data revenues 3Q09 (EUR million)	67.86
SMS revenues 3Q09 (EUR million)	n/a
Messaging revenues 2010 (EUR million)	n/a
Messaging ARPU 2010 (EUR)	n/a
Content ARPU 2010 (EUR)	n/a

MOBILE OPERATORS DATA

	T-MOBILE	ORANGE	TELEFONICA O2 SLOVAK REPUBLIC
Total subscriptions 3Q09	2,301,000	2,869,000	463,000
Market share 3Q09	40.85%	50.93%	8.22%
Prepaid subs 3Q09 (%)	40.03%	38.50%	66.09%
Postpaid subs 3Q09 (%)	59.97%	61.50%	33.91%
Growth rate (%) 3Q08 to 3Q09	-0.69%	-0.76%	67.15%
Total net additions in 3Q09	-22,000	-7,000	46,000
WCDMA net additions in 3Q09	1,700	124,100	n/d
3G EV-DO net additions in 3Q09	n/d	n/d	n/d
Blended ARPU 3Q09	19.00	21.83	0.00
Prepaid ARPU 3Q09	6.00	0.00	7.53
Postpaid ARPU 3Q09	28.00	0.00	24.21

MOBILE OPERATORS VALUE ADDED SERVICES

	T-MOBILE	ORANGE	TELEFONICA O2 SLOVAK REPUBLIC
SMS			
Push SMS	Yes	Yes	Yes
Toll free SMS MO	Yes	Yes	Yes
Premium SMS MO	Yes	Yes	Yes
Premium SMS MT (subscription)	Yes	Yes	Yes
MMS			
Push MMS	No	No	No
Toll free MMS MO	No	No	No
Premium MMS MO	No	No	No
Premium MMS MT (subscription)	No	No	No
Maximum MMS weight	No	No	No
WAP			
Operator portal	WAP.T-Zones.sk	WAP.orangeworld.sk	n/a
Billing type	n/a	n/a	n/a
Pay per Use	n/a	n/a	n/a
Subscription	n/a	n/a	n/a
O-rate URL / Wholesale datacharge	n/a	n/a	n/a
Maximum WAP Gateway download	n/a	n/a	n/a

INDUSTRY ASSOCIATIONS, REGULATORS & CODES OF PRACTICE

	NAME	WEBSITE
Goverment (Ministry)	Ministry of transport, post and telecommunications	www.telecom.gov.sk/index/index.php - lang=sk

SLOVENIA

COUNTRY INFORMATION

Population in 2009	2,000,250
Gross domestic product 2009 per capita, current prices	16,919
Penetration rate (%) 3Q09	103.65%
Language (s)	Slovene
Currency	Euro (EUR)

MOBILE TELECOMMUNICATIONS MARKET

Total subscriptions 3Q09	2,073,320
3G WCDMA subscriptions 3Q09	345,600
3G EV-DO subscriptions 3Q09	n/d
Total revenues 3Q09 (EUR million)	167.69
Service revenues 3Q09 (EUR million)	161.34
Blended montly ARPU 3Q09 (EUR)	25.09
Data revenues 3Q09 (EUR million)	32.58
SMS revenues 3Q09 (EUR million)	n/a
Messaging revenues 2010 (EUR million)	n/a
Messaging ARPU 2010 (EUR)	n/a
Content ARPU 2010 (EUR)	n/a

MOBILE OPERATORS DATA

	MOBITEL	SI.MOBIL	TUS MOBIL
Total subscriptions 3Q09	1,328,020	580,300	165,000
Market share 3Q09	64.05%	27.99%	7.96%
Prepaid subs 3Q09 (%)	28.42%	31.36%	65.58%
Postpaid subs 3Q09 (%)	71.58%	68.64%	34.42%
Growth rate (%) 3Q08 to 3Q09	-3.55%	5.09%	85.58%
Total net additions in 3Q09	-10,130	-1,500	12,800
WCDMA net additions in 3Q09	20,000	10,600	n/d
3G EV-DO net additions in 3Q09	n/d	n/d	n/d
Blended ARPU 3Q09	26.00	23.00	n/a
Prepaid ARPU 3Q09	8.00	8.10	n/a
Postpaid ARPU 3Q09	30.00	29.80	n/a

SLOVENIA

MOBILE OPERATORS VALUE ADDED SERVICES

	MOBITEL	SI.MOBIL	TUS MOBIL
SMS			
Push SMS	Yes	Yes	n/a
Toll free SMS MO	n/a	n/a	n/a
Premium SMS MO	Yes	Yes	n/a
Premium SMS MT (subscription)	Yes	Yes	No
MMS			
Push MMS	Yes	Yes	n/a
Toll free MMS MO	n/a	n/a	n/a
Premium MMS MO	n/a	n/a	n/a
Premium MMS MT (subscription)	Yes	Yes	n/a
Maximum MMS weight	n/a	n/a	n/a
WAP			
Operator portal	Planet.si	Vodafone Live!	n/a
Billing type	WAP	MT SMS	n/a
Pay per Use	No	No	n/a
Subscription	Yes	Yes	n/a
O-rate URL / Wholesale datacharge	n/a	n/a	n/a
Maximum WAP Gateway download	n/a	n/a	n/a

MOBILE CONTENT PRICES (Prices in EUR)

	PAY PER USE	SUBSCRIPTION
Sound		
Polyphonics	0.83-2.49	0.83-2.49
True Tones	1.5-2.49	0.83-2.49
MP3	1.5-2.49	0.83-2.49
Images		
Wallpapers	0.83-2.49	0.83-2.49
Videos	0.83-2.49	0.83-2.49
Games & Lottery		
Voting . Participation TV	0.1-2.49	n/a
Instant Win. quiz	0.4-2.49	0.4-2.49
Java games	2.5-4.49	1.99-2.49
Community	0.1-2.49	0.83-2.49
Chat	0.1-2.49	0.83-2.49

INDUSTRY ASSOCIATIONS, REGULATORS & CODES OF PRACTICE

	NAME	WEBSITE
Electronical communications regulator	Agencija za pošto in elektronske komunikacije Republike Slovenije	www.apek.si
Terms and Regulations (Mobitel-largest operator)	Terms and regulations for service providers	http://eng.m-vrata.com/terms-conditions/mvrata/
Legislation regarding prize games	Office for Gaming Supervision	www.uradni-list.si/1/content?id=42367
Advertising	Slovenian Advertising Chamber	www.soz.si/
Consumer protection	Consumer Protection Office of the Republic of Slovenia	www.uvp.gov.si/en/
Government (Ministries)	Government of the Republic of Slovenia	www.vlada.si/en/news/

SOUTH AFRICA

COUNTRY INFORMATION

Population in 2009	49,077,000
Gross domestic product 2009 per capita, current prices	3,459
Penetration rate (%) 3Q09	101.02%
Language (s)	English, Afrikaans, Zulu, Xhosa + others
Currency	South African Rand (ZAR)

MOBILE TELECOMMUNICATIONS MARKET

Total subscriptions 3Q09	49,576,240
3G WCDMA subscriptions 3Q09	5,758,740
3G EV-DO subscriptions 3Q09	2,500
Total revenues 3Q09 (EUR million)	1,780.15
Service revenues 3Q09 (EUR million)	1,679.89
Blended montly ARPU 3Q09 (EUR)	11.89
Data revenues 3Q09 (EUR million)	275.69
SMS revenues 3Q09 (EUR million)	117.38
Messaging revenues 2010 (EUR million)	n/a
Messaging ARPU 2010 (EUR)	n/a
Content ARPU 2010 (EUR)	n/a

MOBILE OPERATORS DATA

	VODACOM	MTN	CELL C	NEOTEL SOUTH AFRICA	TELKOM
Total subscriptions 3Q09	25,506,000	16,419,000	7,640,000	2,500	8,740
Market share 3Q09	51.45%	33.12%	15.41%	0.01%	0.02%
Prepaid subs 3Q09 (%)	84.18%	82.01%	74.07%		34.32%
Postpaid subs 3Q09 (%)	15.82%	17.99%	25.93%	100.00%	65.68%
Growth rate (%) 3Q08 to 3Q09	11.45%	1.52%	31.29%		
Total net additions in 3Q09	-659,350	-812,000	440,000	2,500	1,440
WCDMA net additions in 3Q09	200,000	150,000	n/d	n/d	1,440
3G EV-DO net additions in 3Q09	n/d	n/d	n/d	-550,000	n/d
Blended ARPU 3Q09	11.43	12.60	9.45	n/a	n/a
Prepaid ARPU 3Q09	5.49	8.82	0.00	n/a	n/a
Postpaid ARPU 3Q09	39.88	31.68	0.00	n/a	n/a

MOBILE OPERATORS VALUE ADDED SERVICES

	VODACOM	MTN	CELL C
SMS			
Push SMS	Yes	Yes	Yes
Toll free SMS MO	n/a	n/a	n/a
Premium SMS MO	Yes	Yes	Yes
Premium SMS MT (subscription)	Yes	Yes	No
MMS			
Push MMS	Yes	Yes	Yes
Toll free MMS MO	n/a	n/a	n/a
Premium MMS MO	n/a	n/a	n/a
Premium MMS MT (subscription)	n/a	n/a	n/a
Maximum MMS weight	n/a	n/a	n/a
WAP			
Operator portal	Yes	Yes	n/a
Billing type	OBS	OBS	n/a
Pay per Use	Yes	Yes	Yes
Subscription	Yes	Yes	No
O-rate URL / Wholesale datacharge	n/a	n/a	n/a
Maximum WAP Gateway download	n/a	n/a	n/a

NETSIZE OFFER

	VODACOM	MTN	CELL C
SMS			
Push SMS	Yes	Yes	Yes
Toll free SMS MO	n/a	n/a	n/a
Premium SMS MO	Yes	Yes	Yes
Premium SMS MT (subscription)	Yes	Yes	No
MMS			
Push MMS	No	No	No
Toll free MMS MO	No	No	No
Premium MMS MO	No	No	No
Premium MMS MT (subscription)	No	No	No
Maximum MMS weight	No	No	No
WAP			
Operator portal	Yes	Yes	Yes
Billing type	OBS	OBS	n/a
Pay per Use	Yes	Yes	Yes
Subscription	Yes	Yes	No
O-rate URL / Wholesale datacharge	n/a	n/a	n/a
Maximum WAP Gateway download	n/a	n/a	n/a

MOBILE CONTENT PRICES (Prices in ZAR)

	PAY PER USE
Sound	
Polyphonics	10
True Tones	15
MP3	20
Images	
Wallpapers	15
Videos	20
Games & Lottery	30 (games, no lottery)
Voting, Participation TV	1.50 - 2.00
Instant Win, quiz	Standard rates are advised
Java games	50
Community	1.5 - 2.0
Chat	2

OPERATOR MOBILE CONTENT PRICES (Prices in US$)

	VODACOM	MTN
Community	Handset client (downloadable): 0.27 / MB. Other data-pricing options available. No content charge.	n/a
Music	Ring-back tones: 1.33 / tone for 3 months. Set-up costs by call ZAR1.50/min and by text ZAR0.50 / message. Browsing free. (Voice) - Ring tones: 0.66 / download - 1.66 / download - 1.33 / download (OTA) - Full-tracks: 2.00 / download (OTA)	Ring-back tones/Ring tones/Full-tracks: 1.33 / bundle. No traffic browsing or downloading charges on MTN Loaded portal. - 2.66 / bundle. No traffic browsing or downloading charges on MTN Loaded portal. - 4.00 / bundle. No traffic browsing or downloading charges on MTN Loaded portal. (OTA/Voice) - Ring tones: 0.40 / download - 0.66 / download - 1.33 / download (OTA) - Ring-back tones: 0.66 / tone, + three-monthly renewal charge of ZAR5.00. (Voice)
TV & Video	Video-on-demand: 1.96 / download - 0.45 / download - 0.65 / download - 1.31 / download - 1.31 / wk - 4.59 / month (Download) - Mobile TV: 1.31 / day (Streamed)	Mobile TV: 1.31 / month, + data charges. (Streamed) - Video-on-demand: 0.65 / day to access all content - 2.62 / month to get youth and music content - 3.93 / month to get Afrikaans-oriented content. - 3.28 / month to get drama and news content (Downloaded/streamed)
Location Based Services	Family locator/ Friend finder: 1.47 / month, + charge / location request: via USSD, ZAR0.20 / 20 seconds; via SMS, ZAR1.84 / SMS; via MMS, ZAR2.89 / MMS (incl. map). (Cell-ID)	Family locator: 1.57 / month. + ZAR2.00 / request to locate someone via SMS or USSD. Via MTN website or via WAP it costs ZAR1.00. Costs ZAR0.86 to become a bearer and bearer must pay ZAR0.86 when someone tries to locate them via SMS, or ZAR0.21/20seconds via USSD. (Cell-ID) - Distress alarm: 1.57 / month. One free distress message / month ZAR2.00 / use thereafter. (Cell-ID)

INDUSTRY ASSOCIATIONS, REGULATORS & CODES OF PRACTICE

	NAME	WEBSITE
Self Regulator	WASPA	www.waspa.org.za
Operator	MTN	www.mtn.co.za
Operator	Vodacom	www.vodacom.co.za
Operator	Cell C	www.cellc.co.za

SOUTH KOREA

COUNTRY INFORMATION

Population in 2009	48,552,250
Gross domestic product 2009 per capita, current prices	10,457
Penetration rate (%) 3Q09	98.92%
Language (s)	Korean
Currency	South Korean Won (KRW)

MOBILE TELECOMMUNICATIONS MARKET

Total subscriptions 3Q09	48,027,400
3G WCDMA subscriptions 3Q09	n/a
3G EV-DO subscriptions 3Q09	5,790,000
Total revenues 3Q09 (EUR million)	4,365.27
Service revenues 3Q09 (EUR million)	3,208.63
Blended montly ARPU 3Q09 (EUR)	22.21
Data revenues 3Q09 (EUR million)	625.45
SMS revenues 3Q09 (EUR million)	n/a
Messaging revenues 2010 (EUR million)	1,496.04
Messaging ARPU 2010 (EUR)	2.99
Content ARPU 2010 (EUR)	6.53

MOBILE OPERATORS DATA

	SK TELECOM	KT CORP	LG TELECOM	KT POWERTEL
Total subscriptions 3Q09	24,137,000	14,904,000	8,619,000	367,400
Market share 3Q09	50.26%	31.03%	17.95%	0.76%
Prepaid subs 3Q09 (%)	0.05%	0.63%	1.03%	
Postpaid subs 3Q09 (%)	99.95%	99.37%	98.97%	100.00%
Growth rate (%) 3Q08 to 3Q09	5.51%	4.52%	5.88%	4.71%
Total net additions in 3Q09	306,110	191,000	91,510	7,380
WCDMA net additions in 3Q09	n/d	n/d	n/d	n/d
3G EV-DO net additions in 3Q09	-1,010,000	2,500	n/d	n/d
Blended ARPU 3Q09	24.04	20.37	20.28	n/a
Prepaid ARPU 3Q09	0.00	0.00	0.00	n/a
Postpaid ARPU 3Q09	0.00	0.00	0.00	n/a

MOBILE CONTENT SERVICES

	TOTAL REVENUES 2010 (EUR MILLION)	CONTRIBUTION AS % OF TOTAL REVENUES
Mobile music market	486.91	12.23%
Mobile games market	206.23	5.18%
Mobile images market	80.99	2.03%
Mobile TV market	346.24	8.70%
Mobile video market	102.65	2.58%
Mobile internet market	1,261.47	31.69%
Mobile messaging market	1,496.04	37.58%

INDUSTRY ASSOCIATIONS, REGULATORS & CODES OF PRACTICE

	NAME	WEBSITE
Telecom regulator	Korean Communication Commission	http://www.kcc.go.kr/user/ehpMain.do

SPAIN

COUNTRY INFORMATION

Population in 2009	44,851,500
Gross domestic product 2009 per capita, current prices	21,166
Penetration rate (%) 3Q09	119.97%
Language (s)	Spanish
Currency	Euro (EUR)

MOBILE TELECOMMUNICATIONS MARKET

Total subscriptions 3Q09	53,807,400
3G WCDMA subscriptions 3Q09	22,014,000
3G EV-DO subscriptions 3Q09	n/d
Total revenues 3Q09 (EUR million)	4,872.29
Service revenues 3Q09 (EUR million)	4,476.49
Blended montly ARPU 3Q09 (EUR)	27.15
Data revenues 3Q09 (EUR million)	789.48
SMS revenues 3Q09 (EUR million)	333.62
Messaging revenues 2010 (EUR million)	1,862.62
Messaging ARPU 2010 (EUR)	4.12
Content ARPU 2010 (EUR)	4.89

MOBILE OPERATORS DATA

	TELEFÓNICA MÓVILES	VODAFONE ESPANA	ORANGE	YOIGO	EUSKATEL
Total subscriptions 3Q09	23,993,200	16,130,200	12,366,000	1,318,000	n/a
Market share 3Q09	44.59%	29.98%	22.98%	2.45%	n/a
Prepaid subs 3Q09 (%)	37.44%	36.93%	50.00%	54.10%	n/a
Postpaid subs 3Q09 (%)	62.56%	63.07%	50.00%	45.90%	n/a
Growth rate (%) 3Q08 to 3Q09	2.27%	4.72%	5.76%	74.34%	n/a
Total net additions in 3Q09	277,600	73,700	247,000	131,000	n/a
WCDMA net additions in 3Q09	800,000	441,280	450,000	131,000	n/d
3G EV-DO net additions in 3Q09	n/d	n/d	n/d	n/d	n/d
Blended ARPU 3Q09	28.00	29.30	22.58	27.78	n/a
Prepaid ARPU 3Q09	13.20	11.70	7.25	0.00	n/a
Postpaid ARPU 3Q09	37.00	41.10	34.33	0.00	n/a

MOBILE OPERATORS VALUE ADDED SERVICES

	TELEFÓNICA MÓVILES	VODAFONE ESPANA	ORANGE	YOIGO	EUSKATEL
SMS					
Push SMS	Yes	Yes	Yes	Yes	Yes
Toll free SMS MO	Yes	Yes	Yes	Yes	Yes
Premium SMS < 1,20 €	Yes - From € 0.30 € to €1.20	Yes - From € 0.15 € to € 1.20	Yes - From € 0.30 € to €1.20	Yes - Up to €1.20	Yes - Up to €1.20
Premium SMS > 1,20 € (Doubble opt-in)	Yes - From € 1.21 € to € 6.00	Yes - From € 1.50 € to € 6.00	Yes - From € 1.29 € to € 6.00	Yes > € 1.20	Yes > € 1.20
Premium SMS MT (subscription)	Yes - Up to € 1.20	Yes - Up to € 1.20	Yes - Up to € 1.20	Yes - Up to € 1.20	Yes - Up to € 1.20
MMS					
Push MMS	Yes	Yes	Yes	No	No
Toll free MMS MO	No	No	No	No	No
Premium MMS MT < 1,20 €	Yes - From € 1.05 to €1.20	Yes - € 1.00 and €1.20 only	Yes - From € 0,90 to €1.20	n/a	n/a
Premium MMS MT > 1,20 €	Yes - From € 1.21 to € 6	Yes - From € 1.50 to € 6	Yes - From € 1.29 € to € 6.00	n/a	n/a
Premium MMS MT (subscription)	Yes - From € 1.10 to €1.20	n/a	Yes - From € 0.70 € to € 1.20		
Maximum MMS weight	n/a	n/a	n/a	n/a	n/a
WAP					
Operator portal	Emoción	Vodafone live!	Orange World	SurfPort	n/a
Billing type	WAP	WAP	WAP	WAP	n/a
Pay per Use	Yes - Up to €7.00	Yes - Up to €8.62	Yes - Up to €6.00	Yes - Up to €6.00	n/a
Subscription	Yes - Up to €5/day - and €25/month	Yes - Up to € 25,86 /month	No	Yes - Up to 30 € day and service /60 € month	No
O-rate URL / Wholesale datacharge	No	No	No	No	No
Maximum WAP Gateway download	n/a	n/a	n/a	n/a	n/a

NETSIZE OFFER

	TELEFÓNICA MÓVILES	VODAFONE ESPANA	ORANGE
SMS			
Push SMS	Yes	Yes	Yes
Toll free SMS MO	Yes	Yes	Yes
Premium SMS < 1,20 €	Yes - From € 0.30 € to €1.20	Yes - From € 0.30 € to €1.20	Yes - From € 0.30 € to €1.20
Premium SMS > 1,20 € (Doubble opt-in)	Yes - From € 1.50 € to € 6.00	Yes - From € 1.50 € to € 6.00	Yes - From € 1.50 € to € 6.00
Premium SMS MT (subscription)	Yes - from € 0.20 to € 1.20	Yes - from € 0.20 to € 1.20	Yes - from € 0.20 to € 1.20
MMS			
Push MMS	Yes	Yes	Yes
Toll free MMS MO	No	No	No
Premium MMS MO	No	No	No
Premium MMS MT (subscription)	No	No	No
Maximum MMS weight	n/a	n/a	n/a
WAP			
Operator portal	emoción	Vodafone live!	Orange World
Billing type	WAP	WAP	WAP
Pay per Use	Yes - Up to €7.00	Yes - Up to €8.62	Yes - Up to €6.00
Subscription	Yes - Up to €5/day - and €25/month	Yes - Up to € 25,86 /month	No
O-rate URL / Wholesale datacharge	No	No	No
Maximum WAP Gateway download	No limit	No limit	No limit

MOBILE CONTENT SERVICES

	TOTAL REVENUES 2010 (EUR MILLION)	CONTRIBUTION AS % OF TOTAL REVENUES
Mobile music market	194.88	5.37%
Mobile games market	114.76	3.16%
Mobile images market	35.04	0.96%
Mobile TV market	59.53	1.64%
Mobile video market	39.48	1.09%
Mobile internet market	1,325.43	36.50%
Mobile messaging market	1,862.62	51.29%

MOBILE CONTENT PRICES (Prices in EUR)

	PAY PER USE	SUBSCRIPTION
Sound		
Polyphonics	2.00 - 4.00	0.50 - 1.50
True Tones	2.00 - 4.00	0.50 - 2.00
MP3	5.50	0.90
Images		
Wallpapers	1.00 - 4.00	0.50 - 1.50
Videos	4.00 - 6.00	1.50 - 2.00
Games & Lottery		
Voting, Participation TV	1.20	n/a
Instant Win, quiz	0.90 - 1.20	n/a
Java games	3.00 - 5.50	1.5

OPERATOR MOBILE CONTENT PRICES (Prices in US$)

	TELEFÓNICA MÓVILES	VODAFONE ESPANA
Community	GPRS/WAP/SMS/MMS: 0.30 / SMS - 1.50 / MMS - 0.02 / KB. Other data-pricing options available. No content charge. - Handset client (downloadable): 0.02 / KB. Other data-pricing options available. No content charge.	GPRS/WAP: 1.62 / wk of data use. Other data-pricing options available. No content charge. - Variable Depending on app (standard data charges apply)
Music	Ring tones: 2.18 / download (lowest price) - 2.91 / download (highest price) (OTA) - Full-tracks: Information not available / download - 8.72 / month (OTA) - Ring-back tones: 2.53 / tone, + €1.2 monthly subscr. charge (prices incl VAT). (Voice)	Ring tones: 2.91 / download (OTA) - Ring-back tones: 1.45 / tone (Voice) - Full-tracks: 2.18 / download (OTA/Streaming)
TV & Video	Mobile TV: 7.46 / month - 5.97 / month (Streamed)	Mobile TV: 2.98 / wk for prepaids. - 8.95 / month for postpaids. - 1.48 / day - 8.95 / month - 2.24 / wk for prepaids. - 5.97 / month for postpaids. (Streamed) - Video-on-demand: 8.95 / month for unl. mobile Web usage. (Streamed)
Location Based Services	Navigation: Not applicable Cost of service bundled in with certain mobile Internet/iPhone flat-rate data plans. (GPS) - Fleet management: 0.13 / location fix for up to 500 of them a month, gradually dropping in price according to volume to a minimum of 0.05 for more than one million a month. addit.ly, customers pay upfront connection fee of €1,000 and monthly service fees of €500. (GPS)	Navigation/ Local search: 11.89 / month anywhere in Iberia (Spain, Portugal, Andorra and Gibraltar) incl. VAT. - 25.09 / month anywhere in Europe (incl. VAT). - 118.07 / year anywhere in Iberia (Spain, Portugal, Andorra and Gibraltar) incl. VAT. - 255.33 / year anywhere in Europe (incl. VAT). (GPS)

INDUSTRY ASSOCIATIONS, REGULATORS & CODES OF PRACTICE

	NAME	WEBSITE
Telecom regulator	Comisión del Mercado de las Telecomunicaciones (CMT)	www.cmt.es
Industry association	Asociación de Empresas de Servicios a Móviles (AESAM)	www.aesam.org

SWEDEN

COUNTRY INFORMATION

Population in 2009	9,211,250
Gross domestic product 2009 per capita, current prices	27,260
Penetration rate (%) 3Q09	130.79%
Language (s)	Swedish
Currency	Swedish Krona (SEK)

MOBILE TELECOMMUNICATIONS MARKET

Total subscriptions 3Q09	12,047,500
3G WCDMA subscriptions 3Q09	4,662,000
3G EV-DO subscriptions 3Q09	n/d
Total revenues 3Q09 (EUR million)	950.97
Service revenues 3Q09 (EUR million)	858.76
Blended montly ARPU 3Q09 (EUR)	20.17
Data revenues 3Q09 (EUR million)	189.40
SMS revenues 3Q09 (EUR million)	n/a
Messaging revenues 2010 (EUR million)	n/a
Messaging ARPU 2010 (EUR)	n/a
Content ARPU 2010 (EUR)	n/a

MOBILE OPERATORS DATA

	TELIASONERA SWEDEN	TELE2	TELENOR SWEDEN	HI3G	SVENSKA UMTS-NÄT
Total subscriptions 3Q09	4,353,000	2,353,000	1,958,000	997,000	2,365,000
Market share 3Q09	36.13%	19.53%	16.25%	8.28%	19.63%
Prepaid subs 3Q09 (%)	55.00%	63.49%	16.70%	17.42%	15.43%
Postpaid subs 3Q09 (%)	45.00%	36.51%	83.30%	82.58%	84.57%
Growth rate (%) 3Q08 to 3Q09	-0.59%	-5.79%	6.59%	30.84%	32.68%
Total net additions in 3Q09	-12,000	47,000	12,000	61,000	160,000
WCDMA net additions in 3Q09	n/d	n/d	50,000	61,000	160,000
3G EV-DO net additions in 3Q09	n/d	n/d	n/d	n/d	n/d
Blended ARPU 3Q09	17.21	18.94	21.61	33.65	n/a
Prepaid ARPU 3Q09	7.21	0.00	7.44	10.50	n/a
Postpaid ARPU 3Q09	24.90	0.00	29.41	33.24	n/a

SWEDEN

MOBILE OPERATORS VALUE ADDED SERVICES

	TELIASONERA SWEDEN	TELE2	TELENOR SWEDEN	HI3G
SMS				
Push SMS	Yes	Yes	Yes	Yes
Toll free SMS MO	No	No	No	No
Premium SMS MO	Yes - Up to SEK 200	Yes - Up to SEK 200	Yes - Up to SEK 200	n/a
Premium SMS MT (subscription)	Yes - Up to SEK 200 month	Yes - Up to SEK 200	Yes - Up to SEK 200	Yes - Up to SEK 200
MMS	Yes	Yes	Yes	Yes
Push MMS	Yes	Yes	Yes	Yes
Toll free MMS MO	No	No	No	No
Premium MMS MO	Yes - Up to SEK 200	Yes - Up to SEK 200	Yes Up to SEK 200	Yes - Up to SEK 200
Premium MMS MT (subscription)	Yes - Up to SEK 200 month	Yes - Up to SEK 200	Yes Up to SEK 200	Yes - Up to SEK 200
Maximum MMS weight	300 kb	300 kb	300 kb	1 mb
WAP	Yes	Yes	Yes	Yes
Operator portal	Telia SurfPort	mobil.tele2.se	mobil.telenor.se	Planet 3
Billing type	WAP billing	WAP billing	WAP billing	WAP billing
Pay per Use	Yes - Up to SEK 200	Yes - Up to SEK 200	Yes- up to SEK 200	Yes- up to SEK 200
Subscription	Yes - Up to SEK 200 month	Yes - Up to SEK 200	Yes- up to SEK 200	Yes- up to SEK 200
O-rate URL / Wholesale datacharge	Wholesale datacharge	Wholesale datacharge	Wholesale datacharge	Wholesale datacharge
Maximum WAP Gateway download	Unlimited	Unlimited	Unlimited	Unlimited

NETSIZE OFFER

	TELIASONERA SWEDEN	TELE2	TELENOR SWEDEN	HI3G
SMS				
Push SMS	Yes	Yes	Yes	Yes
Toll free SMS MO	No	No	No	No
Premium SMS MO	Yes - upto SEK 50	Yes - upto SEK 50	Yes - upto SEK 50	n/a
Premium SMS MT (subscription)	Yes - upto SEK 200	Yes - upto SEK 200	Yes - upto SEK 200	Yes - upto SEK 200
MMS				
Push MMS	Yes	Yes	Yes	No
Toll free MMS MO	No	No	No	No
Premium MMS MO	Yes - upto SEK 200	Yes - upto SEK 200	no	No
Premium MMS MT (subscription)	Yes - upto SEK 200	Yes - upto SEK 200	no	No
Maximum MMS weight	n/a	n/a	n/a	n/a
WAP	WAP	WAP	WAP	WAP
Operator portal	Telia SurfPort	mobil.tele2.se	mobil.telenor.se	Planet 3
Billing type	WAP billing	WAP billing	WAP billing	WAP billing
Pay per Use	Yes - Up to SEK 200	Yes - Up to SEK 200	Yes- up to SEK 200	Yes- up to SEK 200
Subscription	Yes - Up to SEK 200 month	Yes - Up to SEK 200	Yes- up to SEK 200	Yes- up to SEK 200
O-rate URL / Wholesale datacharge	Unlimited	Unlimited	Unlimited	see above
Maximum WAP Gateway download	No limit	No limit	No limit	No limit

MOBILE CONTENT PRICES (Prices in SEK)

	PAY PER USE	SUBSCRIPTION
Sound		
Polyphonics	15.00- 30.00	50-200 per week
Real Tones	15.00- 30.00	50-200 per week
MP3	15.00- 30.00	50-200 per week
Images		
Wallpapers	15.00- 30.00	50-200 per week
Videos	15.00- 30.00	50-200 per week
Games & Lottery		
Voting , Participation TV	15.00- 30.00	50-200 per week
Instant Win, quiz	15.00- 30.00	50-200 per week
Java games	30.00-50.00	50-200 per week
Community		
Chat	9.90	n/a

INDUSTRY ASSOCIATIONS, REGULATORS & CODES OF PRACTICE

	NAME	WEBSITE
Swedish electronic communications and postal sectors Authority	Post- och Telestyrelsen (PTS)	www.pts.se
The swedish gaming board	Lotteriinspektionen	www.lotteriinsp.se
The ethical council	Etiska rådet	www.etiskaradet.se
Industry organization MORGAN	Morgan	www.morganforum.com/

SWITZERLAND

COUNTRY INFORMATION

Population in 2009	7,545,250
Gross domestic product 2009 per capita, current prices	43,200
Penetration rate (%) 3Q09	118.74%
Language (s)	French, German, Italian
Currency	Swiss Franc (CHF)

MOBILE TELECOMMUNICATIONS MARKET

Total subscriptions 3Q09	8,959,000
3G WCDMA subscriptions 3Q09	2,821,000
3G EV-DO subscriptions 3Q09	n/d
Total revenues 3Q09 (EUR million)	1,040.57
Service revenues 3Q09 (EUR million)	957.93
Blended montly ARPU 3Q09 (EUR)	34.80
Data revenues 3Q09 (EUR million)	234.03
SMS revenues 3Q09 (EUR million)	113.44
Messaging revenues 2010 (EUR million)	n/a
Messaging ARPU 2010 (EUR)	n/a
Content ARPU 2010 (EUR)	n/a

MOBILE OPERATORS DATA

	SWISSCOM MOBILE	TDC SWITZERLAND	ORANGE SWITZERLAND
Total subscriptions 3Q09	5,543,000	1,850,000	1,566,000
Market share 3Q09	61.87%	20.65%	17.48%
Prepaid subs 3Q09 (%)	40.03%	39.78%	35.41%
Postpaid subs 3Q09 (%)	59.97%	60.22%	64.59%
Growth rate (%) 3Q08 to 3Q09	4.90%	13.78%	2.35%
Total net additions in 3Q09	65,000	20,000	-2,000
WCDMA net additions in 3Q09	132,000	35,570	14,000
3G EV-DO net additions in 3Q09	n/d	n/d	n/d
Blended ARPU 3Q09	33.57	34.10	39.92
Prepaid ARPU 3Q09	8.56	0.00	0.00
Postpaid ARPU 3Q09	50.03	0.00	0.00

MOBILE OPERATORS VALUE ADDED SERVICES

	SWISSCOM MOBILE	TDC SWITZERLAND	ORANGE SWITZERLAND
SMS			
Push SMS	Yes	Yes	Yes
Toll free SMS MO	No	Yes	Yes
Premium SMS MO	No	No	No
Premium SMS MT (subscription)	Yes - Up to CHF10.00	Yes - Up to CHF10.00	Yes - Up to CHF5.00
MMS			
Push MMS	Yes	Yes	Yes
Toll free MMS MO	No	Yes	Yes
Premium MMS MO	No	No	No
Premium MMS MT (subscription)	Yes - As Premium SMS	Yes - As Premium SMS	Yes - As Premium SMS
Maximum MMS weight	300 KB	100 KB	300KB
WAP			
Operator portal	Vodafone live!	Sunrise live	Orange World
Billing type	WAP + PSMS MT	WAP + PSMS MT	WAP + PSMS MT
Pay per Use	Yes - Up to CHF10.00	Yes - Up to CHF10.00	Yes - Up to CHF5.00
Subscription	Yes - Up to CHF10.00	Yes - Up to CHF10.00	Yes - Up to CHF5.00
O-rate URL / Wholesale datacharge	No	No	No
Maximum WAP Gateway download	n/a	n/a	n/a

NETSIZE OFFER

	SWISSCOM MOBILE	TDC SWITZERLAND	ORANGE SWITZERLAND
SMS			
Push SMS	Yes	Yes	Yes
Toll free SMS MO	No	Yes	Yes
Premium SMS MO	No	No	No
Premium SMS MT (subscription)	Yes - Up to CHF10.00	Yes - Up to CHF10.00	Yes - Up to CHF5.00
MMS			
Push MMS	Upon request	Upon request	Upon request
Toll free MMS MO	No	Upon request	Upon request
Premium MMS MO	No	No	No
Premium MMS MT (subscription)	Upon request	Upon request	Upon request
Maximum MMS weight	300 KB	100 KB	300KB
WAP			
Operator portal	WAP + PSMS MT	WAP + PSMS MT	WAP + PSMS MT
Billing type	Upon request	Upon request	Upon request
Pay per Use	Upon request	Upon request	Upon request
Subscription	Upon request	Upon request	Upon request
O-rate URL / Wholesale datacharge	No	No	No
Maximum WAP Gateway download	No limit	No limit	No limit

MOBILE CONTENT PRICES

	PAY PER USE	SUBSCRIPTION
Sound		
Polyphonics	2.00 - 4.00	1.50 - 6.00/week
True Tones	3.50 - 4.95	3.30 - 6.00/week
MP3	2.00 - 5.00	1.20 - 2.00 6.00/week
Images		
Wallpapers	2.00 - 4.00	1.50 - 9.90/week
Videos	3.00 - 5.00	3.30 - 9.90/week
Games & Lottery		
Voting, Participation TV	1	n/a
Instant Win, quiz	1	n/a
Java games	5.00 - 9.00	5.00 - 9.90/week
Community		
Chat	n/a	n/a

INDUSTRY ASSOCIATIONS, REGULATORS & CODES OF PRACTICE

	NAME	WEBSITE
Telecom regulator	Office fédéral de la Communication (OFCOM)	www.bakom.ch
Telecommunication Law	Loi sur les Télécommunications (LTC)	www.admin.ch/ch/f/rs/c784_10.html
Price indication Law	Loi sur l'Indication des Prix (OIP)	www.admin.ch/ch/f/rs/c942_211.html
Regulation Laws	Code Pénal Suisse (CPS)	www.admin.ch/ch/f/rs/c311_0.html
Regulation Laws	Loi contre la Concurrence Déloyale (LCD)	www.admin.ch/ch/f/rs/c241.html
Telecom regulator	Ordonnance sur les Ressources d'Adressage dans le domaine des Télécommunications (ORAT)	www.admin.ch/ch/f/rs/c784_104.html
Codes of practices	Code de conduite relatif aux services de téléphonie mobile à valeur ajoutée (CoC)	www.mobiletechnics.ch/files/downloads/CodedeconduiteV.2_FR_Juin06.pdf

THAILAND

COUNTRY INFORMATION

Population in 2009	64,806,250
Gross domestic product 2009 per capita, current prices	2,802
Penetration rate (%) 3Q09	99.41%
Language (s)	Thai
Currency	Thai Baht (THB)

MOBILE TELECOMMUNICATIONS MARKET

Total subscriptions 3Q09	64,421,140
3G WCDMA subscriptions 3Q09	n/a
3G EV-DO subscriptions 3Q09	n/d
Total revenues 3Q09 (EUR million)	1,046.67
Service revenues 3Q09 (EUR million)	999.20
Blended montly ARPU 3Q09 (EUR)	4.47
Data revenues 3Q09 (EUR million)	124.57
SMS revenues 3Q09 (EUR million)	n/a
Messaging revenues 2010 (EUR million)	n/a
Messaging ARPU 2010 (EUR)	n/a
Content ARPU 2010 (EUR)	n/a

MOBILE OPERATORS DATA

	AIS	DTAC	TRUE MOVE	HUTCHISON-CAT	CAT	TOT
Total subscriptions 3Q09	28,282,300	19,271,000	15,365,000	1,041,400	416,300	45,140
Market share 3Q09	43.90%	29.91%	23.85%	1.62%	0.65%	0.07%
Prepaid subs 3Q09 (%)	89.98%	87.90%	92.34%	61.09%		92.82%
Postpaid subs 3Q09 (%)	10.02%	12.10%	7.66%	38.91%	100.00%	7.18%
Growth rate (%) 3Q08 to 3Q09	5.63%	5.81%	12.36%	-4.81%	367.23%	-3.71%
Total net additions in 3Q09	380,300	70,840	118,000	200	58,200	-1,420
WCDMA net additions in 3Q09	n/d	n/d	n/d	n/d	n/d	n/d
3G EV-DO net additions in 3Q09	n/d	n/d	n/d	n/d	n/d	n/d
Blended ARPU 3Q09	4.81	5.62	2.38	7.88	n/a	n/a
Prepaid ARPU 3Q09	3.96	4.58	1.85	0.00	n/a	n/a
Postpaid ARPU 3Q09	12.44	13.64	8.75	0.00	n/a	n/a

MOBILE OPERATORS VALUE ADDED SERVICES

	AIS	DTAC	TRUE MOVE
SMS			
Push SMS	Yes	Yes	Yes
Toll free SMS MO	Yes	Yes	Yes
Premium SMS MO	Yes	Yes	Yes
Premium SMS MT (subscription)	Yes	Yes	Yes
MMS			
Push MMS	Yes	Yes	Yes
Toll free MMS MO	n/a	n/a	n/a
Premium MMS MO	n/a	n/a	n/a
Premium MMS MT (subscription)	Yes	Yes	Yes
Maximum MMS weight	Yes	Yes	Yes
WAP			
Operator portal	n/a	n/a	n/a
Billing type	WAP - Direct Billing	WAP - Direct Billing	Wap - Online
Pay per Use	Yes	Yes	Yes
Subscription	Yes	Yes	Yes
O-rate URL / Wholesale datacharge	n/a	n/a	n/a
Maximum WAP Gateway download	n/a	n/a	n/a

NETSIZE OFFER

	AIS	DTAC	TRUE MOVE
SMS			
Push SMS	Yes	Yes	Yes
Toll free SMS MO	No	No	No
Premium SMS MO	No	No	No
Premium SMS MT (subscription)	No	No	No
MMS	No	No	No
Push MMS	No	No	No
Toll free MMS MO	No	No	No
Premium MMS MO	No	No	No
Premium MMS MT (subscription)	No	No	No
Maximum MMS weight	n/a	n/a	n/a
WAP			
Operator portal	n/a	n/a	n/a
Billing type	WAP - Direct Billing	WAP - Direct Billing	No
Pay per Use	Yes - Up to THB300	Yes - Up to THB300	No
Subscription	Yes - Up to THB300	Yes - Up to THB300	No
O-rate URL / Wholesale datacharge	No	No	No
Maximum WAP Gateway download	No limit	No limit	No limit

INDUSTRY ASSOCIATIONS, REGULATORS & CODES OF PRACTICE

	NAME	WEBSITE
Telecom regulator	National Telecommunications Commission (NTC)	http://eng.ntc.or.th/

TURKEY

COUNTRY INFORMATION

Population in 2009	72,791,750
Gross domestic product 2009 per capita, current prices	5,486
Penetration rate (%) 3Q09	87.62%
Language (s)	Turkish
Currency	Turkish Lira (TRY)

MOBILE TELECOMMUNICATIONS MARKET

Total subscriptions 3Q09	63,783,000
3G WCDMA subscriptions 3Q09	2,400,000
3G EV-DO subscriptions 3Q09	n/d
Total revenues 3Q09 (EUR million)	1,755.61
Service revenues 3Q09 (EUR million)	1,740.31
Blended montly ARPU 3Q09 (EUR)	8.64
Data revenues 3Q09 (EUR million)	264.81
SMS revenues 3Q09 (EUR million)	119.15
Messaging revenues 2010 (EUR million)	n/a
Messaging ARPU 2010 (EUR)	n/a
Content ARPU 2010 (EUR)	n/a

MOBILE OPERATORS DATA

	TURKCELL	AVEA	VODAFONE
Total subscriptions 3Q09	36,000,000	12,100,000	15,683,000
Market share 3Q09	56.44%	18.97%	24.59%
Prepaid subs 3Q09 (%)	74.72%	64.46%	86.30%
Postpaid subs 3Q09 (%)	25.28%	35.54%	13.70%
Growth rate (%) 3Q08 to 3Q09	-0.83%	3.42%	-9.68%
Total net additions in 3Q09	-300,000	-300,000	718,000
WCDMA net additions in 3Q09	1,400,000	400,000	600,000
3G EV-DO net additions in 3Q09	n/d	n/d	n/d
Blended ARPU 3Q09	9.24	8.71	7.17
Prepaid ARPU 3Q09	5.88	4.45	6.00
Postpaid ARPU 3Q09	19.66	15.64	14.75

TURKEY

MOBILE OPERATORS VALUE ADDED SERVICES

	TURKCELL	AVEA	VODAFONE
SMS			
Push SMS	Yes	Yes	Yes
Toll free SMS MO	No	No	No
Premium SMS MO	Yes	Yes	Yes
Premium SMS MT (subscription)	Yes	Yes	Yes
MMS			
Push MMS	Yes	Yes	Yes
Toll free MMS MO	No	No	No
Premium MMS MO	Yes	Yes	Yes
Premium MMS MT (subscription)	Yes	Yes	Yes
Maximum MMS weight	n/a	n/a	n/a
WAP			
Operator portal	GNC	Patlican	Live!
Billing type	MSISDN Forwarding	MSISDN Forwarding	MSISDN Forwarding
Pay per Use	Yes	Yes	Yes
Subscription	Yes	Yes	Yes
O-rate URL / Wholesale datacharge	No	No	No
Maximum WAP Gateway download	n/a	n/a	n/a

NETSIZE OFFER

	TURKCELL	AVEA	VODAFONE
SMS			
Push SMS	Yes	Yes	Yes
Toll free SMS MO	Upon request	Upon request	Upon request
Premium SMS MO	No	No	No
Premium SMS MT (subscription)	Yes	Yes	Yes
MMS			
Push MMS	Yes	Yes	Yes
Toll free MMS MO	No	No	No
Premium MMS MO	No	No	No
Premium MMS MT (subscription)	Yes	Yes	Yes
Maximum MMS weight	100kb	100kb	100kb
WAP			
Operator portal	Upon request	Upon request	Upon request
Billing type	n/a	n/a	n/a
Pay per Use	Yes	Yes	Yes
Subscription	Yes	Yes	Yes
O-rate URL / Wholesale datacharge	No	No	No
Maximum WAP Gateway download	No limit	No limit	No limit

MOBILE CONTENT PRICES

	PAY PER USE	SUBSCRIPTION WEEKLY
Sound		
Polyphonics	12 SMS	6 - 24 SMS
True Tones	16 - 24 SMS	6 - 24 SMS
MP3	16 - 24 SMS	6 - 24 SMS
Images	12 SMS	6 - 24 SMS
Wallpapers	12 SMS	6 - 24 SMS
Videos	16 - 24 SMS	6 - 24 SMS
Games & Lottery	not permitted	
Voting, Participation TV	1-10 SMS	n/a
Instant Win, quiz	1-10 SMS	n/a
Java games	24-54 SMS	24 SMS
Community		
Chat	1-4 SMS	10 SMS

OPERATOR MOBILE CONTENT PRICES (Prices in US$)

	TURKCELL	AVEA	VODAFONE
Community	3G/Video calling: 0.20 / min to 7505 - MMS: 0.40 / MMS - Handset client (downloadable): 2.67 / month - 8.09 / month - 0.10 / message - 0.40 / picture message	n/a	Handset client (downloadable): 0.00 Data charges do not apply at this point in time. - SMS: 0.15 / SMS - GPRS/WAP: 0.30 / MMS
Music	Ring-back tones: 2.01 / tone for 6 months, + TRY 2.50 monthly subscr. fee. (Voice) - Full-track: 1.85 / download - 2.69 / download (OTA) - Ring tones: 2.35 / download - 2.69 / download - 2.01 / download (OTA)	n/a	Full-tracks: 1.39 / wk for 25 tracks. (OTA)
TV & Video	Video on demand: 2.71 / download (Streamed) - Mobile TV: 3.36 / month for total of 20 hrs viewing, limited to 4 hrs / day. Use byond this costs TRY 0.13 / min. - 13.52 / month (Streamed) - Video on demand: 3.05 / 50 mins - 1.52 / download (Download) - Mobile TV: 4.75 / month - 4.75 / month (Streamed)	n/a	Mobile TV: 3.40 / month - 3.40 / month - 5.10 / month - 6.80 / month - 3.40 / month / program (Streamed) - Video-on-demand: 0.78 / download (Download)
Location Based Services	Self locator/ Local search: 0.40 / location request (GPS) - Local search: 3.34 / month (GPS) - Local search: 0.40 / location request (GPS) - Location-based survey: n/a (GPS/Cell-ID) - Location-based advertising/ Local search: 0.40 / location request (GPS/Cell-ID) - Friend finder: 0.40 / location request (GPS)	n/a	n/a

INDUSTRY ASSOCIATIONS, REGULATORS & CODES OF PRACTICE

	NAME	WEBSITE
Telecom regulator	Telecommunications Authority	www.tk.gov.tr
Telecom regulator	Ministry of Transportation	www.mt.gov.tr

UNITED KINGDOM

COUNTRY INFORMATION

Population in 2009	61,326,500
Gross domestic product 2009 per capita, current prices	22,948
Penetration rate (%) 3Q09	124.75%
Language (s)	English
Currency	British Pound (GBP)

MOBILE TELECOMMUNICATIONS MARKET

Total subscriptions 3Q09	76,506,090
3G WCDMA subscriptions 3Q09	23,674,390
3G EV-DO subscriptions 3Q09	n/d
Total revenues 3Q09 (EUR million)	5,538.69
Service revenues 3Q09 (EUR million)	5,135.27
Blended montly ARPU 3Q09 (EUR)	24.60
Data revenues 3Q09 (EUR million)	1,673.53
SMS revenues 3Q09 (EUR million)	1,041.60
Messaging revenues 2010 (EUR million)	5,435.01
Messaging ARPU 2010 (EUR)	8.63
Content ARPU 2010 (EUR)	4.74

MOBILE OPERATORS DATA

	O2 (UK)	VODAFONE	ORANGE UK	T-MOBILE	HUTCHISON 3G	VIRGIN
Total subscriptions 3Q09	21,980,800	16,590,450	16,560,000	16,608,000	4,766,840	n/a
Market share 3Q09	28.73%	21.69%	21.65%	21.71%	6.23%	n/a
Prepaid subs 3Q09 (%)	61.22%	50.73%	60.96%	75.49%	23.70%	n/a
Postpaid subs 3Q09 (%)	38.78%	49.27%	39.04%	24.51%	76.30%	n/a
Growth rate (%) 3Q08 to 3Q09	9.44%	0.16%	2.96%	-1.15%	19.07%	n/a
Total net additions in 3Q09	290,100	148,950	39,000	20,000	183,340	n/a
WCDMA net additions in 3Q09	559,000	637,470	404,000	179,850	183,340	n/d
3G EV-DO net additions in 3Q09	n/d	n/d	n/d	n/d	n/d	n/d
Blended ARPU 3Q09	25.50	23.66	24.98	21.82	32.16	n/a
Prepaid ARPU 3Q09	12.40	8.61	10.34	8.04	13.99	n/a
Postpaid ARPU 3Q09	42.00	43.19	47.19	47.09	37.78	n/a

MOBILE OPERATORS VALUE ADDED SERVICES

	O2 (UK)	VODAFONE	ORANGE UK	T-MOBILE	HUTCHISON 3G	VIRGIN
SMS						
Push SMS	Yes	Yes	Yes	Yes	Yes	n/a
Toll free SMS MO	Yes	Yes	Yes	Yes	Yes	n/a
Premium SMS MO + Max Price Point	Yes - Up to £1.50	Yes - up to £10.00	Yes - Up to £10.00	Yes - Up to £10.00	Yes - Up to £10.00	n/a
Premium SMS MT + Max Price Point	Yes - Up to £10.00	Yes - up to £10.00	Yes - Up to £10.00	Yes - Up to £10.00	Yes - Up to £10.00	n/a
MMS						
Push MMS	Yes	Yes	Yes	Yes	Yes	n/a
Toll free MMS MO	No	No	Yes	No	Yes	n/a
Premium MMS MO	No	No	Yes	No	Yes	n/a
Premium MMS MT (subscription)	No	No	Yes	No	Yes	n/a
Maximum MMS weight	300kb	300kb	300kb	300kb	300kb	n/a
WAP						
Operator portal	O2 Active	Vodafone Live!	Orange World	T-Zones	Planet 3	n/a
Billing type	Payforit	Payforit	Payforit	Payforit	Payforit	n/a
Pay per Use + Max Price Point	Yes - Up to £10.00	Yes - Up to £10.00	Yes - Up to £10.00	Yes - Up to £10.00	Yes - Up to £10.00	n/a
Subscription + Max Price Point	Yes - Up to £10.00	Yes - Up to £10.00	Yes - Up to £10.00	Yes - Up to £10.00	Yes - Up to £10.00	n/a
O-rate URL / Wholesale datacharge	No	In Trials	No	No	Yes	n/a
Maximum WAP Gateway download	Handset Dependent	Handset Dependent	Handset Dependent	Handset Dependent	No WAP Gateway - xHTML & WAP to xHTML conversion	n/a

NETSIZE OFFER

	O2 (UK)	VODAFONE	ORANGE UK	T-MOBILE	HUTCHISON 3G	VIRGIN
SMS						
Push SMS	Yes	Yes	Yes	Yes	Yes	Yes
Toll free SMS MO	Yes	Yes	Yes	Yes	Yes	Yes
Premium SMS MO + Max Price Point	Yes - Up to £1.50	Yes - Up to £10.00	Yes - Up to £10.00	Yes - Up to £10.00	Yes - Up to £10.00	Yes - Up to £5.00
Premium SMS MT (subscription) + Max Price Point	Yes - Up to £10.00	Yes - Up to £10.00	Yes - Up to £10.00	Yes - Up to £10.00	Yes - Up to £10.00	Yes - Up to £5.00
MMS						
Push MMS	Yes - through VF UK	Yes	Yes - through VF UK	Yes - through VF UK	Yes - through VF UK	Yes - through VF UK
Toll free MMS MO	No	No	Upon request	No	Upon request	n/a
Premium MMS MO	No	No	Upon request	No	Upon request	n/a
Premium MMS MT (subscription)	No	No	Upon request	No	Upon request	n/a
Maximum MMS weight	300kb	300kb	300kb	300kb	300kb	n/a
WAP	Yes	Yes	Yes	Yes	Yes	n/a
Operator portal	O2 Active	Vodafone Live!	Orange World	T-Zones	Planet 3	n/a
Billing type	Payforit	Payforit	Payforit	Payforit	Payforit	n/a
Pay per Use + Max Price Point	Yes - Up to £10.00	Yes - Up to £10.00	Yes - Up to £10.00	Yes - Up to £10.00	Yes - Up to £10.00	n/a
Subscription + Max Price Point	Yes - Up to £10.00	Yes - Up to £10.00	Yes - Up to £10.00	Yes - Up to £10.00	Yes - Up to £10.00	n/a
O-rate URL / Wholesale datacharge	No	In Trial	No	No	Yes	n/a
Maximum WAP Gateway download	No limit	No limit	No limit	No limit	No limit	n/a

MOBILE CONTENT SERVICES

	TOTAL REVENUES 2010 (EUR MILLION)	CONTRIBUTION AS % OF TOTAL REVENUES
Mobile music market	221.42	2.93%
Mobile games market	156.04	2.06%
Mobile images market	90.43	1.19%
Mobile TV market	67.75	0.90%
Mobile video market	65.38	0.86%
Mobile internet market	1,531.60	20.24%
Mobile messaging market	5,435.01	71.82%

MOBILE CONTENT PRICES

	PAY PER USE	SUBSCRIPTION
Sound	1.00-3.00	
Polyphonics	1.00-3.00	n/a
True Tones	1.00-3.00	n/a
MP3	0.99 Full track music downloads	n/a
Images	1.00-2.50	2.5
Wallpapers	1.00-3.00	2.5
Videos	1.5	1
Games & Lottery	2.50 - 6.00	1.00 - 4.00
Voting, Participation TV	n/a	n/a
Instant Win, quiz	n/a	n/a
Java games	1.00-5.00	n/a
Community		
Chat	n/a	n/a

OPERATOR MOBILE CONTENT PRICES (Prices in US$)

	O2 (UK)	VODAFONE
Community	GPRS/WAP: 1.61 / day of data use. Other data-pricing options available. No content charge.	Handset client (downloadable): 0.82 / day of data use. Other data-pricing options available. No content charge.
Music	Full-tracks: 1.57 / download - 6.37 For 5-track bundle (OTA) - Ring tones: 3.98 / download - 5.58 / download (OTA)	Full-tracks: 0.79 / download - 7.90 For bundle - 11.96 For bundle - 3.11 / wk - 11.96 / month (OTA)
TV & Video	Video-on-demand: 0.15 / download - 0.00 / video (lowest price). - 7.95 / video (highest price). - 0.79 / download - 7.95 / month (Streamed)	Video-on-demand: 7.95 / month (Streamed) - Mobile TV: 1.54 / wk - 3.11 / wk - 4.67 / month - 9.33 / month - 7.92 / month - 15.55 / month (Streamed)
Location Based Services	n/a	Navigation/Local search: 8.20 / month. Standard data charges apply. (GPS)

INDUSTRY ASSOCIATIONS, REGULATORS & CODES OF PRACTICE

	NAME	WEBSITE
Regulatory body for all premium rate charged telecommunications services	Phonepayplus	www.phonepayplus.org.uk
Independent regulator and competition authority for the UK communications industries	Office of Communications (Ofcom)	www.ofcom.org.uk
Industry Association	Mobile Entertainment Forum (MEF)	www.m-e-f.org
Industry Association	Association for Interactive Media & Entertainment (AIME)	www.aimelink.org
Industry Association	Mobile Marketing Association	www.mmaglobal.com/uk/
Industry Association	Mobile Data Association	www.themda.org
Industry Association	160 Characters	www.160characters.org

UKRAINE

COUNTRY INFORMATION

Population in 2009	45,431,750
Gross domestic product 2009 per capita, current prices	1,764
Penetration rate (%) 3Q09	111.79%
Language (s)	Ukrainian
Currency	Ukrainian Hryvnia (UAH)

MOBILE TELECOMMUNICATIONS MARKET

Total subscriptions 3Q09	50,789,200
3G WCDMA subscriptions 3Q09	350,300
3G EV-DO subscriptions 3Q09	n/d
Total revenues 3Q09 (EUR million)	540.39
Service revenues 3Q09 (EUR million)	520.91
Blended montly ARPU 3Q09 (EUR)	3.47
Data revenues 3Q09 (EUR million)	73.10
SMS revenues 3Q09 (EUR million)	n/a
Messaging revenues 2010 (EUR million)	n/a
Messaging ARPU 2010 (EUR)	n/a
Content ARPU 2010 (EUR)	n/a

MOBILE OPERATORS DATA

	MTS UKRAINE	KYIVSTAR	LIFE:) (AS-TELIT)	UKRAINIAN RADIO SYSTEMS (BEELINE)	TELESYSTEMS UKRAINE	UKRTELECOM	GOLDEN TELECOM
Total subscriptions 3Q09	17,780,000	22,285,000	7,800,000	2,199,000	359,400	350,300	15,500
Market share 3Q09	35.01%	43.88%	15.36%	4.33%	0.71%	0.69%	0.03%
Prepaid subs 3Q09 (%)	91.76%	92.78%	97.99%	94.00%			54.45%
Postpaid subs 3Q09 (%)	8.24%	7.22%	2.01%	6.00%	100.00%	100.00%	45.55%
Growth rate (%) 3Q08 to 3Q09	-1.72%	-4.99%	23.81%	-8.53%	71.80%	409.90%	-45.04%
Total net additions in 3Q09	0	62,000	-200,000	265,000	37,200	67,000	-3,400
WCDMA net additions in 3Q09	n/d	n/d	n/d	n/d	n/d	67,000	n/d
3G EV-DO net additions in 3Q09	n/d	n/d	n/d	n/d	n/d	n/d	n/d
Blended ARPU 3Q09	3.57	3.66	2.66	3.77	n/a	n/a	n/a
Prepaid ARPU 3Q09	2.45	2.86	0.00	0.00	n/a	n/a	n/a
Postpaid ARPU 3Q09	22.39	13.73	0.00	0.00	n/a	n/a	n/a

MOBILE OPERATORS VALUE ADDED SERVICES

	MTS UKRAINE	KYIVSTAR	LIFE:) (ASTELIT)	UKRAINIAN RADIO SYSTEMS (BEELINE)
SMS				
Push SMS	Yes	Yes	Yes	Yes
Toll free SMS MO	Yes	Yes	Yes	Yes
Premium SMS MO	Yes - 0,5 - 30 UAH incl. VAT	Yes - 0,5 - 30 UAH incl. VAT	Yes - 1 - 30 UAH incl. VAT	Yes - 0,5 - 30 UAH incl. VAT
Premium SMS MT (subscription)	n/a	Yes - 0,5 - 30 UAH incl. VAT (w/o subscription)	Yes - 1 - 30 UAH incl. VAT	n/a
MMS	n/a	n/a	n/a	n/a
Push MMS	n/a	n/a	n/a	n/a
Toll free MMS MO	n/a	n/a	n/a	n/a
Premium MMS MO	no	Yes	Yes	Yes
Premium MMS MT (subscription)	n/a	n/a	n/a	n/a
Maximum MMS weight	1000 Kb	300 Kb	300 Kb	300 Kb
WAP	Yes	Yes	Yes	Yes
Operator portal	WAP.mts.com.ua, wap.jeans.com.ua	WAP.kyivstar.ua, wap.starport.com.ua, wap.djuice.com.ua	WAP.lifebox.com.ua	WAP.beeline.ua
Billing type	n/a	n/a	n/a	n/a
Pay per Use	Yes	Yes	Yes	Yes
Subscription	n/a	n/a	n/a	n/a
O-rate URL / Wholesale datacharge	no	Yes	no	no
Maximum WAP Gateway download	2000Kb	2000Kb	2000Kb	2000Kb

NETSIZE OFFER

	MTS UKRAINE	KYIVSTAR	LIFE:) (ASTELIT)	UKRAINIAN RADIO SYSTEMS (BEELINE)
SMS				
Push SMS	Yes	Yes	Yes	Yes
Toll free SMS MO	Upon request	Upon request	Upon request	Upon request
Premium SMS MO	from 2010	from 2010	from 2010	from 2010
Premium SMS MT (subscription)	No	from 2010 (without subscription)	No	No
MMS				
Push MMS	No	No	No	No
Toll free MMS MO	No	No	No	No
Premium MMS MO	No	Upon request	Upon request	Upon request
Premium MMS MT (subscription)	No	No	No	No
Maximum MMS weight	n/a	n/a	n/a	n/a
WAP				
Operator portal	No	No	No	No
Billing type	No	No	No	No
Pay per Use	No	No	No	No
Subscription	No	No	No	No
O-rate URL / Wholesale datacharge	n/a	n/a	n/a	n/a
Maximum WAP Gateway download	n/a	n/a	n/a	n/a

MOBILE CONTENT PRICES (Prices in UAH)

	PAY PER USE
Sound	
Polyphonics	8.00
True Tones	8.00
MP3	10.00
Images	4.00
Wallpapers	4.00
Videos	10.00
Games & Lottery	5.00
Voting, Participation TV	3.00
Instant Win, quiz	2.00
Java games	16.00-25.00
Community	n/a (only via WAP)
Chat	n/a (only via WAP)

INDUSTRY ASSOCIATIONS, REGULATORS & CODES OF PRACTICE

	NAME	WEBSITE
Goverment	Ministry of telecommunications	www.stc.gov.ua/uk/index

UNITED STATES OF AMERICA

COUNTRY INFORMATION

Population in 2009	312,465,250
Gross domestic product 2009 per capita, current prices	31,871
Penetration rate (%) 3Q09	89.28%
Language (s)	English
Currency	American Dollar (USD)

MOBILE TELECOMMUNICATIONS MARKET

Total subscriptions 3Q09	278,978,030
3G WCDMA subscriptions 3Q09	42,527,660
3G EV-DO subscriptions 3Q09	49,163,000
Total revenues 3Q09 (EUR million)	32,340.07
Service revenues 3Q09 (EUR million)	28,650.52
Blended montly ARPU 3Q09 (EUR)	34.98
Data revenues 3Q09 (EUR million)	8,160.22
SMS revenues 3Q09 (EUR million)	2,477.49
Messaging revenues 2010 (EUR million)	10,449.30
Messaging ARPU 2010 (EUR)	3.42
Content ARPU 2010 (EUR)	6.80

MOBILE OPERATORS DATA

	AT&T MOBILITY	VERIZON WIRELESS	SPRINT NEXTEL	T-MOBILE USA	US CELLULAR	CINCINNATI BELL WIRELESS	IPCS	LEAP WIRELESS	METRO PCS	SPRINT PCS AFFILIATES	OTHER
Total subscriptions 3Q09	81,596,000	89,013,000	46,521,000	33,013,000	6,131,000	536,300	720,100	4,656,360	6,322,270	245,900	10,223,100
Market share 3Q09	29.25%	31.91%	16.68%	11.83%	2.20%	0.19%	0.26%	1.67%	2.27%	0.09%	3.66%
Prepaid subs 3Q09 (%)	6.54%	5.94%	29.31%	19.77%	4.06%	28.49%		2.00%	7.90%	21.72%	
Postpaid subs 3Q09 (%)	93.46%	94.06%	70.69%	80.23%	95.94%	71.51%	100.00%	98.00%	92.10%	78.28%	100.00%
Growth rate (%) 3Q08 to 3Q09	8.98%	25.71%	-6.27%	3.94%	-0.73%	-5.41%	6.78%	34.57%	30.43%	6.63%	10.02%
Total net additions in 3Q09	1,996,000	1,319,000	-1,416,100	-71,100	-53,000	-7,500	9,900	116,180	66,160	3,900	404,010
WCDMA net additions in 3Q09	4,300,000	n/d	n/d	700,000	n/d	4,000	n/d	n/d	n/d	n/d	n/d
3G EV-DO net additions in 3Q09	n/d	2,120,700	100,000	n/d	6,000	n/d	n/d	n/d	n/d	n/d	n/d
Blended ARPU 3Q09	35.83	35.71	34.88	32.89	37.43	30.37	0.00	27.71	28.74	n/a	n/a
Prepaid ARPU 3Q09	0.00	0.00	24.49	13.99	0.00	20.08	0.00	0.00	0.00	n/a	n/a
Postpaid ARPU 3Q09	42.84	36.93	39.18	36.38	0.00	34.47	34.98	0.00	0.00	n/a	n/a

MOBILE OPERATORS VALUE ADDED SERVICES

	AT&T MOBILITY	VERIZON WIRELESS	SPRINT NEXTEL	T-MOBILE USA	US CELLULAR
SMS					
Push SMS	Yes	Yes	Yes	Yes	n/a
Toll free SMS MO	No	No	No	Upon Request	n/a
Premium SMS MO	Yes - max US$29.99/ - chat US$1.99	Yes - max US$9.99/ - chat US$0.99	Yes - max US$9.99/ - chat US$1.99	Yes - max US$9.99/ - chat US$0.99	n/a
Premium SMS MT (subscription)	Yes - max US$29.99/ - chat US$1.99	Yes - max US$9.99/ - chat US$0.99	Yes - max US$9.99/ - chat US$1.99	Yes - max US$9.99/ - chat US$0.99	n/a
MMS					
Push MMS	Yes *	Yes	Yes *	Yes *	n/a
Toll free MMS MO	No	No	No	No	n/a
Premium MMS MO	Yes - max US$15.99	Yes - max US$9.99	Yes - max US$9.99	Yes - max US$9.99	n/a
Premium MMS MT (subscription)	Yes - max US$15.99	Yes - max US$9.99	Yes - max US$9.99	Yes - max US$9.99	n/a
Maximum MMS weight	n/a	n/a	n/a	n/a	n/a
WAP					
Operator portal	MEdia Mall	Get It Now!	SEE (Sprint Exclusive Entertainment)	T-Zones	n/a
Billing type	MSISDN Forwarding + PSMS MT	MSISDN Forwarding + PSMS MT	MSISDN Forwarding + PSMS MT	MSISDN Forwarding + PSMS MT	n/a
Pay per Use	Yes - max US$29.99	Yes - max US$9.99	Yes - max US$9.99	Yes - max US$9.99	n/a
Subscription	Yes - max US$29.99	Yes - max US$9.99	Yes - max US$9.99	Yes - max US$9.99	n/a
0-rate URL / Wholesale datacharge	No	No	No	No	n/a
Maximum WAP Gateway download	No Max	No Max	No Max	No Max	n/a

NETSIZE OFFER

	ALL OPERATORS
SMS	
Push SMS	Yes
Toll free SMS MO	n/a
Premium SMS MO	Q109
Premium SMS MT (subscription)	Q109
MMS	
Push MMS	Upon request
Toll free MMS MO	n/a
Premium MMS MO	Upon request
Premium MMS MT (subscription)	Upon request
Maximum MMS weight	n/a
WAP	
Operator portal	n/a
Billing type	Upon request
Pay per Use	Upon request
Subscription	Upon request
0-rate URL / Wholesale datacharge	Upon request
Maximum WAP Gateway download	No limit

* Each operator has spending limits per month for both PPU & Subscription.

MOBILE CONTENT SERVICES

	TOTAL REVENUES 2010 (EUR MILLION)	CONTRIBUTION AS % OF TOTAL REVENUES
Mobile music market	1,210.23	4.32%
Mobile games market	614.16	2.19%
Mobile images market	242.42	0.86%
Mobile TV market	367.52	1.31%
Mobile video market	266.11	0.95%
Mobile internet market	14,894.36	53.11%
Mobile messaging market	10,449.30	37.26%

MOBILE CONTENT PRICES (Prices in US$)

	PAY PER USE	SUBSCRIPTION
Sound		
Polyphonics	1.49- 1.99	1.05 - 1.25
True Tones	2.49 - 2.99	2.00 - 2.69
MP3	1.29 - 2.99	1.69
Images		
Wallpapers	1.49 - 3.99	1.25
Videos	2.49 - 6.95	0.99 - 2.99
Games & Lottery		
Voting, Participation TV	n/a	n/a
Instant Win, quiz	n/a	n/a
Java games	2.99 - 10.99	2.99 - 4.99
Community		
Chat	n/a	1.99/month - 4.99/month

OPERATOR MOBILE CONTENT PRICES (Prices in US$)

	AT&T MOBILITY	VERIZON WIRELESS
Community	Handset client (downloadable): 0.20 / message sent/received - Variable Depending on app. - GRPS/WAP: 2.00 / MB. Other data-pricing options available. No content charge.	Handset client (downloadable): 5.00 / month for 250 messages. - 10.00 / month for 500 messages and unl. on-net messages - 15.00 / month for 1500 messages and unl. on-net messages - 20.00 / month for 5000 messages and unl. on-net messages - Variable Depending on app.
Music	Ring tones: 2.49 / download - 2.49 / download - 2.49 / download - 1.99 / download (OTA) - Full-tracks: 3.99 For 2 downloads (OTA) - Ring-back tones: 1.99 / tone (OTA) - Full-tracks: 7.49 / month for 5-track bundle. addit. tracks cost US$1.99 / download. Data charges apply. - 7.49 / month for 5-track bundle. addit. 5-track packs cost US$7.49. Data charges apply. (OTA) - Musical cards: 9.99 For 20 credits. Each card costs 4-5 credits. - 19.99 For 40 credits. Each card costs 4-5 credits. (OTA) - Ring tones/ graphics: 5.99 For 15 credits. Each ring tone costs 4-5 credits. - 9.99 For 30 credits. Each ring tone costs 4-5 credits. - 14.99 For 50 credits. Each ring tone costs 4-5 credits. (OTA)	Ring tones: 2.99 / download (OTA) - Full-tracks: 1.99 / download (OTA) - Ring-back tones: 1.99 / tone (OTA)
TV & Video	Video on demand: 15.00 / month (Streamed) - Mobile TV: 15.00 / month - 30.00 / month (Media FLO broadcast)	Mobile TV: 13.00 / month - 15.00 / month (Media FLO broadcast) - Video on demand: 10.00 / month (Streamed)
Location Based Services	Navigation/ Local search: 9.99 / month (GPS) - Family locator: 9.99 / month, to locate up to two users. - 14.99 / month, to locate up to five users. (GPS) - Friend finder: 3.99 / month (GPS) - Local search: 2.99 / month (GPS/Cell-ID) - Fitness tracker: 5.99 / month (GPS) - Location-based game: 5.99 / month (GPS) - Navigation/Local search: 3.99 / month (GPS)	Navigation/ Local search: 9.99 / month (GPS) - Family locator/ Navigation: 9.99 / month (GPS) - Fitness tracker: 1.99 / day - 3.99 / month (GPS) - Family locator: 0.00 app listed as free. (Information not available) - Navigation/ Local search: 4.49 / month (GPS) - Navigation/ search: 1.99 / day - 3.99 / month (Information not available)

INDUSTRY ASSOCIATIONS, REGULATORS & CODES OF PRACTICE

	NAME	WEBSITE
Telecom regulator	Federal Communications Commission (FCC)	www.fcc.gov
Short Code Ordering	Common Short Code Administration	www.usshortcodes.com
Industry Association	Mobile Marketing Association	www.mmaglobal.com

SPECIAL THANKS

Netsize would like to thank all the people who have collectively worked together in producing this guide.

Interviewees
Paul Berney (Mobile Marketing Association), Suhail Bhat (Mobile Entertainment Forum), Jonathan Bulkeley (Scanbuy), Olivier Céchura (SFR), Stanislas Chesnais (Netsize), Andreas Constantinou (VisionMobile), Mark Curtis (Flirtomatic), Dimitri Dautel (Havas Digital Mobile), Christopher David (Sony Ericsson), Susan Dray (Dray & Associates, Inc.), Scott Dunlap (NearbyNow), John Ellenby (GeoVector), Ian Henderson (Sony Music Entertainment), Jamie Gavin, Alistair Hill (comScore), Diana LaGattuta (Nokia NAVTEQ), Valérie Itey (Universal McCann), Maarten Lens-Fitzgerald (Layar), Phil Libin (Evernote), Chiel Liezenberg (Innopay), Jon Mew (Internet Advertising Bureau), Patrick Mork (GetJar), Jim Nalley (EmFinders), Rimma Perelmuter (Mobile Entertainment Forum), Christophe Romei (Memodia), Francesco Rovetta (PayPal Mobile), Elisabeth Trochet (UGC S.A.), Sienne Veit (Marks & Spencers Direct), Mark Wächter (MMA Germany & BVDW Section Mobile)

Partners
Informa Telecoms & Media: Marco Esposito, Thecla Mbongue, Mark Newman, Dexter Thillien, Thomas Wehmeier

mSearchGroove: Peggy Anne Salz

Netsize
Christine Blattes, Emmanuelle Charles, Alexander Vlasblom; Tamas Boros, Eric Brouard, Gérard Burion, Patricia Caurcel, Marouan Darhnaj, Claire Engele, Matthieu Foucher, José Antonio Garcia Martin, Amelia Gonzalez, Roelene Malan, Susie Harris, Malin Jason, Andrew Kaufmann, Anna Neuberger, Raoul Theunissen, Milena Vinci

PHOTOS COPYRIGHT

Getty Images except for the photos supplied by the interviewees and published under their responsibility.
Cover: School of Athens, Raphael, Apostolic Palace, Vatican City

DESIGN & LAYOUT

Christine Blattes

PUBLISHED BY

Netsize S.A.
53, Rue Raspail - 92594 Levallois-Perret Cedex - France
+33 (0)1 41 27 56 00
R.C.S. Nanterre 418 712 477

PRINTED IN FRANCE BY

CIA BOURGOGNE
Z.I. - IMPASSE DU MONTAIS - B.P.3
58320 POUGUES-LES-EAUX

Legal deposit: February 2010
ISSN : 1772-1598
ISBN : 978-2-9523533-5-9

© Netsize 2010. All rights reserved.
The reproduction, duplication, distribution, publication, modification, copying or translation of any of the material contained in this guide, without the express and written authorization of Netsize, is strictly prohibited. Counterfeiting shall be pursued.
Netsize™ is protected by French, EEC and international intellectual property laws.
Data provided by Informa Telecoms & Media for the Country information, Mobile Telecommunications market, Mobile Operators data, Mobile content services (Mobile content revenues), Mobile content prices (Unit Price) are based on Informa Telecoms & Media research is the property of Informa Telecoms & Media.
All other trademarks and copyright material quoted in this guide are the sole property of their respective owners. Where a trademark or a copyright material is quoted in this guide by third parties contributing to it, Netsize does not thereby represent that such third parties have an ownership interest in, or a license to use, any such trademarks or copyright material. No copyright material in this guide may be copied or further disseminated without the express and written permission of the legal holder of that copyright.
While Netsize has attempted to make the information in this guide as accurate as possible, the information in this guide is provided "as is" without any express or implied warranty of any kind. Netsize excludes all liability to any person arising directly or indirectly from using this guide and any information from it.

ABOUT GEMALTO

Netsize is a subsidiary of Gemalto.

Gemalto (Euronext NL 0000400653 GTO) is the world leader in digital security with 2008 annual revenues of €1.68 billion, and 10,000 employees operating out of 75 offices, research and service centers in 40 countries.

Gemalto is at the heart of our evolving digital society. The freedom to communicate, travel, shop, bank, entertain, and work – anytime, anywhere – has become an integral part of what people want and expect, in ways that are convenient, enjoyable and secure.

Gemalto delivers on the growing demands of billions of people worldwide for mobile connectivity, identity and data protection, credit card safety, health and transportation services, e-government and national security. We do this by supplying to governments, wireless operators, banks and enterprises a wide range of secure personal devices, such as subscriber identification modules (SIM), Universal Integrated Circuit Card (UICC) in mobile phones, smart banking cards, smart card access badges, electronic passports, and USB tokens for online identity protection. To complete the solution we also provide software, systems and services to help our customers achieve their goals.

As the use of Gemalto's software and secure devices increases with the number of people interacting in the digital and wireless world, the company is poised to thrive over the coming years.